PROSPECTING
FOR
TROUT

Delta Books of Interest

NIGHT FISHING FOR TROUT
Jim Bashline

THE SPORTS AFIELD TREASURY OF FLY FISHING
Tom Paugh, Editor

OPEN SEASON: Sporting Adventures
William Humphrey

NEVERSINK
Leonard M. Wright, Jr.

PROSPECTING FOR
TR O

UT

*Fly Fishing Secrets
from a Streamside Observer*

TOM ROSENBAUER

Illustrations by Nancy M. Aitken

A Delta Book
Published by
Dell Publishing
a division of
Bantam Doubleday Dell Publishing Group, Inc.
666 Fifth Avenue
New York, New York 10103

Library of Congress Cataloging in Publication Data

Rosenbauer, Tom.
    Prospecting for trout : fly fishing secrets from a streamside
observer / by Tom Rosenbauer.
      p.   cm.
    ISBN 0-385-30816-7 : $14.95
    1. Trout fishing.   2. Fly fishing.   I. Title.
  SH687.R68   1993
  799.1'755—dc20   92-29642
                                                     CIP

Manufactured in the United States of America
Published simultaneously in Canada

Illustrations by Nancy M. Aitken

April 1993

10 9 8 7 6 5 4 3 2 1

RRH

To Margot and my little Brookie

ACKNOWLEDGMENTS

It is said that there is not much new in this ancient sport of fly fishing—just the same material recycled in new and, one hopes, better ways. None of the ideas presented in this book was created in a vacuum, and I have had the enthusiastic help of many fine fly fishermen over the years. I don't think I've ever talked to another fly fisherman, novice or seasoned hand, without learning something new. I'd like to thank the following individuals for their ideas, for critiquing my theories, for posing for photos, and for showing me new places to fish: Tony Acerrano, Bob Bachman, Karl Badenhausen, Richard Banbury, Fred Barberi, Joe Bressler, Mark Bressler, Vern Bressler, Bob Butler, Jim Cannon, Rick Clark, Carl Coleman, Monroe Coleman, Pat Crow, Teri Felizato, Terry Finger, Art Geller, Doug Gibson, Cooper Gilkes, Bob Gotshall, Kevin Gregory, John Harder, Harry Hayden, John Holt, Mark Innis, Ed Jahn, Bob Jones, Alan Kelly, Dave Kumlein, Art Lee, Kris Lee, Brian Lepage, Jim Lepage, Nick Lyons, Jim McFadyean, Tom McMillen, Craig Matthews, Jackie Matthews, Galen Mercer, Don Owens, Margot Page, Dave Perkins, Leigh Perkins, Perk Perkins, Randall Perkins, Johnny Pippicelli, Bill Reed, Neil Ringler, Rick Rishell, Paul Roos, John Russell, Joe Santoro, Ed Schroeder, John Shaner, Sally Swift, Wayne Walts, and Rick Wollum.

CONTENTS

INTRODUCTION

Over the past twenty years there has been a change in the way most of us fish for trout. Beginning with the 1969 reissue of *Art Flick's Streamside Guide*, we have seen a revolution in fly fishing techniques, particularly concerning the way we look at insect hatches. Instead of pulling on waders, slipping into the water, and plunking away with nondescript flies, we have learned to wait for the hatches. Now it's possible for every fisherman who can read to get to the river just in time for the hatch, recognize what fly is emerging, and fish an emerger or nymph at the onset of the hatch, switching quickly to an exact imitation of the bug of the hour.

Books such as Doug Swisher and Carl Richards' *Selective Trout*, Al Caucci and Bob Nastasi's *Hatches*, and Fred Arbona's *Mayflies, the Angler, and the Trout* further refined these techniques by identifying the major mayfly hatches of the entire country. Gary LaFontaine later did an equally impressive job with the second most important order of insects in his book *Caddisflies*.

We became sitters and waiters.

Walk along the banks of many famous trout streams today—the Beaverkill, Henry's Fork, Penn's Creek—and what do you see? Fly fishermen perch on the banks, peering at the water, watching for a glitter of soft-edged triangular wings or the distant whorl of water that produces an atavistic rise of heartbeat—the same effect a glimpse of a deer must have caused in primitive man. There is nothing wrong with fishing this way. I love sitting on the bank, watching swallows grab the first progeny of a hatch, waiting for the sight of a big trout's nose pushing through the surface. It's the most effective way to catch a large trout on a dry fly, because if you wade into a pool before the hatch, you often spook the best trout before they begin to rise. Especially on smooth, slow rivers every step you take sends a ripple of warning to nervous fish.

Those of us who are lucky enough to live on or near trout streams, however, can get locked into this sedentary behavior. Why spend all your time on the river when you can put in a full day's work, put your baby to bed, cut the grass, and then run down for the best fishing of the day? Let the tourists flog the water all day— *you'll* catch almost as many trout on a dry in an hour.

The only trouble is that those tourists, who don't know the local hatches and the prime times, start coming to you with stories of astonishing nice trout taken on poorly chosen flies at the wrong time of the day. You begin to lose the arrogance of the local. When you take a trip to a faraway trout stream, you realize you have lost the ability to fish the water that your father and grandfather had refined to an art. You realize the regular, predictable hatches so glowingly reported in the entomology books are much more the exception than the rule.

Many rivers, like one of my home rivers, the Battenkill, support fine wild trout populations without offering spectacular or predictable hatches. The fish eat much of their food subsurface, picking and nibbling at caddis pupae, mayfly nymphs, midge larvae, aquatic beetles, sculpins, and crayfish, and they are fickle about responding to the sparse hatches that do occur. The 1989 season offered almost no hatches on the Battenkill, and cool weather and high water throughout the spring and summer dampened the trout's interest, even in the usually predictable evening spinner falls. Due to family and work obligations I was unable to spend many evenings on the river; instead I decided to fish in the mornings, before work. The Battenkill has never been a productive morning river for finding rising fish, and I did not have high hopes for catching many trout.

Fishing an average of three mornings a week for a couple of hours each time, I saw exactly three rising fish until the Tricos started in late July. But by using the prospecting techniques I had learned over the years, I had an amazingly productive and educational year.

Many mornings I caught only two or three small fish, but I can't remember ever being completely skunked. Yet if I had fished my usual way, barging around looking for rising trout or waiting on the banks for a hatch, I would barely have gotten my line wet that summer.

May 31, 1989, has an asterisk in my fishing log. I had found a riffle that was usually productive, and on this hazy, damp morning with the promise of rain, I started out with a streamer and fished four different patterns in the fast water above my favorite riffle. Not a touch. I didn't fish the streamer down through the riffle; instead, I carefully got out of the water above and worked back up through with a size 16 Adams dry. That fly pulled four trout from the riffle, including a thirteen-inch brown and an eleven-inch brook trout. After the Adams seemed to lose its charm, I tied on a size 12 Humpy and picked up two fish in the same water. Next I tried a size 14 Ausable Wulff, and when this bushy dry failed to draw a rise, I fished it across and downstream, skating it in some quiet water along the bank. A fifteen-inch brown, a fish I had never seen despite having fished this riffle two dozen times, slammed the fly. When the fish stopped coming to dries, I took two small ones with a Hare's Ear nymph size 12, and finally I took two browns, including one around fourteen inches, on a big, heavily weighted March Brown nymph. It was tough to leave the river and head for work. In a few hours I took eleven trout, yet not once that morning had I seen a fish rise.

I would like to help you fill your empty hours with days like this. Although most of us can have *almost* as much enjoyment on a trout stream without catching any fish, I'm always suspicious of the person who claims not to need to hook trout. With increased demands on our free hours in these busy times, being able to catch trout at all times, not just in the easy hatch periods, is a skill that most fishermen would love to develop.

This book is divided into three parts: trout and their feeding behavior in different kinds of water; special techniques to catch them; and how to put the pieces together and approach the fish. All are equally important in learning to prospect for trout. When you read the book, I hope you learn as much about trout behavior and trout streams as you do about specific techniques to catch them.

Memorizing a technique and using it on the river will help you catch some fish, but you'll be even more satisfied as you learn to modify techniques to fit your own needs on the stream, based on what you know about trout and their behavior. *That's* trout fishing!

TOM ROSENBAUER
East Arlington, Vermont
April 3, 1991

HOW TROUT
FEED

Under normal stream conditions, when trout are not avoiding a flood, waiting out cold weather in a state of almost suspended animation, moving to find cooler water with more oxygen in the stagnation of summer heat, or occupying themselves for a few weeks with the perpetuation of their species, they do nothing but feed and avoid predators. They learn these skills well or they die. We are part of their outside world, the zone above that hosts herons, ospreys, or raccoons. Little in that zone is beneficial to a trout, save the occasional windfall of a beetle or grasshopper that tumbles from a blade of streamside grass. Trout aren't happy if we see them. If they know we are watching, they will, at least, stop feeding. Most of the time they will also run for deep water, a log, or a rock where they feel we are not able to spot them, although sometimes a tail still peeks out, ostrichlike, from under a submerged brushpile.

Thomas M. Jenkins, Jr., a biologist who studied wild trout in two California streams, Convict Creek and the Owens River, wrote a paper that is a milestone in our knowledge of trout behavior: "Social Structure, Position Choice, and Microdistribution of Two Trout Species (*Salmo trutta* and *Salmo gairdneri*) Resident in Mountain Streams." Although the title is less than succinct, one of Jenkins' introductory statements sums up the life of a trout with surgical precision: "Its habits and habitat are perfectly suited to foil observation by both predator and investigator."

1

It is not our world, that place of trout. Without the help of clumsy gear we can't go there and still breathe. Placed in an aquarium, trout soon die because we can't duplicate their delicate surroundings without thousands of dollars worth of artificial environment. Even those biologists who have been able to create artificial streams are not convinced trout behave the same way there as they do in the wild. Although some of our knowledge of trout behavior is inferred from artificial stream studies, the best information has come from work like Jenkins'. He studied trout, with much difficulty, directly in the Owens River in California, and also in an artificially constructed channel that used Convict Creek's natural flow, food supply, and wild trout. Bob Bachman spent three thousand hours in a tower above Spruce Creek. He filmed trout, recorded their movements and feeding patterns, and later made computer graphics of their daily and seasonal use of bottom structure, yet he admits that much of what he knows of trout comes from talks with perceptive fishermen. "Most biologists don't listen to fishermen," he told me, "but I always listen to the guys who really look at what's going on. They spend more hours on the water observing than do most biologists, and they're less apt to disturb the fish than a bunch of guys sloshing around with electroshocking gear."

Most fishermen, even the successful ones, know little about the daily rhythms of trout. We know volumes about insects, though, particularly mayflies. Most fishermen can tell you what an *Ephemerella subvaria* is likely to be doing at 1:55 P.M. on May 15, but if you ask what they think the trout are doing, they'll move a few pebbles of gravel around with the toes of their waders and mumble something about swimming. Bugs are easier to study than trout. When you peer at them in the water or watch a mating swarm over a riffle, they don't run away. Turn over a few rocks, take some home in a bottle, and you'll be able to write a fairly decent bug biography. Some thick fishing books have been written this way.

A Trout's Day

The best way for me to teach you about how trout live and feed is for both of us to climb a tree or sit on a cliff overlooking a trout and watch him for a day. Let's say it's June, the water temperature ranges from 55 degrees in the morning to 70 in late afternoon, the water is low and clear, and there are lots of different kinds of insects in the river. We'll make the trout a brown around thirteen inches long—a threshold size for most stream trout, as we'll learn later. The water here is about three feet deep. We are in a spot directly over the trout. From the vantage point we would have if we were fishing, the glare and depth of the water would not let us see anything of the trout because of his near-perfect camouflage. From our spot, however, we can see everything that goes on.

As the first light hits the river, we see the brownish yellow pebbles of the stream bottom and a few larger rocks. Staring at the bottom, we notice something out of place: Just downstream of the trailing edge of a rock the size and texture of a cantaloupe, there is a thin shadow. Abruptly, as if in one of those picture puzzles where you pick out the shape of an animal in a bunch of dots, a tail materializes. So does a dorsal fin, the trailing edge of a gill plate, and finally a head. Now we can clearly see a trout, one that has been there all the time, and it seems hard to believe we could have missed it at first. But if we turn away for a minute, we'll have to work to place it again. Even from a perfect spot for viewing, it is difficult to find a trout. If we were down below, trying to peer through slightly riffled water, it would be nearly impossible.

The trout's tail is swaying almost imperceptibly, like a drunk standing at a bar, trying to appear sober as he talks to his wife. It is this movement that allowed us to spot the fish at first. The trout's head is just barely touching the trailing edge of the rock, like the tips of the drunk's fingers surreptitiously using the barstool for support. The trout, however, is anything but inebriated. It is as alert as an animal can be, constantly scanning the water ahead for food and the air above for predators. This is what it will do, without interruption, for the next fifteen hours.

As we watch the trout, we see a slight quickening of the tail motion as he spots something drifting his way, and he tips his head up, slides upward using the force of the water for lift, opens his mouth, and then tips his head down again, using the current to force him toward the bottom. The current has pushed him back about a foot, and with several beats of his tail he returns to his original position. This return to position is the first time the trout has

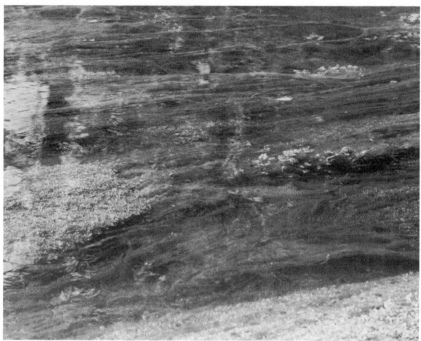

A wild brown trout lying just above a clump of weeds. Can you spot it?

had to swim, as the movements to intercept the food were merely adjustments to the hydraulics of the current. He moved upward about eight inches, staying well below the surface, and there was no lateral movement at all.

Thirty seconds later the trout's tail motion again betrays his interest in something, and this time he darts to the side, simultaneously moving upward with a tip of his head. A single beat of his muscular body propels him a foot sideways to take a piece of food. He returns to position in the same way. We notice a slight chewing motion, which people who have studied the feeding behavior of trout call "handling time." The bigger the item of food, the longer the handling time. Biologists have determined that with an average aquatic insect, plentiful food, and an active trout, the maximum rate of capture is .67 pieces of food per second (a handy piece of trivia to whip out at your next cocktail party). A few seconds later the trout moves forward six inches, this time without raising his head;

he stares at the bottom for a second, wiggles his snout between two rocks, and plucks something directly off the gravel.

Is Selectivity So Mysterious?

We have just seen the three main feeding strategies of a drift-feeding trout. Jenkins and others noticed that the first technique is by far the most common, with the sideways dart less common, and direct feeding off the bottom the least common of the three. This hierarchy of feeding strategies makes perfect sense, because a successful trout will use as little energy as possible to capture his food. Precise casting to where you think a trout may be is essential when fishing blind, because your fly has a slim chance of being eaten unless it is drifting directly in front of a trout.

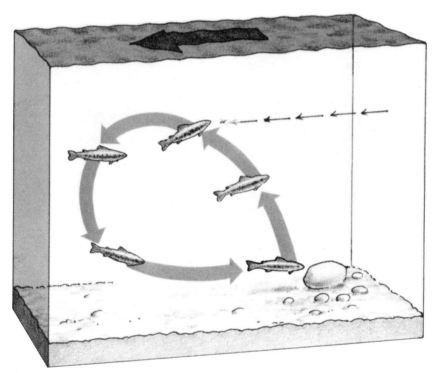

A trout is lying in his position at A. He rises to a piece of food at B, eats it (or refuses it) at C, and drops down at D. The only time he swims is between E and A.

What has our trout been eating? If we could get closer to the water without spooking the fish, we'd see many kinds of objects drifting in the current, including bits of decaying vegetation, twigs, small pebbles rolling along the bottom, midge pupae, caddis larvae, and various mayfly nymphs ranging from a size 20 Blue-Winged Olive to a meaty size 10 March Brown. In June the March Brown nymphs are abundant in the current because they are hatching during the day, and this flattened nymph leaves its sanctuary under flat rocks and migrates into the shallows in preparation for hatching. Some are drifting free in the current, wiggling with pitiful motions that seem to get them nowhere; others are clambering along the bottom.

Contrary to what you read about what trout select as food, our trout is not eating the smallest insect drifting on the current. Trout can and do eat small insects: studies have shown that they will choose insects as small as 2mm (smaller than a size 28 hook). But they prefer to eat the largest abundant and recognizable food, so our fish is choosing the March Brown nymphs. It is also eating size 14 caddis pupae. Right now, though, it is ignoring the smaller Blue-Winged Olive nymphs, not because it doesn't like them or they are not abundant enough, but because there is larger food available. D. M. Ware, a biologist who studied the influence of hunger, prey density, and prey size on the feeding activity of rainbow trout, found a positive correlation between the size of prey and the distance from which they were approached. As long as insects or other pieces of food are of recognizable shape, size, and perhaps color, trout will notice the larger ones first and may just ignore the smaller ones. Ware also found that fish can elevate their reactive distance, the distance from which they notice a food item and begin to move for it, if they acquire sufficient experience with a particular prey. Let's watch our trout for a moment and see how this works in the real world.

Imagine we can not only see the trout but also identify every piece of stuff drifting in the current. Here comes a twig, just a little larger than the March Brown nymphs and about the same shape and color. The trout eats the twig and in a flash spits it out. Trout have excellent sensors inside their mouths, and the stiff, hard feel of the twig is immediately recognized as unpalatable. When fishing with artificial flies, you must strike immediately, because as soft and natural as some of our flies look to us, they are certainly not as soft as insects. Nor do they taste like insects, and a trout's taste buds are also highly refined. Trout make mistakes in feeding because the only way they can switch from one food to another is to experiment, but you can be sure this trout has learned from the experience and will recognize the next twig as something to pass up.

Neil Ringler, an often-quoted biologist who has spent much of his life studying brown trout feeding behavior, saw that trout in a laboratory environment don't always feed on the largest or most abundant food, but they will select a combination of different foods that maximize the number of calories they ingest. Trout also constantly sample new foods, which may help them find untried prey that are even more efficient. They can also select foods by recognizing unpalatable ones. When Ringler fed trout both mealworms and caterpillars, even when he increased the number of caterpillars the trout saw, they greatly preferred the smaller—and less abundant—mealworms.

There is a tendency by fishermen to distrust laboratory tests like this, but I've taken Ringler to difficult pools on the Battenkill for years, ever since he tried to drill the fundamentals of population dynamics and vertebrate ecology into my skull almost twenty years ago. I can assure you that anyone who wields a bamboo fly rod and size 16 Adams the way Ringler does is not about to lead us fishermen astray.

Behavioral scientists have found that the physical features of prey are as important to a feeding trout as size and abundance. Although our trout now faces a conundrum that seems to be too much for his tiny brain—namely how to distinguish the March Brown nymphs from similar-looking twigs—happily for him trout are quite good at this, and it's suspected that one of the ways they do it is to look for movement in the prey. March Brown nymphs have distinctive gills that undulate constantly like the legs of a centipede, so our fish will look for this feature every time it moves for a March Brown. It is not afraid of the twigs—it just ignores them after a quick inspection. You have just seen selectivity at work, the same process that makes a trout ignore your fly if it is not close enough to what the trout recognizes as food. The trout that ignores your fly does not associate it with you, the dangerous predator; it just does not recognize your fly as something good to eat. If a trout didn't use this selection process, it would soon starve to death by wasting its energy eating twigs.

Most of the time, however, we fishermen overestimate the selection process. We act as if trout sit and wait for major hatches, as if they mimic our sitting on the bank, waiting for the Hendricksons or the Pale Morning Duns. In extreme cases we act as if they only eat March Brown nymphs underwater. But trout are opportunists; they must feed almost constantly, and if they ignore all species of insects to the exclusion of a single type, they can't survive. Only during a major hatch, when one insect is abundant and easy to capture, do they pursue a single-minded feeding strategy. And that kind of opportunity is not as common as fishing books and magazine articles lead you to believe.

Returning to our trout, we see him eat a couple of March Brown nymphs and then a caddis pupa, which is large enough to attract attention and is a food that it recognizes from past experience. Looking ahead of the trout, we see two small Blue-Winged Olive nymphs drifting down beside a March Brown, and the trout takes the March Brown, ignoring the smaller flies. If we leave the stream to have some breakfast and come back in two hours, we'll see that the March Brown nymphs are no longer drifting in the current; the daily migration usually ends as soon as sunlight hits the water, and on this stream the nymphs don't hatch until midafternoon. The trout is still eating a few caddis pupae, but he's now started to notice the Olives, and he's eating them with the same interest he showed in the March Browns earlier. He is still ignoring the much smaller midge pupae.

Looking upstream of the trout, we see a large, size 8 stonefly nymph drifting toward him. It drifts about two feet to his left side, and as it gets closer the fish darts over and eats it. This is the farthest he has moved to eat all morning. Because the nymph was large and had a form he recognized, he took the chance of wasting a considerable amount of energy to move those two feet. This is an example of an elevated reactive distance, and it argues for using the largest recognizable food form when fishing blind. If you're enticing a trout to move five feet, your Woolly Bugger or Wulff had better be large

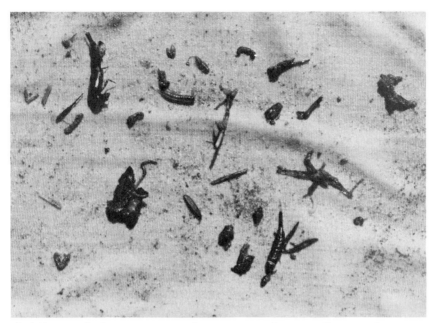

A drift sample from a stream. It contains a few mayfly nymphs, some midge larvae, and a great deal of inedible junk. Can you pick out the nymphs?

The trout from page 4 takes a nymph under the surface. Can you see the white flash as he opens his mouth?

enough to be worth the trout's while. At the same time it shouldn't be bigger than something he is used to eating, and its form should be one the fish recognizes as a tasty prey.

Ten feet from our trout and next to the bank is a shallow place teeming with young-of-the-year trout, dace, and chubs. Why doesn't he take a spin through the shallows and eat some of these high-energy morsels? Adult trout can sense, through experience and inherited behavioral patterns, whether a particular prey can be captured without wasting too much energy. A threshold level of capture must be achieved before a trout will persist in a particular hunting pattern, and the trout knows that a minnow in clear water and in bright daylight has a significant speed and maneuverability advantage. Under the right circumstances a trout can hunt minnows with deadly precision, but right now our trout is better off behind his rock.

A pair of mergansers flies up the river, low to the water. As they pass over the trout, twin shadows flank him, and he darts with the speed and practice of a tight end running for the goalpost to a submerged log six feet upstream. You can tell he's done it before. Huddled next to the log, the trout is nearly invisible from above, protected from anything that might dive onto him. He stays there, motionless, for fifteen minutes, and then he begins to drop down-stream, tail first, swaying his body to steady himself in the current, until he reaches the same rock he has occupied all morning. He finds it without really looking.

How Their Senses Keep Them Safe and Well-Fed

Of all the trout's senses vision is by far the most important. They have a highly refined olfactory sense, but thankfully for fly fishermen they seldom seem to use it except in muddy water (can you imagine what a freshly tied fly, reeking of head cement, smells like to a trout?). Fish can "hear" vibrations quite well, using motion sensors that lie along their lateral line, and this sense comes into play in dark or dirty water. But vision is the sense they rely on most. In their retinas trout have special receptor cells that are sensitive to move-ment, cells that are common in many predator and prey species but lacking in humans. They also have special nerve cells that perceive new objects in their visual field, pretty handy for spotting food drifting into view, or for watching for predators above.

Recent studies have shown that trout see color almost exactly as we do. This knowledge enables us to choose flies that match what we see hatching or on the bottom of a river. If you seine a river and see a lot of brownish olive nymphs in your sample, you can safely assume that the nymph in your fly box most similar to the natural in size and color will appeal to the fish. A trout's eye has an aperture much larger than a human eye, and just like an f1.2 lens it lets in more light. As a result they can see better in the dark than we can. In fading light a trout's cone cells, used for daytime color vision, move back into its retina, while its rod cells, used for monochromatic vision in dim light, move toward the surface. So the color of your fly is much more important during the day than in the early morning, evening, or night.

When focusing on an object two feet away, a trout sees clearly to infinity, at least to the limits of the physical properties of water and air. When it starts to focus on something closer, such as a nymph drifting by or a floating insect, its depth of field shortens. A trout focusing on an object one foot away sees clearly only from eight inches to two feet, and a trout concentrating on tiny Trico spinners two inches in front of his nose sees only a fraction of an inch before and behind the bug. If we ignore the refractive properties of water for a minute, this means that a trout looking at your Woolly Bugger two feet in front of him can also keep sharp vision peeled for predators—like you—and still move in for the fly. If he were hovering just under the surface, concentrating on flies in front of his snout, you might not be in focus, but he has other receptors that detect motion. Unless you move slowly and do all sorts of contortions, he's going to spot you.

A trout's head can't turn independently of its body, so having our puny 180-degree field of vision would be inconvenient and probably fatal. Seeing independently with each eye, trout have 330 degrees of horizontal vision and 160 degrees of vertical vision. They use a narrow cone of binocular vision in front for most of their feeding, which makes sense because only within this limit do they enjoy depth perception. (Imagine trying to eat mayflies in front of your nose with one eye closed.) This knowledge is a great advantage

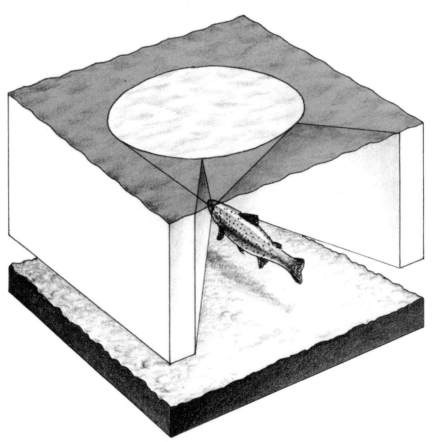

A trout's cone of vision and the blind spot behind it.

in nymph or dry-fly fishing. If you plop a fly directly beside a spotted fish, where it is sure to be outside his binocular vision, sometimes he'll bolt in fright, but often he will turn on a reflex, and without ever really having seen your fly, he will take it with a fury.

A trout can't see far underwater, nor can any animal, because water, even distilled water, scatters light rays much more than air. Add to this the effect of air bubbles in a riffle, plus the suspended matter that is always in trout steams to one degree or another, and it's unlikely a trout can see any submerged object more than twenty feet away. Smaller objects that require high resolution need to be much closer. In most trout streams a few feet is probably the limit for spotting a size 12 fly underwater, especially if there is any turbidity. This is why prospecting for trout requires precise casting skills. By learning how to read the water well, you can eliminate unproductive casting and put your fly where the trout will see it.

Now I touch on a subject that I view with distrust and distaste: the famous Window. I do so with trepidation because I don't think that a trout cares that the wings of a fly are the first to enter into his above-water vision because he can *always* see the parts that are resting on and under the surface, before he sees the rest of the fly. I think a lot of talented fishermen have spent too much time peering up through bathtubs (oh, you've done it, too!). Anyway, this isn't a book about hatches, so we don't have to dwell on what I think is one of the more pedantic theories in an otherwise fascinating sport. Did you really want to read about Snell's Law and see some formulas full of cosines?

A trout's window, or view of the world above, is always studied as if the water's surface were smooth. In most trout streams, however, the surface is so riffled that a fly at window's edge is hard for a trout to discern. What is important about the window is how it affects a trout's perception of danger, and how we can use that perception in our approach. Because light rays entering water bend at different angles depending on their angle of incidence, a trout's view of the outside world is distorted. Light entering the water from directly overhead to about 35 degrees above the horizon suffers little distortion, but below 35 degrees light is compressed into an increasingly narrow zone to a point where trout can't discern objects. Light entering the water from 5 degrees above the horizon is distorted 2,000 percent. Since the laws of optics are fixed, a trout carries the same window wherever it goes, and although it is thought that a fish that is deeper in the water can see more of the outside world, in fact the fish's view is just less distorted. Trout can always see the entire area above the water, but a fish in shallow water has tremendous distortion and compression of events near the horizon. A trout in deep water, especially clear, unriffled water, sees the outside world with less distortion, so it can also see your fly from farther away. When fishing over deep holding water, long casts and careful approach are advised.

The Olives that have been drifting all morning have begun to hatch. We see a few break their nymphal shuck at the surface, and coal black wings appear, shrunken stubs that seem to puff up like inflatable toys, the dark color changing to dun gray as the fly worms the rest of its body free. The adult flies, caught by waves of turbulence, whirl like helicopters out of control, then lift off in a stately flight, as if the thought of leaving the water they have lived in for a year returns their composure. You would think our trout would instantly rise to the occasion (if you'll excuse the pun). He does not. The trout continues to feed underwater, ignoring the hatch.

How many times have you seen this, standing in the water, screaming for the fish to respond to a hatch?

When Do They Rise?

Just as trout key in to the shape and size of their preferred prey, they also develop single-minded preferences about what layer of the water column to feed from. The speed of a river's currents vary greatly from top to bottom. The bottom velocity can be around one foot per second (the speed most trout prefer to lie in); the midwater velocity can be four or five feet per second (a speed that brings trout enough food to keep them interested); and the surface velocity can be over ten feet per second. Moving up through the water column wastes energy and exposes trout to predators as much as moving to the side. It just doesn't look like much of a risk to us because we see trout from above. Dr. Neil Ringler, studying wild trout brought into the laboratory from the Au Sable River system in Michigan, found that trout alter their feeding level in the water column based on a certain rate of prey capture. In other words, at the height of the hatch, when most of the nymphs that were drifting in the current are floating, the fish's interest in subsurface feeding will wane because he is not capturing enough food. He begins looking else-where—like at the surface. In another study rainbows were found to lose interest in subsurface feeding when the rate of insect capture fell to fewer than 3.5 prey per minute. This behavior in the water column is one of the important reasons why trout don't always respond to a hatch, why prospecting with a dry fly in deep water is not a good idea, and why even a perfectly tied weighted nymph fished right on the bottom can go uneaten.

How do trout first notice surface food if they have their noses glued to the bottom? Let's return to our trout for the next five minutes to find out. There he is, monotonously grazing Olive nymphs from the drift. One of the nymphs he has moved for rises

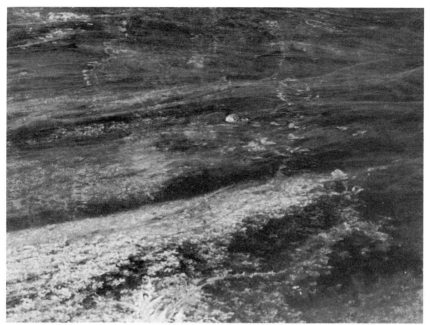

Our brown trout rises to take a fly. Notice how much easier it is to spot him.

quickly, though, and the trout takes it just as it reaches the surface. A rise. The first one we have seen this morning. Now the trout knows that food can be had up above, and a couple more passes at an emerging fly might tempt him to switch to plucking duns off the surface.

Even though this trout has eaten hundreds of nymphs, if we had been standing at water level the rise would have been our first indication he existed. Wouldn't we have seen the trout flashing underwater as he ate the nymphs? Probably not. I've seen them flash when they are spooked, or when they are chasing a minnow or streamer. I see suckers flash all the time when they feed, and trout sometimes hold behind schools of suckers, picking up nymphs the suckers uproot. Friends who fish spring creeks tell me trout sometimes roll on their sides when rooting out scuds from under weedbeds. Trout are so well camouflaged, and their movements are so economical, that a sideways flash seems as likely as a smile from an IRS auditor.

Our trout continues to feed on the Olive nymphs and the duns, alternating between a few nymphs and a rise to the surface when a floating fly catches his attention. It is not a heavy hatch. The fish also takes caddis pupae when they drift by, as they are still recognized as food. After an hour the Olive hatch dwindles, and the trout loses interest in food near the surface because he no longer achieves the threshold level of capture. A beetle falls into the water about two feet to the trout's side, out of his binocular vision, but the sound is a tempting splat, and the fish whirls and quickly scoops the insect from the surface.

A fisherman approaches. We assume the trout is an easy mark and will take any reasonably presented fly. The fisherman has seen the rise and approaches the trout from downstream, kneeling and casting sidearm to avoid spooking the fish. He makes a cast with an ant imitation, a wise choice since it is a form the trout will recognize—and we know the trout is on the lookout for terrestrial insects. He casts two feet upstream of the fish, and the trout sees the fly pushing against the mirrored surface of the water, at the edge of his window. Unseen by the fisherman, the trout moves for the fly, but as it approaches it begins to drag slightly, as the leader is pulled by a contrary current. The trout turns away and the fly passes unmolested. On the next cast the trout again sees the ant but recognizes it as something unnatural. Because of the drag on the previous cast the trout is not afraid of the ant; he just does not view it as food. The fisherman makes a third cast, dumping the line on top of the fish. Fins quivering nervously, the trout settles deeper in the water; if left this way undisturbed he will not feed for about another five minutes. But the fisherman moves, and as he does his leg pushes some waves upstream, which the fish feels with his lateral line. The trout again bolts to the protection of the upstream log. The fisherman stays put and changes flies a half-dozen times, casting over a void. He finally gives up and climbs up the bank, muttering about the wisdom and selectivity of the trout in this stream. We know better.

Knowing About Territory Can Help You Catch Bigger Trout

After a half hour the trout returns to his position and continues feeding, eating several different kinds of food, including some ants that are falling into the water, some March Brown nymphs, one big, fluttering March Brown dun that catches his attention, and some caddis pupae. Despite the absence of a major hatch he is feeding steadily. After an early dinner we return about six o'clock to find that our trout is no longer in the same spot. He is not hiding in his log refuge, either. If we had been around twenty minutes ago, we would have seen him slip over to a different rock, about five feet to his left and downstream. Another, smaller trout was occupying the spot our fish wanted, and he approached the smaller fish from the side, body stiff and fins erect, bristling like a cat with its neck hairs up. The smaller fish took the message, turned, and moved downstream to an alternate site. Trout, especially the dominant fish, usually have several sites that they use thoughout the day. They move from one to the other depending on light conditions, food availability, and the presence of other fish. These sites are seldom more than ten feet apart. I hesitate to use the word territory, because unlike many animals a trout carries his "territory" with him when he moves.

This information comes in handy when you're fishing for visible trout, because sometimes you'll see a fish move and you may think you spooked it. It's best to hang around for a while to see if he resumes feeding. You may have made him just nervous enough to switch positions but not to stop from feeding or to bolt for cover. If you have spotted the precise position of a trout, then the next time you return to try for him, it's better to assume he may be anywhere within a corresponding room-sized area.

It's also vital to know that a trout defends a lobe-shaped area in front of him that corresponds to his field of view. The smaller trout that our friend displaced can return directly behind our fish, but the minute the subdominant fish comes up alongside, the larger fish will drive him off. If you are fishing a pocket that you suspect contains a good fish, such as a deep slot in a riffle, you will most often find the largest trout in the uppermost position, with smaller fish trailing off behind in decreasing order of size. This position is an adaptive mechanism that assures the strongest fish first crack at the food supply.

In trout populations with high densities you'll see various kinds of territorial bouts, which are called agonistic encounters. The most

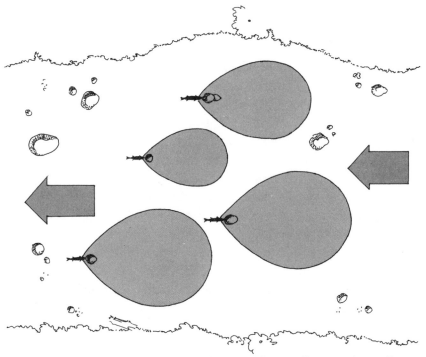

Lobe-shaped territories in front of trout. They will carry these "territories" with them if they move.

common is the erect fin display. Because trout can't afford to waste energy competing directly, this is usually all that is needed. Sometimes, however, the dominant fish will slowly back downstream toward the smaller fish, driving it away. In severe encounters, when the smaller fish won't take the hint, the dominant fish will give chase, using cross-body blocks, and in the most extreme case will actually bite. You usually see this only during spawning.

Jenkins saw four main advantages to territorial behavior in trout. While knowing why trout are territorial may not give you a clue as to what fly to use on the third of June in the Beaverkill, it provides a succinct overview of some of the behavioral tactics we've seen in our trout. First, territoriality improves the chances of dominance in agonistic encounters. In other words the first trout to occupy a choice place has squatter's rights and will be harder to remove even if the invader is bigger or more aggressive. Second, a trout that stays in a familiar place always knows where to find his escape hatch—his log or the big rock he hides under when danger threatens. If he's in an unfamiliar place and has to run for cover, the extra seconds it takes to find a hideout may turn him into tomorrow's heron droppings. Third is the advantage of more efficient feeding, or learned energetics. A trout that remains in one place maximizes its energy intake by learning which currents carry the most food, and when it might be worth the risk to eat from the fast current lanes. Finally, there might be unknown dangers upstream or downstream. A trout does not grow old by taking risks.

How Important Are Sunlight and Temperature?

This day is hot and the sun is bright. As a result few insects drift in the current or on the surface. The water temperature has risen to almost 70 degrees. Our trout does not see any more food in his second spot, so he moves to yet a third location: over near the bank, at the outside edge of the shadow of an overhanging maple. Trout have no eyelids, and their pupils cannot constrict to limit the amount of light entering, so our fish may be more comfortable in the shade. There are conflicting theories about how much light a trout can tolerate. At times they appear to avoid bright light, yet Bob Bachman says he has seen plenty of large brown trout right out in the open, at least when the feeding is good. Apparently the discomfort associated with bright light can be overcome by the lure of an easy meal. Although a trout that has moved into the shade may not be feeding as actively as one out in the open during the day, it still might be induced into taking the right fly.

Brown trout seem to be more sensitive to bright light than rainbows or cutthroats. In a study that compared brown trout to Apache trout (a subspecies of cutthroat), cans were placed on the bottom of a study stream. When exposed to bright light, browns spent 88 percent of the time hiding in cans, but Apaches in the same stream used the cans only 6 percent of the time. The browns also appeared to frighten more easily; although they outnumbered the Apaches twenty to one, fishermen caught fifty-five Apaches for every four browns. These findings confirm my observations and those of most fishermen. In streams that contain browns in addition to brook trout, cutthroats, or rainbows, you'll catch the other species all day long in bright sunlight. At dusk the brown trout seem to come out of nowhere to feed.

Temperature is as important as any other environmental factor in determining when and how much a trout will eat. Seventy degrees approaches the discomfort range for brown trout, and although I have had wonderful dry-fly fishing with the water as high as 75, it takes abundant food to get them to feed at that temperature. As temperatures climb above the 70-degree mark, a trout's metabolism speeds up so much that no amount of food can compensate the energy expended trying to get it. At the same time the amount of oxygen that water can hold decreases. Somewhere approaching 80 degrees a trout literally suffocates. At the other end of the scale, below 50 degrees a trout's metabolism is very slow, almost in suspended animation. From 55 to 65 degrees is an optimal temperature range for brown trout, and at these temperatures they sometimes seem to eat everything in sight.

These temperature rules are not without exceptions. In some icy rivers, where the water never gets above 60 degrees, trout feed

In the lush meadows of midsummer a stream that gets too warm can suffocate trout.

happily at temperatures well below optimum, while in the thermal areas of the Firehole in Yellowstone Park, rainbows feed at close to 80 degrees. Local races of fish can adapt to extremes in temperature. There are differences among species as well: rainbows, in my experience, feed actively through a broader temperature range. In one of our local rivers that supports wild rainbows and browns, I catch rainbows a full week earlier in the spring, and during the summer heat they are eager while the browns are sulking in the shade and at the mouths of cool springs. Brook trout and cutthroats are both creatures that evolved as glacial relicts; when the Wisconsin glaciers retreated, these two species adapted to colder water temperatures remaining in high mountain lakes and headwater areas. They start to feed in colder water than browns (around 45 degrees), stop feeding before the water hits 70, and die at about 75.

I have had inconsistent fishing in very high and very low water temperatures. On mornings before a heavy hatch of early season flies like Hendricksons or Olives, the fishing is sometimes unusually slow, even when there are nymphs drifting in the current. When this happens, sticking a thermometer into the water almost always shows that the water temperature is below 50 degrees. The same thing often happens when the water is above 70. An English biologist named Elliott, studying the relationship between feeding by brown trout and temperature in a Dartmoor stream, concluded that feeding is erratic at either temperature extreme. The amount of food eaten increased from 37 to 55 degrees, remained constant and high from 55 to 65, and decreased rapidly from 65 to 79. Trout were inactive and reluctant to feed below 43 degrees, and very active but reluctant to feed above 65 degrees. The high activity above 65 degrees might be a function of an avoidance mechanism: when the water gets too warm, trout move until they find a cool spring or feeder stream.

Temperature-related behavior is important to understanding why you don't catch trout sometimes, especially in the early and late season. In the optimum temperature range trout wait for food, constantly look for it, seek it out, and when you fish at these times they seem to be in an agreeable mood. If the water is too cold or too hot, however, there must be plentiful food: your single fly passing by their noses may not induce them to feed. You need that stimulus of hundreds of pieces of food drifting in front of them when

In cold water like the Bighorn in November you'll have to use some special techniques.

they're inactive, and even repeated casting to the same spot may not be enough to pull trout out of their torpor. I'll tell you about some ways to catch trout even if they're almost frozen to the bottom, and before we're through I'll also give you more scientifically legitimate excuses for getting skunked.

The Evening Hatch—and After

The sunlight is touching only the tops of the hills surrounding our stream, and in minutes the sharp rays will be replaced by softer, indirect light; March Brown duns will start to emerge from the bottom of the river, and spinners of the same species will come out from under streamside leaves, where they have been hiding from the desiccating rays of the sun. The spinners begin migrating up-stream, with a bending and swaying that hints of more intelligence and caprice than a bug's brain can produce. Shortly we'll see how our trout responds to the evening hatch with behavior that appears to contradict the stark logic of his daytime behavior.

Our fish begins the evening by feeding on the March Brown nymphs now rising to the surface, just as he did for the morning. There are many March Brown duns fluttering on the surface, but so far he has not made a move toward any of them, although smaller trout all around have begun to take the duns with splashy rises that reveal their eagerness and inexperience. The noise of the smaller fish makes our larger trout take notice. He can hear their rises through his lateral line. He takes one of the March Brown duns with a deliberate motion that makes no splash, and as he is looking for another dun he sees a couple of spinners lying spread-eagle on the surface, easier prey than the fluttering duns that are about to take off.

Three things happen: First, he starts to look for spinners, as he has had much experience with this kind of insect and knows it provides an easy meal. His instincts are good: spinners are rich in protein because of the egg-laden bodies of the females. Trout are able to learn the cycles of abundance of their food and to take advantage of instances like this. Second, he changes his search pattern in the water column and looks only at the surface, ignoring food drifting underwater. Third, he moves into a slower, shallower spot, and instead of lying on the bottom and rising up for each spinner, he hangs just under the surface, sipping the insects without missing a beat, so that the rings from one rise intersect with the next.

Smaller fish are all around him now, well within his lobe-shaped territory, and he makes no move to chase them away. Territory collapses during periods of food abundance, and he'll let those smaller fish stay around until the spinner fall ends. During a heavy hatch trout often concentrate in a spot with slow current—a place that offers especially efficient use of energy—to hang below the surface and feed. With what you have just learned, you'll realize why it's so easy to catch trout during the evening hatch. The other trout near him give him confidence and comfort, the fading light makes it harder for him to see predators (and harder for predators to see him), his window on the outside world is smaller because he is so close to the surface, and his depth of field is shallow because

The evening hatch is when a trout breaks the daytime rules.

he is focusing on objects an inch or so away. The abundance of food may also make him preoccupied with feeding and less concerned with predators. It's no wonder we love the evening hatch so much—everything is in the fisherman's favor.

In the next hour our trout eats several hundred spinners, and as it gets completely dark he moves back to the spot where we first saw him in the morning. He chases several smaller fish away from his territory. A few spinners remain on the water, and our trout can still see them (even though we can't), but he is satiated. At a certain point trout do get full, and stretch receptors in their stomachs tell them to stop feeding. Elliott, observing brown trout feeding on small mayflies, found that satiation took anywhere from 20 minutes with a small trout to 150 minutes with a larger one. With satiation comes a stop in feeding and a resumption of territorial behavior.

Trout feed at night, especially the larger ones and especially brown trout. At thirteen inches our trout is at a turning point in his life, where drift feeding alone will barely balance the amount of energy expended with the amount of energy obtained. To break out of this size class and continue to grow, he'll have to change his feeding strategy dramatically, because most trout rivers don't have enough insect life to support *drift-feeding* trout larger than thirteen inches. In the Owens River, Jenkins saw some very large brown trout that never fed on insects in the drift; in fact he never saw them feeding at all. These fish did not get large and could not stay large without great amounts of food, so they must have been feeding at night. Most other students of trout populations have seen, like Jenkins, that the bulk of stream trout are mostly sedentary, smaller fish that stay in one place and let food come to them. There is a smaller population—less than 10 percent—that is mobile and hunts for food, and if it is a brown trout population much of this hunting is done at night.

I have done a lot of night fishing for trout, and by night fishing I don't mean staying after the hatch for a few minutes and pounding a dry fly into the darkness. During a heavy hatch or spinner fall at dusk I've caught rainbows and brook trout under a bright moon, but never on a cloudy night or during a new moon. On nights when I didn't even put on my waders until just before midnight, I have caught only browns. It's thought that brown trout have a higher concentration of rod cells in the retina, which helps them pick out food in low light. A study of night feeding habits of brown trout and Apache trout found that Apaches needed bright moonlight to feed after dark, while browns could feed when there was no moon, using the pale light of distant stars.

Our trout has not yet reached that predatory, night-fishing stage, but if he grows larger than fourteen inches he will. Now he will spend the night hugging the bottom, in the semialert state that passes for sleep in fish, and he will begin to feed on drifting nymphs again tomorrow morning before it is light enough for us to see him. By now you're itching to get on the stream and apply your new-found knowledge of trout behavior, but bear with me. Before we start to look at ways of catching trout in between those easy hatch times, we need to explore the environment in which trout live. In the next chapter we'll learn how to predict where trout will be found, and how to choose a fishing strategy just by looking at the water.

RICH AND POOR TROUT STREAMS

Let me tell you about a couple of my favorite trout streams. One is Armstrong's Spring Creek, on the O'Hair Ranch in the Paradise Valley of the Yellowstone River in Montana. You stop at the ranch house and pay an obscenely low fee (fifteen dollars in April, thirty during the summer) to fish one of the world's richest little trout streams, in both insect life and trout population. You can wade across its transparent riffles and barely get your ankles wet, yet every day of the year a trout over twenty inches is a possibility on a small Pheasant Tail nymph or Blue-Winged Olive dry.

The other stream flows right through my town; let's just call it Manchester Brook (loose lips crowd small streams). Manchester Brook flows with about the same volume of water as Armstrong's Spring Creek, and it is about as wide, yet the largest fish I have taken in fourteen years of fishing it was just shy of thirteen inches. Where every pool in Armstrong's holds scores of rainbows and browns over fifteen inches long, with many more small fish as well, a decent pool in Manchester Brook will offer one brook trout of ten inches, maybe an eleven-inch brown, and a half-dozen more trout of both species that, laid end-to-end, might total a couple of Armstrong's average fish.

In Manchester Brook you can blind-fish with a Hare's Ear nymph

Ed Jahn fishing Manchester Brook in August low water. I took him there only when I found he was leaving town.

or the buggy dry fly of your choice: Humpies, Irresistibles, Haystacks, and Ausable Wulffs will catch trout all season long, any time of day. Yet if you try the same tactics in Armstrong's, you're guaranteed to draw a blank. In Armstrong's you have to go two or three fly sizes smaller, and the successful flies will be of a different type from those you can get away with in Manchester Brook. If you try to prospect or blind-fish with a dry fly in Armstrong's, you'll spend much of your day looking at an unmolested fly. In general trout in rich streams won't come for a dry fly if there is nothing of interest hatching, while trout in infertile streams will come to a dry almost all day long, even if there are no insects on the water's surface. The difference between the two is geology, and nothing more.

Geology determines the entire character of a trout stream. A glance at the surrounding terrain can tell you how big the trout will grow, how much food is available to them, and how they will be distributed in the stream; it also helps you predict their feeding behavior and even what flies will work. Trout streams are made from water and rock, or rock particles like sand and silt. The chemical composition of the water comes from compounds leached from surrounding rock. These compounds encourage or discourage the growth of algae, diatoms, insects, crustaceans, and rooted aquatic plants, which form the food chain that supports a trout population. Surrounding vegetation also contributes to the food chain, as aquatic invertebrates feed on dead and decaying shore plants, but even this part of the chain is dependent on the geology of the stream's banks. The slope of a stream, which dictates its riffle-to-pool ratio, is a function of bedrock. The types of rock determine the size of the particles in the bed of the river, which in turn fixes not only the number and type of aquatic invertebrates but also the number of places trout have to live.

Armstrong's Spring Creek. It has about the same volume of flow as Manchester Brook in April, and probably ten times the trout population. John Holt photo.

If you intend to fish only to rising fish during hatches, geology and a knowledge of stream reading are unimportant. You need only sample the drift to find out what flies will work, and you know where the fish are because you can see them feeding. But when you prospect without the benefit of hatches, you need other clues to help you select flies and find fish. The relative richness of a river, which you can usually determine with a few minutes of observation, is one of the most important clues.

Manchester Brook begins high in the Green Mountain massif, which is composed of Precambrian gneiss and quartzite. The metamorphic rocks that make up its bed offer little enrichment because these rocks are mostly insoluble silica. The water is much the same as rainwater runoff—on the acidic side with little of the dissolved calcium found in richer streams. The stony, thin, acidic soil also encourages the growth of conifers, especially hemlock, which, as the early settlers of New England found, is a source of tannic acid. The water has the tea-stained look of tannin, which comes directly from the hemlocks and from humic acid formed in bogs by the decomposition of organic matter.

Now if you look at a geological map of the Paradise Valley, just north of Yellowstone Park where Armstrong's Spring Creek flows, you'll see a band of Paleozoic Madison limestone and dolomite. This band crosses the Yellowstone River valley just south of Livingston, exactly where the three famous spring creeks—Armstrong's, DePuy's (actually the lower end of the same spring source as Armstrong's), and Nelson's—flow out of the ground and into the Yellowstone. Elsewhere in Paradise Valley, where the Yellowstone flows through basement rock of gneiss, granite, and schist, the tributaries are stony, with wide channels that indicate frequent spring floods. In midsummer the stream channels are often dry, or nearly so. But where the Yellowstone cuts through the ten-mile-wide strip of limestone, the character of the feeder streams changes dramatically. The soft limestone bedrock is dissolved by the acidity in rainwater and groundwater, and pressure on the water table from the high mountains on either side of the river valley squirts water up through holes in the wormy bedrock, forcing water to the surface in artesian springs and making the feeder streams run bank-full throughout the season.

One immediately apparent difference between the two streams is stability. Manchester Brook rises and falls and rises again from rainfall to rainfall. Snow melting in the spring in the mountains above raises the water level to the edges of the banks and beyond, while during a dry summer the brook shrinks to a tenth of its former volume, only to rise to early spring levels with a summer cloudburst. On the other hand Armstrong's is monotonously constant, and when I fished it during the unprecedented dry summer of the Yellowstone Park fires, I could see no appreciable difference in flow from wet late Aprils during years of heavy runoff. This difference in stability partly explains the difference in growth rates of trout, and it also helps you figure out which flies and techniques to use in the two streams. Armstrong's never floods, so the concomitant loss of food supply, heavy mortality of young trout, and expenditure of a lot of energy by adult trout evading floodwaters don't occur. In Manchester Brook heavy mortality of both the food supply and the trout population is a yearly occurrence. Where Manchester Brook's water temperatures range from the mid-30s in winter to the mid-70s in summer, Armstrong's seldom waver from the 50s even in the dead of winter, because the water comes directly from the ground, and groundwater reflects the mean temperature of its latitude. Trout don't feed and grow when the water temperature gets below 45 or above 70, so the trout in Armstrong's are eating and putting on inches in mid-January, when the fish in Manchester Brook are in suspended animation.

There are other factors that make streams running through limestone richer than those running through quartzite, sandstone, or gneiss. Even streams that are not spring-fed but that run through limestone or other calcareous rock are much richer than those that run through mostly silicate rock. Penn's Creek in central Pennsylvania is a good example. It is hardly a model of stability—in fact, every time I have tried to fish this famous river, it has been chocolate brown and over its banks. Yet even though it does not have the rich, clear, weedy character of a spring creek, because it flows through limestone bedrock it is much richer in insect and crustacean life than similar-appearing, silicate-bedded streams.

Given smaller seasonal stability and runoff pattern, a "hard" water stream will be richer than one with "soft" water. Any rock composed primarily of calcium or magnesium carbonate will leach into water, thereby "hardening" the water and giving you a richer trout stream. The most important such rocks for our purposes are limestone, composed primarily of calcium carbonate, dolomite, or calcium magnesium carbonate, and marble, composed of metamorphosed limestone or dolomite. Many empirical studies have proven that trout grow faster and behave differently in hard water streams. A Pennsylvania study of three soft water and three hard water streams with similar drainage patterns showed that trout's growth rate was directly related to specific conductivity, which is a measure of dissolved calcium and magnesium salts in the water. Another study, in England, proved that limestone stream trout have a much lower seasonal variation in diet than those from soft water streams, and they grow faster as a result.

Before you think we're going off on a tangent far removed from learning to catch trout when there are no hatches, let's take a look at how rich streams differ from less fertile ones, and at some practical ideas that surface as a result. Assume for the time being that soft water streams are not as rich as hard water streams—you'll learn how you can eyeball the relative richness of trout streams.

Predicting a Trout's Feeding Habits

Rich trout streams have a steady, constant food supply. At the height of the richness scale are spring creeks, which differ little throughout the world. The LeTort in Pennsylvania, Armstrong's in Montana, and the Test in England have virtually the same food supply as spring creeks in Argentina and New Zealand. Twelve months a year the fish feed on midge pupae, small Blue-Winged Olive nymphs, scuds, and sow bugs. I grew up fishing a small spring creek in upstate New York, and the fly box I used when fishing this stream has served me well on spring creeks elsewhere. Although, if I fish a spring creek in midsummer, I add a couple of ant and beetle patterns, for the most part I can use the same half-dozen patterns in November or April.

Medium-rich streams like the Beaverkill, the Madison, or the Battenkill lack the constant water temperature and water level of spring creeks, but they still offer trout an almost endless buffet. The difference is that the kind of food changes throughout the season, and a nymph that trout climb all over in late April may be ignored in July. If I planned to fish a medium-rich trout stream like the Deschutes in Oregon, a river that I've never seen but hope to someday, I would not have the same confidence in the contents of my fly box, and I'd have to read up on the river, hire a guide, or stop in to a local fly shop before I chose my flies.

Relatively infertile streams offer a small and inconsistent food supply. Think of the upland brooks or mountain streams you have fished—the bouldery kind common in New Hampshire, North Carolina, Vermont, Montana, or California. Or imagine one of those boggy, tea-colored streams punctuated with beaver ponds that run through the lowlands of Maine, Michigan, and Wisconsin. Infertile streams are usually smaller—larger rivers run through wider valleys

The Ausable in New York State is relatively infertile, and as a result most of its trout are small.

and pick up nutrients from rich bottomland sediments. If a larger river runs through rocky canyons, however, it too may offer a sparse food supply. Examples would be the Gallatin in Montana, the Ausable in the Adirondacks, or the Penobscot in Maine. It can be argued that the Ausable or the Gallatin offers good hatches for the fisherman, but the day-to-day food supply, the stuff that puts inches around a trout's waist, is not as abundant as in rivers that flow through more fertile valleys.

The bad news is that you'll have trouble predicting what kinds of food are prevalent in an unfamiliar infertile stream. The good news is you probably won't have to. Further good news is that the flies you can get away with will be larger. Trout in infertile rivers don't have the luxury of being selective, because they don't see enough of any one insect to get picky about which one they choose. Either they eat every piece of food that looks remotely edible or they starve. In most infertile rivers the quantity of aquatic insect larvae available to the fish by midsummer is insignificant, and they depend on terrestrial insects that fall into the water for a great part of their food. Since they never see many of the same kind of aquatic insects, and the terrestrials they feed on are a stew of all shapes, sizes, and colors (and we've seen in the last chapter that, all else being equal, trout prefer to eat the largest morsel of food available), all you have to do is turn over a few rocks or shake the bushes and decide what is the largest edible insect they are likely to recognize.

In more fertile rivers you have to pay greater attention to what's on the menu. The trout are used to seeing multiple foods at any given time, and although they are not usually selective to a given species of insect, most of their food falls into specific parameters of size, shape, and color. If you go outside of that realm, you won't draw as many strikes. Here the largest available food item might be rare enough that trout don't recognize it. In the Battenkill, for example, most of the nymphs are small, skinny, and brownish olive—dull. If you turn over enough rocks, though, you'll sometimes find a couple of those giant black stoneflies that trout go crazy over in the Rocky Mountains. I have tried size 6 stonefly nymphs in the Battenkill year after year, with never even a touch. Not only do the trout not eat them, I bet if I could look underwater I'd see them bolting for cover when that ugly nymph rolls into the neighborhood.

I've found that in richer rivers, smaller flies are more effective. I'm not exactly sure why. Perhaps it's because smaller insect life is more abundant, and the fish are more likely to take a fly that's similiar to what they're eating, while the fish in an infertile stream grab almost anything that looks edible. On the Beaverkill in mid-June, blind-fishing during the middle of the day when hatches were sparse, I once had to go down to a size 18 caddis to catch trout even in the riffles. Big Wulffs, variants, and other attractor flies didn't even draw splashy refusals. I decided to explore a nearby tributary, which by the look of the water was nowhere near as rich as the Beaverkill. Tired of straining to see the tiny caddis, I put on a size 10 Ausable Wulff, more to enjoy watching the fly bouncing on the riffles than anything else. You know the rest of the story. In every pool there were a couple of trout eager to take the bushy fly as soon as it hit the water. This was less than a hundred yards from trout that wouldn't even look at a fly larger than a 16. Since that day I've noticed that on rich streams like the Bighorn or the Battenkill, I seldom do well blind-fishing with a fly larger than size 16 (except for streamers and during grasshopper time). On small streams or on rivers like the Ausable or the Gallatin, for between-hatch periods I can get away with size 10 or 12 nymphs and dries—although during hatches of smaller flies I still use the tiny stuff.

One of the most important clues you can get from eyeballing the richness of a river is a sense of how the trout are distributed. When you don't have the benefit of rising fish to tell you where they are, knowing where they should be saves you from fishing over unproductive water. There is nothing more frustrating than blind-fishing a piece of water, wondering if there are any trout at all underneath your fly. When I fish a stream I have never seen before and start to doubt the presence of trout anywhere near my fly, my confidence erodes and I lose concentration. As a result I can get sloppy about what I'm doing. If you know that feeling too, read on for a confidence booster.

The first time I fished the Missouri River was a lesson in the value of fishing water I would have passed up on other rivers. The Missouri is a productive tailwater, and its currents carry a rich soup of insect life all the time. Paul Roos, who was guiding my wife Margot and me, kept talking about looking for "collectors." At first I

A "collector" on the lower Henry's Fork in Idaho, similar to those on the Missouri.

couldn't figure out what he was talking about, but Paul has guided on the Missouri for over twenty years, so I kept my eyes open and my mouth shut. When Paul finally pointed out a collector, I realized he meant the slow, barely swirling backwaters along the bank and behind islands in the river, where trout waited to collect flies that had drifted out of the main current. The trout could lie just under the surface without expending much energy because the currents were nearly imperceptible. Paul used the term collectors to describe both the places and the fish, and we soon found ourselves gazing with intense concentration at water we wouldn't have given a second glance on other rivers. The Missouri is so rich fish can thrive on the extra food that peels off from the main current. I suspect that on the Missouri the bigger fish are found in the collectors: their energy expenditure is at a minimum, so they can grow bigger, faster.

There were trout in the main currents as well, but because we were fishing a Trico hatch it was easier to spot the trout in the slow water. There is no reason to think that if we were fishing blind the trout would not have been in the same spots. Trout in rich rivers are evenly distributed, all over the place, because there is enough food to support them everywhere. Even in shallow sloughs with a mud or sand bottom, spots that look more suitable for minnows or frogs, trout can be found. In fact I've noticed that large brown trout in spring creeks seem to prefer these places over the deeper channels. On the other hand, in infertile rivers trout distribution is spotty. They will not be found in backwaters because it might be an hour's wait for a piece of food to drift by, even at the height of a heavy hatch. So trout in rivers that aren't so rich frequent the logical spots, the places that scream for a well-placed cast with an Adams or Hare's Ear nymph. These logical places are the areas protected from the heaviest flow of water, but close enough to the main current so a sideways tip will allow trout to intercept food. At the edge of seams, at the tail of a pool, in front of and behind rocks, and where the head of the pool spills over a shelf—these are all logical places, and we'll talk more about them in the next chapter on stream reading.

Applying Richness to Your Fishing Strategies

This knowledge, then, can help you form a fishing strategy. On rich streams, cover all the water. Never assume that a trout won't be right in front of you, and concentrate on covering the water closest to you with repeated casts, changing flies or techniques often if you aren't getting any strikes. Armstrong's Spring Creek offers about a mile of water on the O'Hair Ranch, and they divide it among up to fifteen fishermen a day. One fifteenth of a mile of water seems like fishing in a closet until you get around a bend where you can't see any other fishermen and you stare at the water. If the trout are rising or it's sunny enough to see into the water, you won't ever want to move, unless you must stretch your legs. I've often wished that someone would tie me to a cattle stile and make me fish twenty feet of water on Armstrong's. I would be a better fisherman for the ordeal, and I would not be wanting for targets.

If you tied me to one of the hemlocks along Manchester Brook,

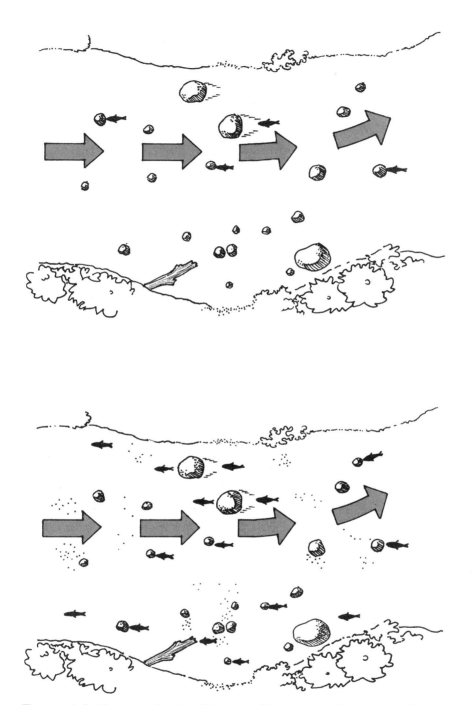

Trout in infertile rivers (top) will be found in the main flow, while those in rich streams (bottom) will be found throughout the channel, even in near-stagnant sloughs.

though, I'd be ready to gnaw through the rope in five minutes. On infertile rivers, pass up much of the water, the stuff that doesn't look fishy. Move faster between spots, then concentrate hard on the best-looking water. You can also move faster on infertile rivers because the fish don't agonize over fly patterns—so neither should you. Trout in infertile rivers will move farther for a fly, so unerring casts are not as important here, and if your fly lands within a foot of where you think a trout is lying and floats drag-free (or swings properly if you're fishing a wet or streamer), make a few more casts and move on. I don't want to suggest that you get sloppy, but many times I have seen trout in unproductive streams move five feet for a dry fly. The only time a trout will move this far on a fertile river is when there are large, meaty flies like salmon flies (a huge, size 4 or 6 stonefly that hatches on western rivers) or grasshoppers on the water.

Remember I said I was going to give you some great excuses for getting skunked? Here's one that relates to the richness of a trout stream: In fertile rivers trout appear to feed in spurts, with periods in between when they seem uninterested in any food and can't be tempted with any fly. There are exceptions: although some biologists have observed these slack periods, Bob Bachman's Spruce Creek fish never stopped feeding in the daylight hours when he could see them. Generally speaking, however, there are slack feeding periods in rich streams—not only in winter or the early season, when *nobody* argues with the fact that trout feed for only a couple of hours when the temperature climbs above 50 degrees, but during the height of the season, when water temperatures are perfect and insects are in the drift all day long. In streams that aren't so rich trout feed even at high noon and in late afternoon (times when trout from richer waters most often take a siesta). Because they never get enough food, they are on the alert all the time. As we saw in the last chapter, though, trout learn to anticipate cycles of abundance, and trout in richer streams may be able to kick back for a couple of hours in the afternoon, knowing there will be a spinner fall in the evening.

If I'm fishing a biologically productive river like the Delaware or the Bighorn and I go without a strike for a couple of hours, I don't brood, because I know the trout will switch on later. (This is assuming I have confidence in the fly I've tied on and the way I'm fishing it.) But if I fish over two pools in an infertile river without a strike, I look for another explanation. The fly I've chosen may be so far off that the trout won't look at it or someone may have just fished through the pool and spooked all the fish. I may not be fishing the fly deep enough (often the case in high, cold water), or there may be no trout in these two pools. Another possibility is that *I* may have spooked the trout with clumsy wading and sloppy casts. In any case, if the situation arises, I either pack up and move, or sit on the bank and make adjustments to my tackle and my approach.

How Many Trout Are in That Stream?

The number and size of trout a stream can support are always limited by something, but almost never by fishing pressure or other predation. Populations are usually limited by the physical features of the stream, and you can make predictions about how many trout a stream holds by an estimation of its richness. Infertile streams have little migration, stunted adults, and many juveniles. Rich streams, on the other hand, are space-limited. Trout can get enough food anywhere in the stream, and the total number of trout is limited by the number of available places to hold and feed without wasting an inordinate amount of energy. A rich stream with a bottom covered with rubble of different-sized rocks offers lots of nooks and crannies to break the force of the current, and it can hold many more trout than a stream of equal richness with a sand or gravel bottom. A spring creek with many weedbeds offers protection from the current and places to hide when danger threatens, and it can hold more trout than an equally rich stream that has been widened, shallowed, and trampled by cattle.

A food-limited stream hosts trout of many different sizes, with frequent interactions among individuals (in competition for space) and net migration downstream. This migration, usually of the largest individuals in a population, can help you find some interesting fishing on today's crowded waters. The lower reaches of many of our richest and most famous trout streams offer fishing for big trout in water usually thought to be the home of bass, northern pike, walleyes, and even carp. These lower-river trout seldom respond to

Can you spot all the trout in this photo? A spring creek offers enough food to keep all of these fish happy, even though they're in close proximity.

hatches, if indeed there are any in such warm-water habitats, so prospecting techniques will help you find them. I've explored the lower Beaverkill and Delaware in the Catskills, well out of the famous trout water, and the lower Battenkill, and I've found surprisingly good fishing for large brown trout. Friends tell me about equally good fishing well out of the supposed trout range on the Madison, Bighorn, and Missouri.

Spawning conditions are poor in these places, and most of the trout ascend to the upper river to spawn, or they use a tributary stream. As you might suspect, water temperature is the main limiting factor for trout populations in these places. You can confine your search to the mouths of tributary streams, especially in the summer, and that is a relief because the lower reaches of these rivers are often huge. On one mammoth river in the Northeast (I would be risking the attention of a hit man if I used the name), there is a tight-lipped group of local fishermen who fish a deep, wide stretch of water a hundred miles below what is considered by the local chamber of commerce to be trout water. At the mouth of each cold-water tributary stream is a whirlpool, and just before dark these fishermen launch float tubes into the whirlpools and slowly revolve into the sunset. In a stretch of water known for walleyes and smallmouth bass, they catch rainbows that average about twenty inches long.

Why Are Some Streams Richer than Others?

Now that you know some advantages to learning to gauge richness, let's explore the reasons for these differences in productivity. Calcium compounds, found in many sedimentary and metamorphic rocks, counteract acidity. The amount of biomass in a stream, particularly the pounds per acre of trout flesh, is directly related to the pH. The more bicarbonate in solution, the more acid is neutralized, and the higher the pH. The higher the pH, the more productive the trout stream. Calcium in solution is also suspected to benefit the physiology of trout directly. Apparently it helps the fish fight off toxins in the water. Plants can also pull a molecule of carbon dioxide directly off calcium bicarbonate in solution, so streams with high calcium content support more plant life. More plants mean more insects. And fatter trout.

The amount of calcium in a stream also determines the supply of one type of organism that is extremely valuable as a trout food—crustaceans. The outer shell of these animals is made from a compound high in calcium, and because they absorb it directly from the water, the abundance of crustaceans in a stream is directly related to the concentration of calcium bicarbonate. Crayfish, sow bugs, and amphipods (or scuds, as fishermen call them) are a high-energy source of food year-round. These animals do not hatch out of a river as aquatic insects do, so toward the season's end and throughout the winter, when mature insects have flown away and mated and their offspring are too small to be of much use, full-sized, adult crustaceans are available. Crustaceans are easy to capture and high in protein and fat. Wherever they are found in great numbers, you will find lots of corpulent trout. Nymph fishing is superb in

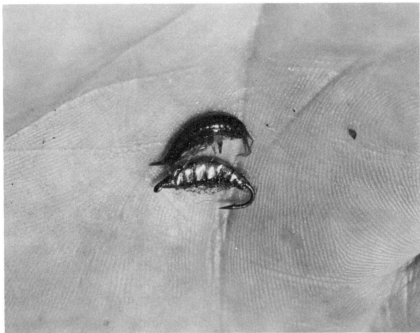

Aquatic crustaceans like this scud, shown here with an imitation, indicate rich water.

Water that looks like this will be calcium-rich, and full of aquatic insects and crustaceans.

streams with large populations of crustaceans, to the point where trout often ignore heavy mayfly hatches because crustaceans give them a source of high energy without the costly risk of surface feeding. The chapter on nymphs will give you some ideas on how to take advantage of this opportunity.

A Brief Field Guide to Rich and Poor Trout Streams

Two minerals form the bulk of freshwater buffering systems: calcite and dolomite. Calcite is pure calcium carbonate, and dolomite is mostly calcium magnesium carbonate with various impurities. Limestone is the most common source of these minerals, and the most productive trout streams in the world flow through limestone. You can spot limestone bedrock by its sedimentary layers and its brown or yellowish color. Because limestone occurs in flat layers, rocks along the banks of a river with limestone are flat plates, as opposed to the rounded igneous or metamorphic rocks of less fertile streams. Sandstone and shale, sedimentary rocks that don't contribute much to the fertility of a stream, can be distinguished instantly from limestone or dolomite with a couple of drops of vinegar or dilute hydrochloric acid. Rocks that contain calcite or dolomite effervesce or fizz when you put the weak acid on them. Did you ever think you could predict how to fish a trout stream by carrying a vial of vinegar with you?

Gypsum and marble also buffer trout streams and make them richer because they contain calcium carbonate. You can tell them from other whitish rocks, such as quartz, because they lack the large, crystalline grains you see in rocks that contain quartz. They also usually have a crumbly look, which comes from their solubility in the weak acid of rainwater. Marble is metamorphosed limestone or dolomite, and because of the heat and pressure it has undergone, it is not as soluble as limestone (sometimes you have to pulverize it before it will fizz with weak acid), but marble still offers strong buffering properties. The Battenkill flows through a valley flanked by insoluble granite and gneiss to the east and marble bedrock to the west. Its pH fluctuates from around 5 below tributaries or springs entering from the east to more than 7 downstream of tributaries entering from the west. Trout in the brooks on the eastern slope will

These limestone ledges along the Madison in Montana betray its richness at a glance.

take a big dry fly all day long, regardless of the insects hatching or the time of day, but if you hop over to the other side of the valley, the trout often ignore a blind-fished dry fly. You have to use smaller flies that look more like the insects that are hatching during the current week, and the trout seem to have periods of lockjaw when no fly will work. The trout in the western tribs are also bigger and fatter.

Rocks composed mainly of silica contribute nothing to the productivity of a trout stream because they release no carbonates into the water. Silica rocks in streams can be recognized by their smooth, rounded shapes and crystalline structure. The ones you commonly see making up the beds of unproductive trout streams are gneiss, sandstone, quartzite, and various forms of granite.

Seldom do I predict the richness of a trout stream solely by staring at the rocks. It's easier and more accurate to eyeball other clues in and around a stream and use the geology as one piece of the puzzle. For example, the color of the water can often be a dead giveaway to its richness. The tea-colored water so common in the north country indicates an infertile stream, where trout will be small, slow-growing, and eager to take almost any fly pattern. In the limestone belt of Pennsylvania many of the streams have a gray or white tint due to undissolved calcium carbonate, and the trout are well-fed, pickier about what nymph they take, and less inclined to come to the surface for a blind-fished dry fly. Water with no apparent color is not much of a help—it can indicate either a stream where all the brownish humic acid has been neutralized by carbonates, or, as in many high-altitude streams in the Rocky Mountains, water that has few dissolved minerals of any kind. Crystal-clear water can indicate purity, but absolutely pure water is less productive than water that contains some dissolved nutrients.

Civilized Richness

This is a hard pill for most of us to swallow, but water polluted with human or animal waste is always more productive than pristine water. H. T. Odum, one of the world's leading ecologists, once wrote, "Polluted streams are possibly the areas of highest primary productivity on the planet." The Bow River in Alberta is one example. Above the city of Calgary the Bow is relatively infertile and can be easily blind-fished. Below the city, where the waste of over a million people enters the river, it is fertile beyond comparison in that part of the country, and the trout show the pickiness, reluctance to feed at certain parts of the day, and hesitance to come to the surface that are common among well-fed fish. Studies in Michigan and Pennsylvania have shown that removing domestic sewage can dramatically reduce the productivity of a trout stream, while adding it can make an infertile stream rich. The same goes for water that flows through agricultural land. Sewage and agricultural fertilizer are rich in phosphates and nitrates, and the lack of these nutrients often limits plant growth in streams, so when you add them to a stream you get the same effect as when you sprinkle 5-10-5 on your sweet corn in the spring. A study in Wisconsin found that runoff from one hectare of agricultural land puts 7.7 kilograms of nitrate per year into a trout stream. This beneficial effect walks a fine line because pollutants can also increase the biological oxygen demand of a stream, especially in hot weather, and too much

Rounded quartzite boulders tell you this stream is not rich, and the trout will behave accordingly—and they'll be easy!

organic material without cool water and a lot of riffled water can suffocate trout.

Weeds in the water always indicate higher productivity, and as a result more invertebrates for trout to feed on. Watercress and stonewort thrive in alkaline environments rich in carbonates, and long, thin, bright green strands of filamentous algae tell you either that the water is rich in carbonates or that sewage or agricultural effluent is present. In a stream that runs through a town or city, you'll often notice that the bottom of the river is clean above town, while below town the rocks have a coating of algae or long strands streaming from them. The water will be richer below town, as it is in the Bow, but you should be aware that not all rivers have the head of cool water to compensate for the increased oxygen demand during the summer.

You can predict the richness of surrounding trout streams by taking a shower in a nearby house or inspecting the owner's plumbing. (You thought it was bad enough that normal people ridiculed you when you walked around in trout streams with a butterfly net. Now you're going to be knocking on doors asking for a cup of vinegar and a look at the bathroom sink.) Calcium carbonate in the water is the same stuff that causes "lime" in your plumbing. If the local water supply contains a high concentration of carbonates, chances are the nearest trout stream does, too.

Tailwaters Are Usually Rich, Too

I lied when I told you that spring creeks are the richest trout environments in the world. They are the richest *natural* trout environments. As a class tailwaters are the richest trout streams in the world, and when you think of the waters fishermen dream to wade in, you have trouble leaving out the Henry's Fork, Madison, Bighorn, Missouri, Delaware, White, Green, South Platte, or Frying Pan. All of these rivers famous for their imposing trout and plentiful hatches are made rich by the still waters above them. Dams, if they release water from the bottom of the reservoir above them, as most

Tailwaters like the South Platte can be as rich or richer than spring creeks, and the banks usually show stability, with no sign of frequent flooding.

of the famous ones do, stabilize both flow and temperature by being miserly with spring runoff and doling it out throughout the summer. Floods are reduced, temperature extremes are moderated, and growth is easier. Nutrients are concentrated in the impoundments behind dams. Trout also benefit in tailwaters because plankton is washed directly into the rivers and eaten by insects and crustaceans. Natural streams have little plankton because it's hard to maintain a population if you keep getting washed downstream, so invertebrate life in tailwaters enjoys a tremendous bonanza found in few natural environments.

How Valuable Is Rock Flipping?

You might be thinking I've left out the most obvious way of determining the richness of a river—picking up a couple of flat rocks and looking at the insects waddling madly to get away. Unless you're prepared to set up a seine, however, and trash a couple of square feet of stream bottom to get a representative sample, and then compare this sample to other streams, I don't think you will get a fair idea of richness from rock turning. You may miss the right part of the riffle and pick up rocks that are barren just by chance. You might be looking late in the season, when most of the larger insects have hatched and their offspring are too tiny to be noticed. Many of the insects in a river cannot be found by turning over rocks—you'll only find the clinging and crawling species and will miss the burrowers and swimmers. Sculpins, other forage fish, and crayfish are food chain supplements, ingredients that support big trout, but you'll seldom see them when you turn over rocks in the shallows unless you look at the place the rock *was* rather than what is clinging to it. Also these animals usually live in deeper water than you want to reach your arm into.

Looking at rocks helps you pick a nymph pattern, particularly in richer streams where the pattern choice may be important, and although it can give you a hint at a river's diversity, diversity is not as important as richness when it comes to working out a fishing strategy. Gauging the richness of a river is like "pre–stream reading": a way of looking at the river as a whole system before you start gazing at current patterns and rocks.

R EADING THE WATER

Some water that is easily fished during a hatch is tough to blind-fish with consistent success. Stream reading is a vital skill for prospecting, but you should approach a day of fishing with the philosophy that not all places in a stream hold trout, and others that may hold trout cannot be blind-fished easily.

When you cast to rising fish, you know exactly where each fish is, you have a good idea what they're eating, and you stalk one fish at a time. You know the fish are willing to feed, and if your casting is accurate you know they can see your fly. On the other hand, when blind-fishing, you must constantly keep two questions in mind: Can he see my fly, and can he see *me*? If he sees you before he sees your fly, the fish will be spooked, and even if he doesn't bolt for cover he won't be interested in eating. You must have confidence in your ability to locate unseen fish, and you must be able to make a decent presentation to the narrow range where a suspected fish can see your fly.

In general slow water is the hardest water to fish blind, for a number of reasons. Slow water is more difficult to read, because in big pools you don't have the benefit of differing currents to narrow the possibilities of where you may find a trout. In a riffle or run much of the water is too fast for a trout holding in place, and some of the water is also too shallow. Trout will be found in narrow, easily recognizable bands where fast water meets slow, deep water meets shallow, or rocks or shelves offer relief from the current. It is difficult

A giant slow pool, like this one on the Delaware, is difficult to read and to prospect for trout in.

to cover slow water without spooking the fish, because fish in slower currents get a much better look at the outside world and the food they're eating. In a riffle you can drop your line right on top of a trout without spooking him, so a thirty-foot drift will effectively cover thirty feet of water. In slow water, though, a thirty-foot drift will cover a maximum of fifteen feet, the length of the longest leader most of us can handle, and the trout lying under the fifteen feet of fly line will probably be spooked. Frankly most of us lack the patience to blind-fish slow water. The fly drifts so slowly that we lose interest and confidence in what we are doing.

You've seen fish rising in your favorite pool on another day when there was a good Sulphur hatch, so you know exactly where they are lying, right? Sorry. Those fish may be lying below the same spot you saw them rising, but in slow water, especially during a heavy hatch or spinner fall, trout often move from their normal lies into places where they can capture floating food with greater ease.

Prospecting is much easier in this kind of riffled water.

There *are* ways of finding trout in slow water, which we'll explore a little later in this chapter, and there are methods of fishing that work in slow water, which I'll talk about in later chapters. Vermont's Battenkill has miles of slow, deep water that I have tried to blind-fish with a nymph or dry during every month of the season, but I find myself spooking an entire pool before I can get a fish to look at my fly. Where a riffle punctuates the slow water, I'll do fine, but between the infrequent fast water I find myself relying on streamers, which can be fished independent of the current and for which trout will move from ten or even twenty feet away. On the other hand, when conditions are right in faster water, I can take trout on dries, wets, nymphs, or streamers.

So prospecting for trout relies heavily on riffles, runs, and pocket water, which is fine because in a heavily fished stream this is the water most fishermen ignore. When there are no hatches, I always start fishing at the head of a pool or run, in pocket water, or in a riffle, and then I graduate to the slower water if I can figure out what is going on. Fish in rough water are less easily disturbed, and they're also less wise to the dangers of artificial bugs. Trout fishing is supposed to be challenging, but I am quite content with the dumbest, least neurotic trout available if there is no hatch to even the odds.

Why Trout Need Special Places

When Thomas Jenkins built his artificial channel in Convict Creek, he found that different trout introduced into the channel separately used virtually the same feeding positions, even if a whole new group of trout replaced a previous group. The positions used didn't offer more food than the unused sites, but Jenkins thought the sites used offered better *energetics*—in other words, the fish could obtain their food without wasting more energy than they were gaining. Energetics is the basis of learning to read a stream. Trout need enough food passing by their position to have an almost constant supply, yet they need to lie in areas where the current velocity is nearly zero.

Bob Bachman has determined that brown trout prefer to lie in water with a speed from one-quarter to one-half foot per second and feed in water running about two feet per second. Rainbows generally feed in faster water, up to about six feet per second, while brook trout and cutthroats like about the same current speeds as browns. In a stream that offers all four species you'll often find the rainbows at the head of a pool and the other species in the middle and the tail of the pool, or in places where a large object slows the current. The current at the surface of a tumbling mountain stream might be ten feet per second, the fastest water in an average riffle-and-pool lowland stream six feet per second, and the middle of a slow pool at low water approaching that magic half a foot per second. This is why you'll see trout hanging just below the surface in the middle or tail of a pool during a good hatch or spinner fall at low water—the current is slow enough that the fish can comfortably lie and feed in the same place.

The usual scenario, though, is for trout to lie in slower current and dart into faster current to grab a piece of food. A fish might lie behind a rock and move to the side, where food is washed around the rock. Another fish might lie on a rubble-strewn streambed and slide up into the faster water just above the bottom. The places to look for trout are areas where fast water meets slow, adjacent to the main current. How do trout find these places? One theory is that they "hear" a particular chord of sounds with their lateral line. Apparently every place in a stream has a unique sound fingerprint.

You can find the main current by watching the line of bubbles and debris that snakes its way through a pool or run. Look up to the head of a pool and find the fast water spilling into it, then trace its path through the pool to find the places where trout anchor themselves. Understanding stream richness will help you determine how close to the main current trout will be found—in an infertile stream they will be locked onto its edges like cars waiting on a highway entrance ramp. As richness increases they will be found farther and farther away, in the side streets and alleys.

Fishermen call these current-speed transition zones seams, and if you know nothing else about reading the water, you can find trout by looking for them. If you board a drift boat with a guide, the first thing he'll tell you is to hit the seams. Loosely defined, almost any place a trout feeds is a seam, because trout almost always lie in slow water and feed in faster adjacent currents. But seams formed by two currents of different direction and velocity are especially useful because they can help you find trout where there are no bottom obstructions to break the current, or where you can't see the obstruction on the bottom. When two currents meet, there is always a pocket of relative calm within the turbulence, and often it is enough to form a place where trout can lie and feed in comfort, even when there are no rocks, logs, or shelves. Seams like this form between the slow water next to a bank and the main current, below an island where currents re-form, or along the edges of a fast chute.

Less obvious than horizontal differences in current are the vertical ones. Anytime water encounters an object, friction slows the current and causes turbulence. Water that flows through a smooth pipe is nearly laminar, meaning most of the water molecules are running in the same direction. A trout stream never approaches

The seam at the head of this riffle is easy to spot.

anything near laminar flow, as the roughness of the streambed, the banks, and objects such as gravel bars and logs slow down the water, deflect the flow from a straight downstream course, and cause turbulence. That is why water in a straight piece of stream is fastest in the center of the river, near the surface. The closer to the banks and the bottom, the greater the friction, the greater the turbulance, and the slower the downstream progress of the water. Not surprisingly, then, in a stream of reasonable velocity without midstream obstructions you find most trout near the banks or on the bottom.

Reading Surface Currents

Reading the water is often spoken about as if it's some kind of voodoo that only grizzled old men who smoke pipes and have many patches on their waders understand. They are supposed to be able to make magic predictions by translating the fingerprints of surface currents into signs that point directly to trout. Stream reading skills do improve with experience, but no good stream reader depends entirely on surface currents; in fact you should only use surface currents if you have no other clues. As a bonefish guide on Christmas Island told me, "Don't look at the water, look into it, look through it." With a decent pair of polarized sunglasses and a little training—teaching your eyes what to look for—you'll be able to see deeper into the water. You'll also be able to spot trout on those rare occasions when they are visible. Don't think it takes vision like The Man of Steel's, either. It just takes experience learning what to look for. My eyesight has always been poor, and I wear strong contact lenses so that I can use polarized sunglasses and still take them off when it rains. A friend of mine, a commercial shell fisherman, can spot a flock of gulls wheeling over the water at least a half mile before I can, yet when we fish together I can spot trout and submerged rocks that he never sees. It's simply a matter of picking up patterns.

There are times, however, when you'll have to depend on reading surface currents: when the water is too dirty to see more than a foot into it; when glare that polarized sunglasses can't block obscures the water, especially in the morning and evening; or in a riffle where bubbles and surface turbulence hide what's underneath.

Midstream Rocks

Perhaps the most overstudied situation involves a submerged rock surrounded by either sand or gravel, so the rock stands out as an obvious trout haven in an otherwise unattractive spot. When water meets an immovable object, some of the water is stopped dead, and the kinetic energy it had is transformed into potential energy. Water gets potential energy by piling itself higher and gaining altitude, and you can see this at the head of a submerged rock. A bump in the water surface shows you where the rock begins; this bump is always slightly downstream of the rock because the current pushes it. It's a comfortable place for a trout to live because the current is slowed considerably, yet food is constantly pushed to him. Sometimes the force of the current digs a hole, giving the trout a place to bolt to when an osprey's shadow darkens the water.

When water rushes over a submerged object, an area of slower water forms just behind the object, and the difference in velocity causes turbulence. If the water is sufficiently shallow and fast, the turbulence carries to the surface and tells us where behind the rock the area of slower current is located. Trout like these places behind rocks, but not always and not everywhere. When you see standing waves or loads of foam behind a submerged rock, you may not find any trout directly behind it. The current's force is too great, the swirly turbulence may make it difficult for a trout to hold his position, and the unpredictability makes it hard for him to see and to intercept his prey. The current behind a large rock or boulder may be so slow that it offers little food. Only when the rock is no larger than a television set and the current moderate enough to form gentle swirls behind it are you likely to find a trout with his nose up against the rock.

Many more trout, and bigger ones, feed at the edges of the current that swirls around a rock and near the tail of the plume that extends downstream. I call the downstream end of the V-shaped plume, where it narrows to a point, the focal point, and the focal point is usually the best spot of all for trout. Lying here, trout can feed from currents coming around both sides of the rock without fighting the violent turbulence that often forms just behind the rock.

Seldom do you find a single rock lying in a riffle or run like a spot on a clean mirror. Usually the mirror is covered with spots of all shapes and sizes, and if most of the bottom is covered with

Trout near midstream rocks, and where the bump above a big rock will appear.

The focal point
behind this rock
is a particularly
distinct one.

boulders and cobbles, fishermen call it pocket water. This stuff is a blind-fisherman's delight: the trout here usually feed all day long. They are easy to approach, and they are not too picky about their fly selection. Stand off to the side and look for places where the focal point of one nice rock intersects the bump in front of another rock, or where a family of rocks form a minipool with its own bump, edges, and focal point. Because trout feed on drift that comes in front of the rock or slides off to the sides, I avoid dropping my fly in the swirly water right behind the rock, even though it's tempting to slam your first cast right there. Try it a couple of times and you'll see why it should be avoided—placing your fly there without dumping piles of slack into the leader will give you almost immediate drag, and a trout may be put off your fly on successive casts, even if they are drag-free. A trout that is lying around looking for food but not preoccupied with a hatch can be spooked much easier by a fly that drags than a trout that is filling his face with bugs. If you begin by placing your fly in front of the rock a few times and then try a drift along each side, it will be easier to get repeated drag-free floats. The water in these places runs uniformly downstream, so it's less likely that a squirrelly current will make your fly go south when the leader is heading north.

If you just can't resist plopping your fly in that gurgling mess right behind the rock, don't use a dead-drifted nymph or dry. Try a streamer, or a skating caddis or spider—something that laughs in the face of convoluted currents.

The Head of the Pool—An Easy Spot for Prospecting

Often the water is too deep for you to pick out individual rocks, or the rocks are too small to be differentiated from the characteristic marks on the surface. Even though trout will key in on certain rocks no bigger than themselves, and fish will lie on top of or just behind certain rocks year after year, no one has come up with a formula for predicting what rocks offer exactly the right hydraulics. I hope they never do. When you can't locate the rocks, you have to use other clues. The head of a pool or run is the first place I go, because the water there is faster than in the rest of the pool, so the fish will be easier to approach and fool. (I never told you we would always force ourselves to do this the hard way, did I?) Water coming into a pool, right in the tongue as it spills over whatever obstruction forms the head of the pool, may often be too fast to hold trout. Without a log or rock to block the current's force, this part of a pool may be sterile. Usually, though, as the current entering a pool starts to flatten and slow (typically just below the standing waves, if there are any), there will be a shelf, with an area of calm water below its lip. Here trout can hold in comfort and have the pick of the current. If you can tell me how to get to them in early spring, when there are four feet of raging current above them, then you should be writing this book instead of me. Once in a while, if you twist enough lead in front of a streamer, toss it above the pool, and strip just as it drops over the lip, you might draw one out of the maelstrom. But in the early season the water generally is too cold for a trout to chase anything moving faster than a crawl, so you're out of luck anyway. You can try those guys under the waterfall in midsummer, when the current barely whispers over their heads. There are easier places at the head of the pool.

Look at the edges of the fast current on either side of the tongue, the place New Zealanders call the "eye" of the pool. If there is a bend in the river at the head of the pool, as there often is (do you know how hard it is to find a "classic" pool with mirror-image seams on either side?), there will be an inside and outside bend. Where most of the trout will be found depends on current speed. In fast current, where the water on the outside bend smashes against the bank, you'll find more trout on the inside. The outside may even be completely sterile. I once coveted a spot on a favorite trout stream where the current plowed up against the far bank, carving a dark undercut. I never saw a trout rise there and never hooked one blind-fishing, so I assumed there was a monster brown in residence. One steamy August day when even bobbing away in an inner tube looked inviting, I put on a diving mask and poked around. I was disappointed. Not only were there no trout in a place I had paid much attention to over the years, the bottom was as smooth as a beach pebble and offered not one place for a trout to get out of the current.

On the other hand, if the current is so slow that leaves and other debris collect on the inside of the bend, you'll find more trout on the faster outside, where the meager current will bring them the most food. In streams with poor to average fertility you would expect to find trout where there is at least *some* current to bring them food, but in a rich river trout can be anywhere, including those neglected backwaters. Also, if the head of a pool is formed by a gentle riffle rather than a slick tongue of fast water, you'll find trout distributed all across the riffle, not just at the seams on both sides of the tongue.

Turbulence is what makes the head of a pool easier to fish. At the tail of a pool, and usually in the middle, the water velocity is

The head of a bend pool. Notice how the flow strongly favors one side.

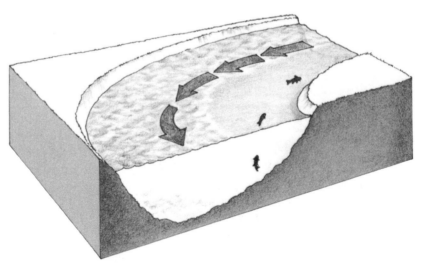

In a fast bend trout may be found more often on the protected inside of the bend.

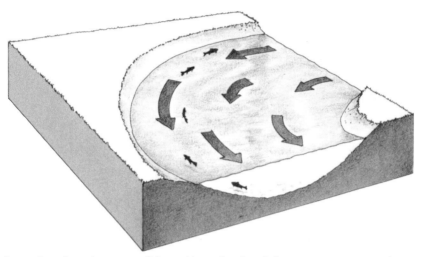

In a slow bend trout will be where the food flow is concentrated—on the outside of the bend.

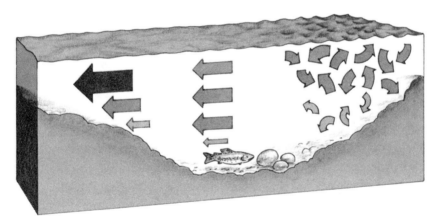

At the head of a pool water velocity is more uniform in a vertical cross section; it stratifies in the middle and tail.

stratified: faster water is at the top, where your fly enters, and much slower water is near the bottom, where the trout lie. When you cast a dry fly upstream in the tail of a pool, the water closest to you is accelerating before it dumps over into the next pool or riffle, so drag sets in almost as soon as your fly lands, making it move unnaturally.

When you cast a nymph upstream, it starts to sink, but the leader and line on top of the water are moving faster, so they begin to pull the fly upward, keeping it out of the productive water below and, again, dragging unnaturally. Your choices include dumping a lot of slack into the cast when fishing a dry or nymph upstream, using a technique that is independent of the current, such as a streamer, or using a technique that uses current to your advantage, like a swung wet fly or a skating caddis. If you're unfamiliar with these techniques, don't worry; I'll describe them in later chapters.

At the head of a pool or riffle, though, turbulence mixes the currents so they're much less stratified. The downstream progress of the water is impeded, making it easier to slip a nymph through the currents or to get a drag-free float with a dry fly. And you can still swing a streamer or wet fly through these currents, so your options are doubled.

Riffles and Soft Spots

Plain, boring old riffles are some of the easiest and most productive places to blind-fish, because the way the water moves conspires against the trout. Current speeds seem uniform both vertically and horizontally: the many cells of turbulence are so small that they produce, for practical purposes, a uniform body of water, lessening drag on a dry fly or a nymph. Contrast a riffle, with its many tiny goose bumps of turbulence showing on the surface, to a boiling slick, where the turbulence cells are larger, big enough to grab your leader and wrench your fly. In a boiling slick the turbulence may even be strong enough to push a trout out of position constantly. Since trout like predictability, if they have to fight for position or they can't accurately take a piece of food, they'll move in a hurry. Unless I'm streamer fishing or I have seen a decent trout rising in them (which is seldom), I avoid boiling slicks like a bank full of worm fishermen.

Datus Proper, in his thought-provoking and iconoclastic book *What the Trout Said*, describes places he calls "soft spots." These are places where almost anything you do will produce a strike— places that Proper takes rank beginners to bolster their confidence. Every stream I fish has some soft spots, which I have found through

A plain, boring—and easy—riffle on the Bighorn. It's a real soft spot.

experience, and I use them for special guests, children, and impatient or discouraged fishing buddies. All of the soft spots I know are in gentle riffles, lacking either strong whorls of current or the rooster tails of standing waves.

A wide expanse of riffle, whether at the head of a pool or in a transition between pools, seems at first to have no features. Look harder. First you'll notice seams at the edge of the riffle, and these are worth much of your time and effort. Out in the middle of the riffle, look for slicks—areas that look as though someone polished and flattened the bumps on the surface. Slicks are formed either when the water is too deep for the turbulence formed by contact with the bottom to reach the surface, or when the water is slowed by a plateau in the streambed or an object on the bottom. If there is enough water, all of these places will hold trout. Depth is a limiting factor for trout abundance only when the water is so shallow that trout feel insecure about holding in it. In a riffle the water may be too shallow to hold adult trout, because as a rule they need to have a foot of water over their backs and a nearby refuge. So look for the places where the water is too deep for you to see the stones on the bottom clearly; when looking at slicks, make sure they are big enough or deep enough that a trout can find a place to hide when you stumble up through the currents. A slick the size of a kitchen sink in the center of a shallow riffle might offer all the food and protection from fast currents a trout needs, but a trout won't stay alive there for long unless the merganser population has flown south for the winter.

If you can find a slick the size of a bathtub with secure cover nearby, you may find a trout that everyone else has missed. I remember one place in a shallow riffle I must have walked through fifty times without a cast. There was an old dead tree trailing in the riffle, and at the downstream end was a tiny pocket, barely deep enough to cover my ankles. I stared and thought I could see bare stream bottom, but I cast a Gray Fox Variant anyway. A brown shape formed seemingly out of the gravel, rose to meet the fly, moved without apparent haste to the tangle of branches, and broke my leader. I have been back to the same place another fifty times and have not seen that trout again.

The result of fishing a nymph in that soft spot on the Bighorn.

The Middle of the Pool

The middle of a pool also often looks featureless, without the obvious seams between fast and slow water that guide you to trout at the head. If there is nothing else to guide me, I can find the best fish the middle of a pool by tracing the main threads of current down through it. Look up to the head and follow the line of bubbles and debris carried by the current, and you'll see the best feeding positions. Even if the places where the main current flows are shallower or offer less cover than water off to the side, you'll find more trout, and especially more feeding trout, where the current brings a constant stream of food.

Look on the bottom for lines of color that show a dramatic change in depth. Trout may hide in the dark depths when you

A soft spot on New York's West Branch of the Ausable.

The featureless middle of a pool. Note the bubble line in the foreground.

stumble through a pool, but deep water doesn't offer much food. If the depth suddenly changes from eight feet to two feet, all the food being carried by the current is forced into a narrow vertical choke point, and a trout here can see all the food that the current carries. In the bottom of a hole he can see only a fraction of it. Look too for rubble on the bottom, as opposed to sand or gravel. The rougher the bottom, the greater the number of nooks and crannies that offer places to hide and pockets of slower water, energy-efficient places for a trout to live and feed. If the water isn't too slow or too shallow, you'll be able to spot these places if you can't "see" into the water by reading the roughness of the surface.

Don't Ignore Springs . . .

In the early and late season a spring or small tributary entering a pool will concentrate the fish. Springs reflect the average mean temperature of a given latitude, and because of the insulating effect of the ground they hold a constant temperature year-round, just as your basement does. So in early spring, when the river water is 45 degrees, the temperature of an entering spring could be closer to 50, a more comfortable temperature that will encourage more feeding. In August, when the temperature of the river is 72 degrees with a corresponding decrease of oxygen, the spring will be around 55 degrees, and it may often be a question of survival rather than mere comfort that keeps trout with their noses stuck into the cold water. The Firehole in Yellowstone Park is a river that suffers from high summer water temperatures because of the hundreds of geysers, mud pots, and boiling water pools that flow into it. One August day I found a cold spring flowing into the Firehole opposite the famous Ojo Caliente hot spring. There were more than twenty trout packed into a shallow, barren flat below the spring, and they were unusually spooky, but I found that a tiny Pheasant Tail nymph dropped into the crowd would get a nod if I rested the pool after the previous fish I'd taken. It was the first time I had fished the Firehole, and had I not wanted desperately to catch a trout there, I would have left them alone, as they were vulnerable and stressed by living in this crowded, exposed environment. Since that day I have avoided cool springs in extremely hot weather, preferring to fish near them only when a couple of trout have moved in for comfort, not when an entire pool has migrated there out of desperation. You're the predator, though, and you can make that decision on your own.

. . . or the Banks

Reading the water by looking at the banks is often ignored, but the banks in many streams (not just meadow streams with undercuts) are the most important fish-holding features. Unless a bank has a shallow slope without cover and is made from fine gravel or the water along it is so shallow that a trout's back would poke out, you'll

Great bank water, with a cobbled bottom as well. You'll find many trout here.

find trout somewhere along this edge. Generally one bank is better than the other. When you're fishing blind, fish are spookier than if they're preoccupied with a hatch, and because you'll have to favor one of the banks when wading up or down (unless the river is so big you have to fish the same bank you're wading), it's important to look over both banks before you enter the water.

If the river is so fast in the middle that it is difficult for you to wade, there is nothing to break the current, and there are no twists to make current seams, you can be certain that any decent trout around will be near one or both banks. Which one should you choose? Just as you evaluated the middle of the pool, look at the head of the pool or riffle to see where the current is directing most of the food. Usually the current will bounce the main volume of water toward one bank or the other. But wait, you say; trout don't need to worry about aquatic insects when they live near the banks because they have plenty of terrestrial insects falling right on top of their heads. It's true that in some rivers terrestrial insects make up the bulk of a trout's diet, but contrary to what most fishermen say and believe terrestrial insects are no more important to trout near the banks than to trout in the middle of the river. I remember casting to a large brown trout rising to leafhoppers and beetles in an upstate New York river one windy day, and I counted thirteen fly changes until I got him to take. He was in the middle of the river, fifty feet from either bank. One early morning on the Madison I walked the bank upstream from the Raynolds Pass Bridge. I rose dozens of big-spotted browns on a hopper right next to the bank, but when I turned my attention to the middle, the rainbows on the seams of the fast water ate the hopper just as eagerly.

There is a simple reason for my not thinking terrestrials are more important to fish living near the banks: An object falling into a river

With standing waves like these on the Madison you can bet most trout will be close to the banks.

is quickly drawn into the center. If a grasshopper or cricket or beetle or ant falls into the water and isn't eaten right away by a trout living next to the bank, it will soon be available to those guys out in the center. In tiny brooks or shallow streams the deeper bank is usually better. You should make sure, however, that some current is getting to the deeper bank, because sometimes the deep bank is an almost stagnant backwater. Huge trout can use these deep places for refuge, but they don't eat there, so trying to get one to take is like pitching to a batter while he's sleeping. If one bank slopes gently up from the river and the other is made from ledge rock or is otherwise steeper, the steep bank is likely to be better. In huge, fast rivers where the current along the deeper bank might be moving at ten feet per second and the water might be twenty feet deep, I'd take a look at the shallower bank first. There *might* be a trout underneath that twenty feet of fast water, but you're not going to have much luck getting a fly to where he'll see it and feel inclined to move for it.

Once you've identified the better bank, make sure as you fish that you keep your eye on where the good water peters out, as often the good water switches from one bank to another. Because you're not looking for rising fish but casting to likely stream features, you can sometimes tighten the blinders too much and wade right through some water you should be fishing rather than blundering through.

Any object that breaks up the outline of the bank will increase its attractiveness to trout. Where a deep riffle runs along a bank, look for a point of land that sticks out. Just like a rock in the middle of a river, the point will form two choice places for trout to lie—one just upstream of the point where the water is backed up to form a dead spot, and another area just downstream. If the point sticks out more than a foot from the bank, you might think that the most or best fish will be found close to the bank in the backwater right behind the point. My experience has shown that most trout, and certainly the bigger ones, prefer to lie just inside the seam behind the point. This place makes sense for trout because it offers protection from the full brunt of the current and easy access to food being carried by the current. If you toss a twig into the backwater behind an object, it will whirl around for many revolutions before it rejoins the current, and some fishermen argue that trout like to be in backwaters because they get multiple looks at pieces of food. I think they are more concerned with getting enough to eat than with admiring their next meal.

I also like to think this is true because getting a fly behind a point of land just inside a fast current and maintaining a natural drift is difficult without throwing piles of slack or adding a six-foot tippet. I'd rather throw my fly into the easier current just outside the point for a longer natural drift and hope the trout just inside can easily slide over and inhale my fly. If he is tucked way back, he may still see my fly and rush over for it. Only after I've attempted every permutation of drifts on the outside will I try the nasty water in the backwater.

Rocky banks are good. A jumble of rocks offers many havens from the current, with plenty of areas of different current speeds and seams. Narrow lanes between rocks concentrate the current— and move the food—into alleys, simplifying feeding. Any kind of vegetation will also make the bank more attractive to trout, even if the vegetation overhangs the water and doesn't break the current. Shrubs hanging over the water offer trout security from predators.

Big boulders along the bank give you excellent water for prospecting.

Luckily for fishermen, if there is a tunnel of alders along the bank, trout will not feed way back inside the tunnel but will lie just to the outside of the brush, using the dark interior only if they are frightened. Logs along a bank, whether parallel or perpendicular to the current, offer protection and breaks from the current.

A tree that has fallen into the water at a right angle to the current, usually with the trunk still attached to the bank, is called a sweeper. The best places near a sweeper are at the outside tip of the branches extending downstream along the seam, and in front of the crotch

Fred Barberi nets one taken off the end of a sweeper in a suburban Connecticut stream.

where the sweeper meets the bank. Both places offer breaks from the current and a steady food supply. Often a line of trout extends below the tips of the branches, with the biggest fish upstream and the size decreasing as you go downstream, because a trout will not tolerate a smaller or less aggressive fish in front of it. Downstream of the sweeper is often barren water. If it contains trout, they'll be much smaller than you'd think, because the sweeper strains food from the current and pushes it to the outside leaving slim pickings to the trout behind.

A log lying parallel to the current will probably hold more trout than a sweeper of the same size, because the entire length of the log offers attractive feeding grounds. When I was a teenager, I fished a productive stream that runs through the limestone bedrock of upstate New York. This river had all the attractive haunts a trout stream could possibly offer, but as far as my sampling could determine, one log in particular held the biggest fish. About fifteen feet long and five feet from the bank, the log always held several small trout; two six-inch nubs were left from branches that had been broken off over the years. And anchored at these nubs were the two best trout in the pool, one twenty inches long and the other nineteen. All these trout fed on the outside edge of the log, and even though there was a good five feet of dark, deep, protected water between the log and the bank, I never saw a trout rise and never caught one there.

The subject of banks brings up the question of cover—the degree trout use it, and the amount they need. Anyone who has studied a piece of trout water for any time has seen trout feeding out in the open, away from obvious cover. The energetics of getting enough food seem to be far more important than safety from predators. But even if you can't see it, you can bet that trout feeding in the open have a place to run to nearby, and that they have memorized the route. Brown trout seem to place more importance than other species on cover, and if they can find a spot that offers food, protection from the current, and cover, they'll stay close to cover. When you hook a brown trout, he will invariably head for the nearest log or rock. The other day I was fishing a stream that holds both browns and rainbows, and out in the middle of a pool I hooked a rainbow that tailwalked in place four or five times, ran upstream, and then grudgingly headed downstream to be released. I cast to another fish rising in almost the same spot, except this trout streaked downstream before *I* even knew he was hooked, and he used a submerged root six feet ahead of me to remove the fly from his jaw as cleanly as popping the top off a beer bottle. He swam past me with an arrogant flip of his tail, and left my fly stuck firmly in the root, all before I could begin to strip in my line. As the fish passed, I saw the dark spots of a brown trout along his back.

Brown trout have even been known to burrow in gravel when frightened, but the behavior of frightened rainbows betrays their lack of concern with overhead cover. Rainbows, when spooked, usually head en masse to the deepest part of a pool, and when you walk by you can observe what biologists call "fright huddles"— groups of rainbows all packed together, fins trembling. You never see browns mixed in with them because all the browns have headed to the bank with its more substantial cover. Brook trout seem to use cover less than browns but more than rainbows, so you will more often find them farther from cover and from the bank than browns. Where cutthroats and brook trout are found together, biologists have seen more use of cover by the brook trout. So if you know a river contains only brown trout, spend more time casting tight to the banks than out in the middle. If it holds only rainbows, bless their

Brown trout will use cover more than any other species of trout.

Rainbows will usually be found in more open water, whether it's riffly like this or slow and smooth.

hearts, you can concentrate on the easier places in the middle of the river. But don't ever completely ignore the banks. The middle of the Railroad Ranch section of Henry's Fork in Idaho is essentially featureless, as most of the water is one long flat without big rocks. The better rainbows are near the banks, possibly because of cover, but more likely because the current along the banks is reduced enough to form areas of slower water with access to the food carried by the current.

The Most Difficult Part of a Pool

Everything I've said about rocks and banks and logs applies to the tail of a pool as well, and in most of the rivers I've fished, the tails hold the largest trout. All the food passing through a pool is channeled at the tail into a vertically and horizontally constricted funnel, and the smooth water here allows a nearly unobstructed view of the outside world, which warns of the approach of all kinds of predators. During a hatch the tail of a pool is the first place I'll go to catch a trout that will pull line off my reel. It is also the *last* place I'll go to prospect. When a trout in the tail of a pool is preoccupied with feeding and you know exactly where he is, approaching him is still difficult; when he is not actively feeding, it is masochistic. Because the tail of a pool is shallower than the middle, look for the deepest place in the tail to hold the most trout, barring any rocks or logs in the water. The place where the tail begins to shallow, where dark water gives way to lighter-colored water, will often be where trout are lined up to feed. If the water close to the banks is deeper than in the middle, and especially when vegetation meets the water, you'll often find more and bigger trout next to the banks than out in the middle.

When you stand at the tail of a pool and fish upstream, following the usual line of attack, the water at your feet is faster than the water you cast into. The water in the tail is always accelerating, particularly in the early season when the current is faster. As soon as your fly lands, drag sets in, and even throwing big piles of slack will not always counteract this problem. You can get a better presentation by casting from upstream or from across-stream and throwing upstream curves, and this works best early in the season when you

Brook trout use cover less than browns but more than rainbows.

The nastiest part of a pool—the tail.

can get closer to the trout without spooking them. In midsummer I find that from above you spook the fish in the tails of most pools, especially in smaller streams or when the water is unusually low.

Because most aquatic insects live in riffles, and everything that hatches in a pool that doesn't fly away will be funneled into the tail (as will any terrestrial insect that falls into the water), trout in the tail of a pool seem more aware of surface food than trout in any other place. If you stand and watch long enough, you will often see them sipping here throughout the day, especially in the low water of late season. This is not really a hatch situation; it is opportunistic surface feeding at every little morsel that drifts by. Sometimes you can watch for twenty minutes before you see a rise, so if you're moving at a normal pace you won't spot the fish, and you'll fish the tail blind. During the summer, when the current has slowed enough, you can often make a short, accurate upstream presentation from a trout's blind spot. But since your drift will still be short before it drags, decide first where you think the trout will be lying—don't just blast away at random. It's a good idea to study the surface currents for several minutes as well. If you can get close enough to where you think a trout might be, and you can figure an angle from which you can get a drag-free float, a terrestrial pattern or small spinner imitation in the middle of the day may rise a trout of a size you would normally see only during the evening hatch.

Even in the same stream at the same time of year, you cannot approach the tail of a pool with the casual tactics that might work in a riffle. If you want to catch trout in the tails of pools, study the last chapter on approach carefully. In the technique chapters that follow, note these techniques that have worked best for me in the tails of pools: actively stripped streamers, swung wets, and skated dry flies.

How the Setting Can Change

Four minutes from where I sit in an office eight hours a day is a tiny stream that is my laboratory, escape valve, and forty-five-minute retreat. I can fish three or four pools on my lunch hour. In one favorite half-mile stretch I know virtually every fish except the unseen brown trout that I suspect inhabit a couple of deep undercut banks at the base of streamside maples. I have never caught one of these elusive browns, but I imagine them sulking in a tangle of drowned roots, oblivious to my flies but capable of eating a six-inch brook trout followed by a three-day fast. At the beginning of each season I mark a couple of gullible brook trout by clipping their adipose fins so I can follow their progress through the season. If I can figure out where they are living, I can almost always catch them. In early spring they are in the deeper, slower pools, and to catch them you need a large nymph fished close to the bottom, with no drag at all. As water temperatures rise above 55 degrees and flies start to hatch, they will be pulled from the pools into shallow riffles. Now a dry fly will work, as will a wet fly or nymph that swings across the current. As water levels fall during the summer, they can be hard to find, and whenever I fail to catch one that has been in the same spot for a couple of months, I start to imagine my brookie in an aluminum-foil coffin in somebody's freezer, or in the belly of a heron or otter. With the lower water levels it's also likely that there are fewer places in this little stream that can hold trout, and my friends were pushed downstream by more aggressive trout. In summer most of the trout are concentrated in only the deepest holes and in the heads of pools—it may be a hundred feet between places that hold trout.

During the winter and early in the season trout are more concerned with avoiding anchor ice and floods than they are with eating. There are few insects in the drift for them to capture, and their metabolisms are slowed to the point where they take little advantage of the food that might be available. Shallow water can be scoured by floating ice and anchor ice, which grows from the bottom of the river, so look for trout in deep-water refuges, out of the main current. When there is no ice, though, I have caught them on sunny days in shallow riffles, and because I doubt trout spend the winter in water like this, I suspect they move into places that are warmed by the sun as spring starts to wake up the river. As the water temperature approaches 50 degrees, and insects begin to drift and hatch, the fish migrate to shallow riffles and the heads of pools to take advantage of insect life at its source. You can gauge the migration time by the first major hatch of the season. In the East, if you blind-fish before the Hendrickson hatch, you'll find most trout in the side eddies and backwaters, but as soon as this first big hatch begins, the trout appear in riffles, in tails of pools, and out in the main current. They're still there on days when the flies don't hatch, and early in the morning on days when flies don't hatch until midafternoon.

There they will stay until low water and high temperatures shrink the comfortable places in a stream and concentrate the trout. As habitats contract, trout don't move far, sometimes just from one side of the pool to another, or from the middle to the head. In the tail of a big pool on the lower Battenkill, I found a pod of a half-dozen large brown trout one late spring evening, and I returned a couple of evenings a week to work them over. By the middle of the summer I had caught and released most of them, including a couple that I fin-clipped. A vacation kept me away from them for ten days, and when I returned the places where they had been feeding were almost dry. I couldn't find a single one. One night I happened to look at the other side of the river, which was deeper but had never produced a fish, I guess because this deeper pocket was out of the main current and did not supply enough food. There were several good fish rising there, and sure enough, over the next several weeks I caught some that I had clipped. As I looked carefully at the water, I saw that their new home was deep enough to keep them secure. The current had shifted because of a newly exposed gravel bar, and by the looks of the bubble line coming down through the pool, most of the food was now funneled to the opposite side of the river.

In the tough late season there are three keys to finding trout: temperature, oxygen, and flow. If you remember them, you will catch trout all day long, even in the noonday heat of August when there is slim chance of any kind of hatch.

Temperature: Look for springs entering the river. Even springs whose surface flow runs dry during the summer usually offer some flow below the dry channel, so a scar of clean rocks along the bank that looks as though it might have been a tributary in early spring may tip you off to some cooler water. In general any entering tributary will be cooler than the main river, so look for trout below the confluence of a smaller and a larger stream. Wade wet to find springs entering the river beneath the streambed.

Oxygen: Water's oxygen content is inversely related to its temperature, so if you can't find the cooler water, which holds more oxygen, look for places where oxygen is forced into the water by physical means. Riffles, runs, pocket water, the bases of dams—trout will move to these places in midsummer, often leaving the rest of a pool barren.

Flow: This important factor of midsummer trout fishing is often overlooked. Trout won't live where they can't eat, and during low water their options are limited, making stream reading easier. Especially in slower pools, don't look for trout anywhere but right under the bubble line, because flow is reduced to a point where only the main current offers enough food. If you can't locate the bubble line or it doesn't seem to help, another way of finding trout is to look at the stones on the bottom. Once when I was fishing a stream known for its wild rainbows, I was in a wide riffle that holds scores of trout during the spring, and I knew some of them had to be around, even though the water looked too shallow. At first the entire riffle looked daunting and I couldn't decide where to start. Then as I stared at the water, I noticed something. Most of the rocks on the bottom

Look for oxygenated water like this in the late season. Margot Page photo.

were covered with a thin film of dusty-looking silt, but in places that were slightly deeper and had a stronger current, the rocks had been wiped clean. That gave me some targets, and by pitching a Flasha-bou Caddis Larva into the narrow lanes of clean stones, I picked up a half-dozen ten-inch fish, more than I would have expected in such a flat, shallow riffle.

At this point you should have a clear idea of what a trout needs to survive, how to tell how rich a trout stream is, what richness tells you about finding trout and selecting flies, and where trout live in streams at all times of year. Now we'll explore the techniques you can use to catch trout when you don't see them rising.

STREAMERS

I have to pull this old cliché on you: If I had but one fly to use for a single season, not for pleasure but to put pounds of meat on the table, it would be a streamer—a Woolly Bugger. There are those who would argue that a Woolly Bugger is not really a streamer but a nymph or a wet fly with a long tail. Let's get the semantics out of the way. In this book any long, skinny fly that is usually given some motion by the angler is a streamer. This includes traditional feather streamers, bucktails, Muddler Minnows, and the Woolly Bugger and its many clones.

The English have a better term for this kind of fly. Our streamer is a lure to an English chalk stream fisherman, who would say the word with a curl of the lip, as if he had just found an American tourist poaching roses from the colonel's garden. Lures, the English believe, are all right for reservoir fishermen or for dredging sea trout out of deep pools in the dead of night, but not for precious chalk streams. Despite some occasional snobbery, however, the English aren't as rigid in their stream fishing rules as we make them out to be. On most waters you are not restricted to dry fly, upstream only—many clubs and leased boats allow nymphs and downstream fishing. They frown on streamer fishing because it isn't necessary. It's seldom that you don't see all the rising fish you can cast to, and slapping a streamer just makes a mess out of a quiet chalk stream. It's also too effective to be any fun.

My wife and I once had a couple of days on the Test and Itchen, and one evening we were on the Test with a young but perceptive

The Woolly Bugger and its variations are some of the most effective prospecting flies.

gilly named Richard Banbury. There was no one around, no voices around the corner. Margot, who usually fishes beautifully, especially for fussy trout, was feeling the effects of jet lag and three days of traveling. She was into one of those downward spirals that only get you more wind knots as you try harder. Dammit, she wanted to catch one of those English trout and right now. Richard peered into the water, by now almost black and inscrutable, and said, "I believe there is a pike over there by the far bank, Margot. Give him a try with this Dog Nobbler."

It's one thing to have a trout predator in natural balance in a wild stream, another to have pike chomping the trout you have carefully introduced into a somewhat artificial ecosystem. When a pike is found in the Test, it is removed by spearing, shooting, or electrofishing—or by the deadly Dog Nobbler.

A Dog Nobbler is a marabou tail, chenille body, and bent hook with a spot of lead molded onto it—a crappie jig if you're from Minnesota. Richard may not have been able to fish streamers or Dog Nobblers when the neighbors were looking, but I was willing to bet he was no virgin, either. Rainbows and browns pounded Margot's lure into submission like Spitfires onto Me 110s. Fish that have never been exposed to streamers can be unbelievably gullible, even selective and spooky brown trout raised in a chalk stream full of food.

Funny—Margot never hooked or even saw a pike.

Why Do Trout Take Streamers?

With all kinds of tiny fish swimming around them, were those trout striking that Dog Nobbler because they thought it was a minnow? This is a common misconception when we decide to use a streamer. It's a carry-over from the hatch-matching mentality. Originally streamers were used in New England as smelt imitations for catching landlocked salmon, and ever since we have been fooling ourselves, thinking that every time a fish takes a streamer he is saying, "Gee, that looks like a minnow. I think I'll eat it." Does a Woolly Bugger look like a minnow to you?

Studies of wild trout populations have shown that once trout, particularly brown trout, reach a certain size they need more than drift feeding on invertebrates to keep growing or even to maintain body weight. In a typical freestone river this size is about fourteen

Margot and Richard, shortly after the Dog Nobbler episode.

inches. If a trout of sixteen inches were to depend solely on sipping duns from the surface or plucking nymphs from midwater currents, he would use up more energy than he obtained and would slowly waste away. Genes refined over thousands of generations make him switch his feeding patterns. Large fish become predators, ambushers. They start to look for bigger chunks of food, and they feed at times when they have a predatory advantage—at dusk, at dawn, throughout the night, and during rainstorms when the water gets fast and dirty and small fish get knocked around and disoriented.

Thomas Jenkins saw some of these fish during his study of the Owens River. He noticed some very large, non-drift-feeding browns that stayed in deep water or brushpiles, occasionally making threatening passes at smaller fish. He was only observing them during daylight hours, but you can bet that after dark they were doing more than making threatening passes. In three thousand hours observing unmolested brown trout in Pennsylvania's Spruce Creek, known for its rich food and big trout, Bob Bachman never saw a fish over fourteen inches drift feeding. In all that time he saw only a couple of trout eat minnows. Nevertheless he believes that the big trout—Bob

Brown trout like this one seldom grow to large size by eating just insects.

calls them sharks—were somewhere, perhaps not in the pool he was watching.

This fourteen-inch size threshold is not etched in stone. Rainbows and cutthroats are able to use the drift more efficiently. They grow well beyond fourteen inches feeding almost entirely on nymphs, crustaceans, and terrestrials. It is also possible to find a brown trout population where the average drift feeder is much larger—if the food supply is sufficient, and especially if energy-rich crustaceans like scuds and sow bugs are plentiful.

On the Bighorn in Montana the average brown trout caught on a dry or nymph measures between sixteen and twenty inches, and these fish are obviously drift feeding. You see them sipping at every bend in the river, even in the winter. Alan Kelly knows the biology of this river better than anyone; as well as running a superb lodge and guide operation on it, he was the U.S. Fish and Wildlife biologist for the river for four years before it was opened to the public in 1981. I remember him talking one cold November day with Jim McFadyean, his head guide. Alan was excited because he was starting to see young whitefish farther up the river than ever before. Alan explained to me that the Bighorn is a trout river still in its infancy, as it was for years a warm-water fishery containing walleyes, catfish, and sauger. When the Yellowtail Dam was built in 1965, the cold water released from it created a superb trout river that threads through the near-desert of central Montana.

Brown trout in the Bighorn are common up to twenty inches and rare above that size, except in the lower river, where marginal water supports a lot of "trash" fish—the kind of goodies that overstuffed brown trout need to live. "We won't get many big browns in the upper river until the whitefish take hold," Alan told me. The upper Bighorn has no sculpins and few other minnow species, and he was hoping the young whitefish would fill this forage niche. The rainbows in the lower Bighorn have less trouble breaking the twenty-inch mark because they continue to grow on the rich soup of invertebrates that slides through the feeder channels.

"The browns, once they reach eighteen inches," Alan said, "try to make forage fish 98 percent of their diet. They may be forced to make up the rest of their diet in insects, though. The rainbows, on the other hand, try to make 98 percent of their diet insects. Big browns will suffer if they can't get enough forage fish."

If you float the upper Bighorn where those young whitefish have yet to appear on the menu every Friday, pounding the water with a Woolly Bugger, Muddler, or Matuka Sculpin can catch you large brown and rainbow trout—but you'll be ignoring perhaps the finest dry-fly and nymph fishing in the world. On the lower Bighorn there won't be many fish rising, but if you fish a streamer thoroughly the few trout you catch will all be fish of a lifetime.

You don't have to travel to Montana to see this. Most trout rivers have lower reaches that are marginal trout water, too warm during the summer heat and without suitable water for spawning. Large trout, those that can hold their own against predatory pike and smallmouth bass, move downstream because the cooler water in the upper reaches won't support the baitfish they need. These large trout stay downstream until warm water and the spawning urge send them back upstream in midsummer; after spawning in the fall, they return to deep-water winter refuges.

So the reason trout take streamers is that trout mistake streamers for smaller fish. Do trout also take streamers thinking they are some other kind of food? And do they eat streamers out of a reflex mechanism that has nothing to do with a specific kind of food? I think the answer to both questions is yes.

Large trout have been known to eat frogs and mice, and in Alaska one of the best flies for drawing explosive strikes imitates a lemming. I think trout in the lower forty-eight mistake our streamers for crayfish as often as they take them for small fish. Where you find crayfish, you find big trout. Since I don't kill trout anymore, I don't get the hard-core evidence that stomach contents give you (one of the biggest drawbacks of catch-and-release fishing). I make a point, though, of asking bait or spin fishermen I know to keep track of what they find in the stomachs of their trout. Crayfish claws, which don't digest quickly, are found as often as parts of fish. Of course, because crayfish claws digest more slowly than anything a trout eats except stones, these results could be biased—but the claws are present often enough to make us pay attention.

You might be asking yourself how a trout could possibly strike a streamer thinking it's a crayfish when your fly is just under the surface, moving as fast as you can strip it. Once I was standing on a bridge, watching a brown trout of about eighteen inches. He was holding just above the bottom, barely swaying in the current, when he abruptly moved upstream a foot and speared his snout into a crevice between two rocks. He missed, and out streaked a crayfish, spurting upstream as fast as I've ever stripped a streamer. But the crayfish didn't look for refuge under another rock right away. Instead it popped up just under the surface of the stream and kept swimming. It didn't get more than two feet before the trout, with a powerful burst, grabbed the crayfish, turned, and scooted back to his place on the bottom, leaving a serious wake on the surface—like the wake a trout leaves when it takes your streamer.

The next time you go fishing, turn over some rocks and watch the crayfish when they swim away. They swim backward, blunt midcarapace first, with claws streaming behind and all those little legs on the underbody folded back. Look like a Woolly Bugger to you? A Marabou Leech or a Zonker? Or even a Dark Edson Tiger, with its brown back and yellow body? To me streamers look much more like escaping crayfish than do the stiff, realistic flies invented

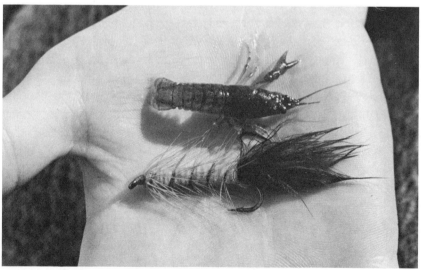

Imagine this Woolly Bugger wet and streaming through the water. Do you think it looks like a crayfish to the trout?

by tyers who have never watched a crayfish swim. And the movement and shape of a crayfish fleeing from danger are more likely the triggering mechanisms for a strike than a stiff pile of hair, plastic, and lacquer.

Despite the importance of crayfish I'm not suggesting you plan your streamer fishing around imitating them. It's better to think of streamer fishing as selecting a lure. Imagine a predator ready to pounce on an animal trying to escape, a piece of food that is panicked and disoriented. Trout feeding on baitfish, crayfish, or even mice are not selective feeders. They don't lie in wait for a black-nosed dace, passing up a long-nosed dace. And even trout that have a couple of years of growing ahead of them before they reach that magic fourteen-inch size will strike a big streamer when conditions are right.

Territorial behavior is another reason trout will chase and often bite a streamer. Fin nipping is a less common response to territorial intrusions than erect fin displays and bluffing, but it is common enough, especially when the intruding fish makes an overt move and doesn't seem to get the message. Studies have shown that active fish nip more often than inactive fish. A trout in water of an optimum temperature, 55 to 65 degrees F, will take a streamer just because it gets in the way. At 45 degrees a trout may ignore little fish invading its space, just as it may lack interest in food.

It's also been observed that trout show increased aggression during food deprivation. At the risk of getting anthropomorphic I can understand that, and Margot can tell you that although I don't resort to fin nipping I am much less tolerant of an invasion of territory before I've had coffee and breakfast. This makes a good case for using a streamer in infertile waters when temperatures are optimal—not only are active trout more likely to nip the fins of an intruder, they are apt to do it with a vengeance.

Prime Streamer Times

Streamer fishing can be as frustrating as any other kind of fly fishing, but there are times when it seems like you can't make a mistake with one, and your uncle Jim who has never held a fly rod in his hand can hook a twenty-inch brown in a hard-fished eastern river.

When water temperatures are optimal and a rainstorm makes the river rise and take on some color, trout, especially bigger ones, seem to lose their caution and prowl for minnows, crayfish, and anything else that falls into the water. Apparently they can even anticipate a change in water level or color, because often the start of a heavy rainstorm prompts trout to break cover in the middle of the day and strike a large, fast-moving fly.

More than once on the Battenkill, a stream where size 18 flies and 6X tippets are what you start out with, not what you resort to in desperation, I have had a Trico hatch interrupted by a summer downpour. The Trico hatch, or spinner fall as it is more properly called, requires at least a size 22 fly, a 7X tippet, much swearing, and the expectation that for every five trout you make a perfect, delicate cast over, four will bolt for cover. A quick, hard rain can change the rules in a hurry. If it rains enough to change the surface from a smooth sheet to a pockmarked surface, you can cut your leader back to 3X or 4X, tie on a streamer a full 600 percent larger than a Trico spinner, and pull trout out of the river with the ease of taking bluegills on a bobber and worm. Those trout may not be the same ones that were feeding on Trico spinners a few minutes before, and you won't hook as many as you saw rising before the rain. But I'm certain you would not have hooked any trout on a streamer if it hadn't started to rain.

Fishing a streamer under these conditions requires little skill in presentation and fly selection. Pattern and color aren't as important as covering a lot of water, moving the fly quickly, and being as obnoxious with the fly as you can. Trout detect the change in conditions either by a change in light or maybe by a change in the chemical makeup of the water that stimulates their olfactory senses. In any case they sense that the advantages prey species have in clear water—being able to see a trout coming, and being faster than a trout—no longer hold true.

If it starts to rain hard, tie on a streamer you have confidence in. Maybe it's a pattern that you've caught trout on before, or one that a fly shop owner recommended, or a fly you read about in a magazine. It's hard to go wrong with a Woolly Bugger, Muddler Minnow, Zonker, or Mickey Finn, sizes 4 through 10. Start by wading on the shallow side and casting to the deeper bank, or if the river is shallow in the middle, wade down the middle and cast to both banks. If the river you are fishing is the bouldery, pocket water type, then try to wade the shallow, gravelly areas and cast to the deep pockets in front of and behind the rocks.

Types of Streamers and When to Fish Them

It's usually not necessary to put on a sink-tip line or attempt to get your fly close to the bottom. Trout can detect moving prey, even in dirty water, especially if the fly makes "noise" that can be heard by the trout's lateral line senses. How do you tell if a fly makes noise? Just a glance will tell you. If it has a palmered hackle like a Woolly Bugger, or a deer hair head like a Muddler or sculpin, it will set up a disturbance in the water. Slim, clean-looking flies like a Grey Ghost or a Black Nose Dace are more subtle, and they're more effective when the water is clear and colorless.

I was once caught in an early morning rainstorm on the LeTort Spring Run in Pennsylvania, a clear stream with stable flows that hardly ever changes color, even after a cloudburst. After trying a couple of different variations of the Muddler Minnow without success, I rooted through my streamer box until I found a long-buried Black Ghost, left over from a landlocked salmon trip. Landlocks prefer slim flies because their main food is smelt, a long, skinny baitfish of northern lakes. That Black Ghost pulled some handsome trout out from the watercress beds where the bulkier flies had failed.

You'll go crazy trying to load up your fly box with the latest streamer pattern you read about in *Fly Fisherman*. Carry noisy ones and some slim ones, in light and dark shades, in sizes 4 through 12. Most should be weighted to get them under the surface quickly, but carry a few unweighted smaller ones for shallow water. Tippets can be on the heavy side, especially for the weighted flies, because strikes will often be violent. Also, because you are moving the fly, you don't have to worry about a flexible tippet to make it look natural. In dirty water with a size 4 fly I wouldn't hesitate to use 0X, and I would never, not even in clear water with a size 12, go below 4X.

Streamer Techniques

After you've chosen your fly and planned your approach, begin by casting so the fly swims broadside to the current in front of every deep pocket, log, weedbed, or boulder. Let's say there is a nice log against the far bank. Wade to a point just upstream of the log and thirty or forty feet out into the current (or whatever distance is comfortable for you to cast while keeping far enough away so you don't spook the fish). Cast as near to the bank as possible, maybe three feet upstream of the log. Now strip—and don't stop stripping until the fly is fifteen feet off your rod tip. A friend of mine, who was once really cleaning up with streamers, told me to strip "like you would for bluefish." Don't worry about the fish not being able to catch the fly. You cannot strip fast enough to pull your fly away from a trout that really wants it, and if you get a swirl to your fly but don't connect, I can guarantee it wasn't because of any physical limitations on the part of the trout.

Experiment with the amount of line you pull with each strip. Most often foot-long strips are best, but if those don't draw any strikes, or the trout continually boil at the fly but don't connect, try six-inch strips or two-foot strips.

Trout that take a fly when you are stripping like this will boil

Carry slim streamers, like the Brown-and-Yellow Marabou and Black Ghost at the top, and noisy streamers, like the Muddler Minnow and Zonker on the bottom.

Foot-long pulls are usually the best way to retrieve streamers. Keep your rod tip low and pointed at the fly.

behind the fly, connecting with a swirl every bit as exciting as a rise to a dry fly. Sometimes they come completely out of the water, seemingly taking the fly on the way down after becoming airborne. Stopping or slowing the fly will usually turn them away, maybe because they get too good a look, or because they lose their resolve. I have trouble with bonefishing for just this reason—I am so used to trout fishing that it unnerves me to hear a guide yelling, "Strip! Stop! Strip. Strip. Strip. Stop." A bonefish may gobble a stopped fly that is sinking toward the bottom, but trout are not usually fond of an erratic retrieve.

Point the tip of your rod at the fly to maintain a tight connection and keep control over the fly. Also keep your rod tip low to the water to avoid slack. Using the rod tip to give the fly action in these circumstances will make it pause too long in between strips—either you'll miss strikes or the fish will turn away. And don't strike until you feel them take—just raise the tip of the rod enough to tighten the line. Striking to every boil will only pull the fly away from the fish.

If you don't get a strike, you can make another cast to the same spot if you want, but I wouldn't. Seldom under these conditions will a second cast work when the first didn't. Instead, take a few steps downstream and cast right to the head of the log. Touch the log with the fly if you can. Strip—fast. Cast again a third of the way down the log. Then cover the rest of the log with a few more casts. Pay particular attention to the log's trailing edge, a real hot spot. And okay, I might even take two casts there.

If you still don't get any strikes, don't wring your hands, worrying about what you might have done wrong. Keep moving downstream, hitting every likely spot in the same way. In pools I fish regularly, in which I have a pretty good idea of the trout population, I may get one follow for every twenty trout. You have to cover a lot of water. That's why I suggest that you work downstream, because covering all the good stuff and playing the percentages gets tiring, especially in heavy current, if you have to wade upstream.

Another exasperation you'll have to deal with is short strikes. On many days, for every trout you hook, two or three will boil at the fly but not touch it. Some fishermen claim it's from streamer wings tied too long, or from patterns that aren't quite right. I don't agree. A trout that boils for a streamer without connecting hardly ever comes to the same fly a second time or to a fly of a different size or pattern. I think it's more a reflexive reaction of the trout to something that looks like food, and he puts on the brakes at the last minute when he decides he really doesn't want to expose himself to chase this thing. The next time a streamer passes in front of him, caution prevails. Trout don't have long memories, but their short-term seems to work fine.

Fishermen often use a streamer to locate trout, then come back to them later, either during a hatch or with a wet fly or nymph. My friends and I used to spend a week every spring on the East Branch of the Delaware, but I hardly ever fished more than four pools. These pools were a quarter of a mile long and full of trout, and they were far enough away from the road that we never saw another fisherman. One May the fishing was dismal for three days, so bad that we resorted to catching frogs in the oxbows with Hendricksons (size 12, in case you ever find yourself in the same position). On the fourth day a heavy rain pushed the river just over its normally stable banks, not high enough to rule out wading, but high enough to make dry-fly fishing unlikely. "I'm going upstream to explore," I yelled to my friends, but they were too busy working a nice pod of leopard frogs to hear me.

Despite ten years of fishing this river hard, I had never tried some pools just a few miles upstream, that friends had told me about, so with nothing to lose I drove up and got into the river. Maybe there were some bullfrogs around. Tying on a size 8 Woodchuck Sculpin, a simple fly with an elk hair head, dubbed body, and woodchuck tail wing, I worked through a pool the way I've described before. I hooked and landed two sixteen-inch browns, not a bad tally for a half hour's fishing. But even more valuable in the long run were the two dozen trout that swirled at the fly but didn't take. When I came back and fished that pool during a hatch, not only did I know it had some nice trout in it—I knew their addresses.

Although the broadside cast is best when they're taking streamers in rising water, you may find spots where that angle is not practical or comfortable. Any other angle, including straight upstream or downstream, can also produce, but the fly is harder to control and you can't present the whole profile of the fly to the fish. Casting straight upstream and retrieving downstream is especially difficult because it is sometimes physically impossible for you to

The deadly Woochuck Sculpin.

keep the fly moving fast enough to interest the trout. And a fly that swims right at them may be threatening, as this is unusual behavior for their prey.

How long does this magic time of rising water last? Depending on water temperature and how full their stomachs were when the feeding spree started, the fish will get satiated after an hour or two, and then the action slows down quickly. It pays to get on the water as soon as it starts raining enough to wash debris and mud into the water, or to tie on a streamer if you're already fishing. The first flush of a spate disorients minnows, dislodges crayfish, and washes worms and terrestrial insects into the river. It doesn't take the trout long to get with the program.

Streamers in the Morning

We've looked at the best circumstances for streamer fishing, but there are many other times when a streamer will be effective. Even under bright sun in clear water it's hard for a good streamer fisherman to work through a pool without at least getting a swirl to his fly. One of the best times for streamers is the morning, before the sun hits the water. I have had heart-stopping mornings casting to steep banks still in shade—from bedrock banks punctuated with cedars on the Battenkill to lush rhododendron slopes on the Willow-emoc. This can often be an exercise in locating trout, with low percentages of connecting. The trout follow the fly out from the shade, turning away when they break into the sunlight. The earlier you get on the river the better, and if you arrive at first light, especially in midsummer, you may latch on to a trout much bigger than you expected.

Other than the fact that you will have a trout stream to yourself in early morning, there is a sound biological reason for fishing a streamer at first light: The trout that eat the most forage fish exhibit high activity levels at this time of day. In their radio telemetry study of eight brown trout between sixteen and twenty-five inches long on the Au Sable in Michigan, Dave Clapp, Rick Clark, and James Diana observed four daily activity peaks in June—one at sunset, two in the middle of the night, and one right before sunrise. The July sunrise peak was almost three times more active than that in June and was

A great place to fish a streamer early in the morning.

the highest level of forage activity observed during the entire 346-day study.

Places to Concentrate On

Where you fish a streamer is as important as when—but not always as easy to choose. Trout on the prowl for large prey do not sit still and wait for it to stumble by. In fact the study of the Au Sable proved these sharks used deep water with heavy logjams for daytime refuge but ranged at night as much as a mile, usually returning to the same refuge site in the morning. This behavior makes sense if you're a fat old trout. Minnows avoid deep, slow water, and to catch them trout have to hunt the shallows. So if you are fishing streamers in the early morning, by all means cast to those impenetrable logjams: the occupant may have just returned from a long night prowling for food. If he was unsuccessful, he might still be looking for a bite.

He may also still be slinking through the shallows, so be careful in your approach. Long, flat areas in the tail of a pool and wide riffles at the head are especially productive places, and I have often seen wakes from spooked trout who departed these places as I stumbled in the shallows. I have also hooked a few when I have been smart enough to kneel down and fish carefully through water I would pass up in bright sunlight.

Daytime Streamers and Float Fishing

You can catch trout on streamers in the middle of the day, even in midsummer, if you're resolved to playing percentages and going through hundreds of casts without a strike. This takes patience, but it still might be more productive than a dry or nymph. Fish close to the refuge areas—so close that your fly touches logs and brush when it lands and, oh yes, hangs up frequently. A trout in bright sunlight may not streak halfway across a pool to nail a minnow, but he might bite if you wiggle it by his nose. And it's not always deep water that is most productive. Most of the float fishing done on western rivers, and on a few large eastern rivers such as the upper Connecticut and the Delaware, is done by casting the fly right to the bank, usually a deep bank or one with some streamside cover like logs, rocks, or brush. Trout in large rivers seem to prefer these places. They'll pounce on a streamer in the snap of a finger, sometimes before you have time to begin the first strip.

The guide may sometimes suggest several casts to midstream boulders or the seam at the head of a pool, but the banks justifiably get the most attention. To watch an experienced guide at work, even with a novice client, is elegance. After watching a few casts, the guide will direct the boat to the exact distance from the bank that is a comfortable cast for the fisherman, and along an irregular bank the guide will weave in and out to maintain this distance. If you concentrate on the fishing, you don't even notice all the guide's machinations; you only notice what a great caster you are. You cast right to the bank, make three or four strips while you glance ahead for the next spot to cast, pick up, and cast again to the next place.

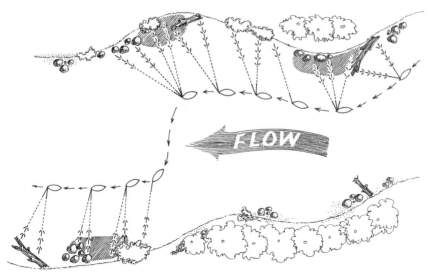

How an experienced guide would row a drift boat through a stretch of river. The shaded areas are the deeper pockets. Dotted arrows indicate strips. Solid arrows indicate the boat's direction.

Float fishing is an efficient way to cover miles of water with a streamer.

Casting ahead of the boat works best, so that by the time you begin to strip, the fly is moving broadside into the current. Casting the fly behind the boat and stripping it downstream is seldom productive unless you're slick enough to throw an upstream curve. If you miss a spot that looks especially interesting, the guide may suddenly dig the oars into the water and hold the boat in the current for another try.

Because you can cover so much water, fishing this way deceives you into thinking there are more fish in a river than there are. (Imagine trying to fish the Madison like this on foot.) No other method of fly fishing allows you to cover as much water as float fishing with a streamer, but you can modify this technique for wading in a river with one fishy-looking bank and one with shallow, easy-to-wade water. Walk downstream slowly, cast your streamer directly to the far bank or just ahead of you, strip, strip, strip, pick

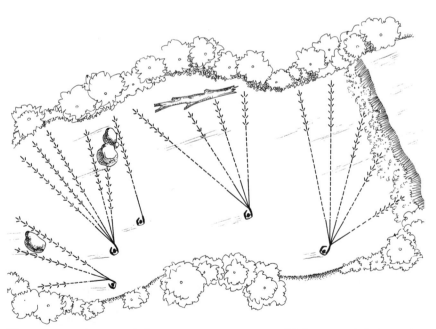

You can work a pool the same way you would from a drift boat by wading, too. The dotted arrows show productive spots to hit with a streamer, and you can work an entire pool in a few minutes.

up, and fire another cast a few feet downstream. Keep moving slowly as you fish. It's a great energy-saving technique to cover miles of water by wading—you don't push any waves because you're moving slowly downstream, and you don't spook many fish, because you stay near the shallow bank. I like to use this method on a river I have never seen before if I don't have a clue where the fish are, or even if the river supports trout at all.

Cold-Water Techniques

I hope I haven't given you the idea you should be inflexible in the way you present streamers. The across-stream, steady-strip method seems to be best when water temperatures are in the most active range for trout—55 to 65 degrees F. But a streamer can be fished at any speed, in any direction, at any time. If you can figure out the right combination, you'll catch trout. In winter (where fishing is legal) and early spring you'll have to modify your technique, mainly because trout are less active in cold water and will not move more than a couple of feet for a fly. You can even fish them upstream, dead-drift, right on the bottom like a weighted nymph, though I have found adding some wrinkles to the dead-drift technique is often a better idea.

Here's one to try when the water is below 50 degrees: Cast upstream and across, using a heavily weighted fly and a nine- or twelve-foot leader. Let the fly sink as it comes back to you, throwing upstream mends if the water is deeper than three feet. As the fly passes directly across from you, give it a strip so it moves a foot or so, then let it drift four or five feet downstream and strip again. As the fly starts to swing downstream, give it another upstream mend and let some of the slack you have retrieved slip out of your hand, so it feeds downstream and keeps the fly from being pulled toward the surface. As the fly continues to swing, gently pump then drop the rod tip every three seconds. Throughout the drift, hold the rod tip relatively high and try to keep as much line as possible off the water, which will again keep the fly near the bottom and drifting downstream in the same current lane. Trout that are not inclined to chase a fly will be attracted by its movement, but it won't move away quickly enough to put them off. Baitfish, especially sculpins

Cold-water streamer techniques worked for Margot on a Wyoming river.

and darters, move this way when they are changing position, darting upward, settling back toward the bottom, and quartering across the current in a downstream direction.

Strikes will usually come when you are stripping the fly. Just to be safe, watch the line carefully; if it seems to stop or tighten, set the hook quickly. Seldom will trout slam a streamer fished like this, and they seem not to hold on to a fly if they are tentative in striking.

The colder the water, the slower and deeper you should fish, and if you're not ticking bottom once in a while, add a split shot or two a foot above the fly. Keep the shot off if you can, because it's miserable stuff to cast and probably interferes with the action of the fly—but I have had many days where it was the only answer. Even though a short leader will make this rig easier to cast, avoid the temptation to use a leader shorter than nine feet. Without a leader at least twice as long as the water is deep, your floating line will pull the fly upward.

Another variation of this technique is to cast up and across and, keeping the rod about 45 degrees above horizontal, follow the fly with the rod tip as it drifts back toward you, continuing as it swings

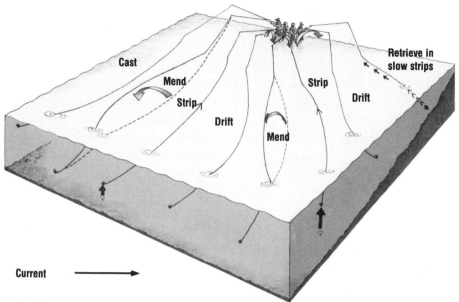

Cold-water streamer technique. You alternate between mends, strips, and drifts, and your fly stays deep yet animated.

below you. This is done without giving the fly any action, and it is much like the traditional way of fishing wet flies—except the fly swings much deeper because it is weighted. It is almost a dead-drift, but you maintain a constant tension with the fly. Keep slack out of the line, and keep as much line as possible off the water—you should feel as though you are steering the fly. The fly will be at the deepest part of its swing when it gets even with you, so position yourself just opposite the spot where you sense the trout are.

The slight drag on the fly is not enough to pull it toward the surface, but the resulting movement is different enough from junk drifting in the current to attract a trout's attention. In Alaska this is the standard way to fish streamers for rainbows and the five species of Pacific salmon—it's usually done with a fast-sinking sink-tip line or a sinking shooting head.

Fall Techniques

Just as the deep swing is attractive to spawning salmon in Alaska, it also works on our lower forty-eight resident trout in the fall, when they are staging for spawning or holding in pools preparing to move. Spawning movements can start as early as August, even though the trout will not begin mating and building redds until November. Trout on the move are less inclined to bother with insect hatches and may slow their feeding, a fact that has often bothered me because it doesn't agree with what I've seen on the river: brown trout of obvious spawning age vigorously feeding on hatching insects. Either a heavy hatch is an irresistible temptation, or perhaps different strains of fall-spawning trout spawn anytime from late summer to early winter. Bob Bachman has done preliminary research on some streams in Pennsylvania that seems to support the second idea.

But many of the browns and brook trout, the fall spawners, won't react to anything near the surface in the fall: you have to drag a streamer in front of their noses. One theory holds that when trout are on the move anything that gets in their way annoys them, and they try to swat it out of the way with the only tool they have—their mouths. Another idea, rooted in behavioral science, holds that it is an adaptive advantage for trout to attack minnows around spawning time. Sculpins and other small fish feed on fish eggs, and a trout that kills or cripples a small fish near the redd saves some of its future genetic material. That slow, deep swing, without any added action, seems to draw the most strikes, perhaps because its deliberate movement threatens with arrogance.

When to Use a Sinking Line

When do you fish a sinking line as opposed to a weighted fly or weight on the leader? I use a floating line as much as possible because it is easier to cast, pick up, and mend. A floater with a long leader works fine in small streams, where you can stand fairly close to where the fly is drifting and you need to get the fly down quickly. But in larger rivers, where you may be wading fifty feet from the fly and it is hard to keep most of the line off the water, a sink tip or sinking shooting head is the best answer. Large rivers offer the luxury of a longer upstream cast, and the line that you can't keep off the water is better off sinking than floating because a floating line pulls the fly up and toward you.

One trick I have discovered with a sinking line is to cast and then, as soon as the line hits the water, lift up sharply with the tip of the rod. This helps the line break the water's surface tension and pulls the fly under quickly.

Incidentally, I feel that full-sinking lines have limited application in stream fishing—they are just too difficult to control in moving water. Sink-tip lines, and sinking shooting heads with a floating running line, will get the fly just as deep. Save your full-sinking lines for still-water fishing.

Sink-tip lines can also be handy in warm, shallow, fast water, especially when float fishing. In fast water a floating line sometimes makes even a weighted fly skip across the surface; despite occasional vicious strikes this usually puts the fish off. A line that pulls the fly under when you strip solves this problem. Regardless of the technique, when you fish a sink tip or sinking shooting head, your leader should be short—a maximum of six feet. A leader any longer will buoy the fly toward the surface. Where the water is dirty, or where the fish are not leader shy, as in Alaska, fishermen often put a perfection loop in a foot of 1X tippet and loop it right to the loop in the fly line. Guides in Alaska have told me they would attach the fly right to the fly line if they could only get the fly line through the eye of the hook!

The Traditional Quartering Downstream Technique

Streamers can also be fished quartering downstream. Although this is considered the traditional way of fishing streamers, it is not often done today. Cast toward the far bank, anywhere from directly across the river to about 45 degrees downstream, and let the fly swing in the current on a tight line until it stops directly below you. This technique can be used with a floating line, best in shallow and slow water, or with a sink-tip line in deeper or faster water. Try it with absolutely no motion on your part, and if that doesn't work, try pumping the rod gently. Small fish changing position will quarter across the current, and apparently this motion of the fly looks lifelike to trout.

The late Tony Skilton and I often fished a pool on the White River in Vermont where one of us could stand on a high roadside shoulder and see the entire pool while the other fished. We called it

The Classroom because you could see every move the fish made. One day I started out fishing a streamer my favorite way, stripping like a madman across the current. The water temperature was about 55 degrees. Tony watched from the observation point, and I didn't even get a follow. We switched positions and Tony used the same fly, except he gave action to the fly by gently rocking the tip of his rod. You could have stared at that pool for hours and not spotted a trout, but on every cast, as Tony's fly came around in the current, I saw the glint of a trout tipping up to look at the fly. Although he only connected on a couple of them, it was like pulling rabbits from a hat.

Apparently in the cold water my strips were moving the fly too quickly to interest the trout. Tony, however, was adding action to the fly without moving it any faster than the current pulling on the line.

Once the fly swings below you, you have a number of options. One is to let it hang there. Sometimes a trout will follow the fly across the river and stare at it, or there might be a trout lying just below where your fly ends up. You can twitch the rod tip a little, or you can retrieve the fly back upstream, experimenting with short and long, fast and slow strips, or a steady hand-twist retrieve. Trout caught by your drawing the fly back upstream will usually be small ones, sometimes not much bigger than the fly.

Streamer Techniques for Difficult Water

In tiny streams that are too narrow to cast anywhere but straight upstream or straight downstream, you can often use the direct downstream presentation. With your profile low, sneak downstream to twenty or thirty feet from one of those bathtub pools that form above a logjam or boulder. Cast to the far side of the tiny pool and let the fly swing across, right in front of the obstruction. Give it a couple of twitches if you want. Then draw the fly back upstream slowly, or let it hang in the current for a while. With this technique you can catch small-stream trout from tangled pools that you couldn't with any method other than a worm or small spinner. Keep the flies on the small, sparse side for this kind of fishing. The good old Woolly Bugger in sizes 8, 10, 12, and even 14 is one to start with, and if that doesn't work, try something bright like a Mickey Finn, especially in waters with brook trout or cutthroats. You'll become convinced that streamers are not just for intimidating rivers and corpulent trout.

You can also use streamers at the base of a waterfall, where it is almost impossible to catch trout on anything except bait—the water is too foamy for trout to see a dry fly, a nymph will not drift properly in the swirly currents, and you can't get a proper swing on a wet fly. Using a weighted streamer or two or three split shot on the leader, cast directly to the base of the falls. At the completion of the forward cast, turn the tip of the rod quickly below the horizontal as if you want to slam the fly into the water. This will drive the fly under the surface quickly and throw some slack line on top of it, so it will sink immediately below the foam. Don't start stripping right away. Give the fly a few seconds to sink, and then begin stripping back toward you. The advantage of using a streamer here is that you can cast from any direction, from the side of the falls or from downstream,

Tough water like this boiling falls pool is tailor-made for a streamer.

and still have the fly swimming in an effective manner. Unlike any other fly a streamer is effective regardless of its direction in relation to the current.

This same advantage—being independent of tough currents—can be used in other places. Tails of pools are difficult to fish with a dry fly or nymph; the water picks up surface speed quickly just before a tail spills over into a riffle, but near the bottom, where the trout are, it does not increase in velocity at the same rate. So a dry presents tremendous drag problems, and trying to drift a nymph naturally with the leader and line picking up speed above causes problems. But you can fish a streamer through this stuff with confidence because *you*, not the currents, are controlling the fly.

One final trick with streamers is a sneaky one that works in clear water, even in the middle of the day when trout will make a pass at a streamer and not connect. Start with a nine-foot 3X or 4X leader and cut the tippet back to about a foot. Tie on a two-foot-long piece of 5X, leaving a six-inch tag end from the heavier end of the leader, so you have a dropper above the tippet. Tie a small, slim baitfish imitation, like a Blacknose Dace or a small weighted Muddler (size 10 or 12), to the dropper, and a size 16 or 18 nymph to the 5X tippet. Now work this combination along the edges of weedbeds, logs, or rocks, or along a shady bank. Move the flies about a foot, then let them drop back or hang in the current. A trout will often follow the streamer, decide not to take, and drop back. The nymph hanging there presents a perfect opportunity for a bite that is less threatening to the fish, and they seem to take it almost as a reflex. You can also try it the other way around, with the nymph on the dropper and the streamer below, so it looks like a small fish trying to catch a nymph.

Streamers are about the most useful flies you can use in non-hatch times. You can fish them in water that doesn't have enough current for a dry or nymph, or in water that is too fast and foamy. They'll catch trout in water too cold for a dry, in the steamy heat of a July morning, or before spawning time, when trout may not be interested in insects. A streamer will draw strikes from tiny yearlings for reasons we don't understand, and from huge browns that have lost their interest in hatches and live in water more suitable for carp.

W ET FLIES

It was a big striped bass that finally convinced me: a fly swung in front of a fish has almost universal appeal.

Holding on to a 10-weight rod with both hands as twenty pounds of silvery muscle combined with the force of the outgoing water from Menemsha Pond, I sweated inside my waders even though it was three thirty in the morning. Recovering a hundred yards of backing and ninety feet of line inch by inch in the darkness gave me a lot of time to think about how I had hooked this fish—with the same technique I would have used for Atlantic or Pacific salmon, steelhead, or plain old stream trout. My friend Cooper Gilkes and I had been prowling the beaches of the eastern end of Martha's Vineyard for many hours in the darkness, searching for schools of striped bass. Coop, a native of the island who knows all the spots, suggested we drive to Dutcher Dock, in the working fishing village of Menemsha. When I asked him why we should hang around a dock in the middle of the night, where floodlights blast into the water, he just growled at me to trust him. We drove out onto a boardwalk where market trucks load fish during the day, and hanging over the side of the planks Coop told me to take a look in the water four feet below. As I approached, I heard a repertoire of barks, purrs, and mutters, and looking over the side I saw a pair of otters noisily munching on fish, contentedly oblivious to the two forms above them.

Coop walked to the other side and said softly, "Now come look over here." As I walked across the boardwalk, I heard a deep thunk, and peering into the brightly lit water, I saw a huge bass slide out

Swinging a classic wet fly in front of a trout may look like something other than a drowned insect. Margot Page photo.

from the shadows under the dock, pluck something from the outgoing tide, and shimmer back into the shadows. He looked like an oversized brown trout sipping a mayfly. Three or four other bass joined him in the next five minutes. I cast a white Deceiver across the current, stripping back in the foot-long pulls that usually work on stripers, without eliciting a bit of interest. Then I got up-current of the fish and began to cast across and down-current, letting the fly swing on a tight line, exactly the way you would for salmon or steelhead. A couple of fish rose to inspect the fly only to sink back into the depths. Finally one latched on to the Deceiver, and I began a half-hour slugging match that would end with me pouncing on the bass while I slipped on the jelly-coated rocks of the jetty, leaving me dripping with fish slime and salt water after I released him.

Although for trout fishing a wet fly is often thought to imitate a drowned or emerging insect, I think the appeal of a wet fly swung in front of a trout carries over much more into the realm of a lure than most of us like to believe. It ties in to fishing without hatches nicely: freed from imitating a specific insect, we can think more about fishing a fly that is appealing or provoking to a trout. Virtually the same techniques that draw strikes from Atlantic salmon, steelhead, smallmouth bass, and any other fish that lives in running water will also catch trout. It's fine to believe that a wet fly suddenly rising to the surface looks just like a hatching insect, but most of the time a wet fly swings *across* different current lanes, and often across strands of current far too strong for an insect to swim. Although some caddisflies swim across currents when they are emerging, most insects swim weakly, if at all. Baitfish swim broadside to the current, but it's hard to believe a trout takes a size 16 or 18 soft hackle as a minnow imitation.

What Do Wets Imitate and Why Use Them?

Why does a fly swung across currents work so well? I don't have the answer, but the idea that a suddenly accelerating fly provokes the hunger or predatory instinct is a valid one. Fish respond to stimuli with a reflex, a knee-jerk reaction, because their brains lack the power to reason. It's been suggested that salmon and steelhead, which are mostly through with feeding during their spawning runs, react to a fly instinctively to protect their eggs from predators; even though they do this far in advance of actual spawning, it's hard for an animal to turn such behavior on and off at will. Male birds sing for months after the breeding season. A fly swung in front of a fish must be one of the most overt, obnoxious stimuli he sees, and it also alerts a fish to the fact that the object whizzing by is more than just another piece of debris.

So when you fish a wet fly for trout, a fly that looks *something* like the insects they have been eating, I think you put two pieces of the puzzle together. The fly reminds them of a recent meal that satiated their hunger, and it also grabs their attention like a piece of string being drawn in front of a cat. I don't think they have the capacity to reason that the two pieces don't fit together.

In this book let's consider any subsurface, insect-appearing fly that you fish on a tight line, cast in any direction other than straight upstream, to be a wet fly. In other words, if you're fishing a Hare's

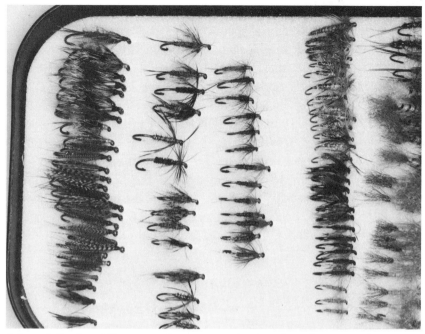

A box full of wet flies can give you a relaxing day of prospecting.

Ear nymph dead-drift upstream, we'll call it a nymph, but if you turn around and fish it swinging downstream, it's a wet fly. The wet-fly techniques discussed here apply to nymphs, soft hackles, flymphs, and Hornbergs, as well as standard winged wet flies.

There are reasons to fish a wet fly that have nothing to do with science or productivity. Little you can do on a trout stream is as pleasant as casting a single wet fly. The fly is not as wind-resistant as a dry or streamer, nor as heavy as a weighted nymph. Seldom do you need to false cast more than once, so the casting motion is satisfying and relaxing. Because of the ease of casting and the fact that you can cover a lot of water by just slapping the fly on the water and letting it swing, fishing a wet fly downstream is an energy-saving technique especially suited for big, featureless water, where trout may be evenly distributed. For example, on big water like the Madison or the Delaware, both of which contain long, even riffles, you'll kill yourself covering all of the good-looking water in a run if you try to place a weighted nymph in exactly the right spot on each cast. But if you work downstream with a wet fly, you can wade with the current without struggling to place your leg every time you move, and you can limit the amount of casting you do by letting the current work the fly, with an occasional mend here and there.

Times and Places to Use Wets

Wet flies work better when water temperatures over 55 degrees favor an active pursuit by the trout. Unlike a weighted nymph fished dead-drift near the bottom, where trout need to move only a short distance to inhale the fly, a wet fly usually swims closer to the surface. Even with a weighted fly, a sinking-tip line, or a section of lead-core line looped to the leader, tension on the fly pulls it upward and across the currents in a pattern a cold fish is reluctant to chase. Wet flies also work better when there are scattered, erratic rises on the river. Have you ever seen a rise once every fifteen minutes or so, never in the same place, and no insects on the water? This is not a situation where a dry makes much sense, because there is no hatch to match and no consistent target to hit. It's a perfect setup for a wet fly, though, because you can cover a great deal of water and you know the trout are willing to chase something to the surface. Activity like this usually portends a caddis hatch later in the day, when you can settle down and pitch to rising fish, but why sit on the bank and wait for something to happen? I've also seen this activity shut off or dribble along all day without a hatch ever occurring. Perhaps the fish are chasing caddis pupae that are trying to break the surface film, but they could also be eating backswimmers, aquatic beetles, or water boatmen—bugs that won't turn into a hatch because they are already in the adult stage.

To be honest with you, I fish a swung wet fly less often than a dead-drifted nymph, and under most conditions I find the nymph far more effective, especially if the water is cold or deep, or if I have seen nothing rising. But one circumstance almost demands a swung fly: when the water is dirty from runoff or a rainstorm. One of our local rivers contains brown trout and some incredibly gullible wild rainbows. This river is a nymphing classroom; nearly any nymph pattern, at any time, will catch at least a few rainbows. A joke among

The Partridge and Orange soft hackle has often saved the day for me in dirty water.

my fishing friends, when shown an ugly, scraggly nymph pattern, is to exclaim, "Boy, that fly would really work on Otter Creek!" The codicil, usually unspoken unless the fly tyer is a good friend, is that *any* nymph will work on Otter Creek. Once I was fishing this river when the water had gotten dingy from a short cloudburst. There was not enough rain to raise the water level so the fish would turn on a streamer, but there was some soil and debris in the water. I fished a Hare's Ear nymph upstream for an hour—a pattern that works in *any* river—without a touch. In desperation I turned around and slapped it across the current without much thought for finesse, and a trout—a nice one—took it on the first cast. Later I switched to a Partridge and Orange soft hackle and took a dozen fish, all on the downstream swing. As soon as I faced upstream and fished the fly without a swing, the fish stopped taking.

Thinking about this experience later, I realized it made sense. When water is full of debris, trout will inhale a lot of junk, most of it inedible. The swing given to a wet fly distinguishes it from the inedible trivia and lets the trout know that it is alive, something under its own power and not at the whim of the current.

A wet fly also works better than a dead-drifted nymph in the tail of a pool. As we've seen in previous chapters, the tail is tough to fish because of the great speed difference between current at the surface, where your line enters the water, and current close to the bottom, where trout are eating. Since it is difficult to sink your fly close to the bottom and get a dead-drift for more than a few inches, why not use the current instead of fighting it? A trout in the tail of a pool is in shallow water anyway, and rather than trying to get a nymph to the bottom, using slack line casts and continuous mends for a questionable or short-lived drift, it's better to use a method that lures trout to a fly under controlled drag.

Spring creeks are often thought of as the premier place to fish upstream, dead-drifted nymphs. In most such cases this kind of subsurface fly will outfish any other technique—and it's a fascinating way to fish, particularly if you can see the fish. It is the way I prefer to fish a spring creek even if there are trout rising. However, there are times when dead-drifting a nymph on a spring creek seems futile. When clouds darken the sky, you can see neither the trout nor the pockets between weedbeds where they lie, and if wind ruffles the surface it can be nearly impossible to keep an eye on your leader for the slight hesitation that indicates a strike. The wind on western spring creeks gets so strong that even a strike indicator can be blown across the surface, ruining the drift of your fly. At times like this a wet fly, normally reserved for freestone riffles, can salvage a day of fishing.

The gentle swing of a wet fly in the slow currents of a spring creek, with fly and leader submerged below the effects of the wind, sometimes works surprisingly well. You'll be able to feel the strikes instead of having to watch your leader, and without a strike indicator your fly will be pulled by the current, not the wind. If your fly has to be yanked around by *something*, better the current, which gives it a more natural movement than the wind. Find a place in a spring creek where there is a touch of current—enough so that when you cast slightly upstream to get your fly to sink, the current will tighten the line and draw the fly across as it comes across from you and below. In dead-slow water I've found that mending *downstream* to increase the swing (in most wet-fly fishing, as you'll see shortly, you'll be trying to mend upstream to decrease the swing) keeps a tight connection on the fly, keeps it moving, and enables you to feel the strike.

Another place a wet fly can work better than any other is where you find brook trout. I fish a stream near my house just because it is full of brookies. I can fish a wet fly, or a couple of them on droppers, and delight in the easy casting motions and the sensual anticipation of feeling the strike while looking at the scenery or daydreaming. All along I know I am fishing the most effective method possible. There is no worrying about watching the end of the line or leader every second, no squinting into the light to pick out a dry fly bobbing through a riffle where every piece of foam resembles the white wings of an Ausable Wulff. Brook trout have evolved in about the most sterile, food-limited freshwater environment in North America—acidic upland streams—and as a result they rise for a dry fly eagerly and take a dead-drifted nymph with abandon. But a wet fly swung across the current, teasingly suggesting that it is alive and good to eat, makes them streak across a tiny pool. Favorite brook trout flies are often full of bright, highly visible colors—not because brook trout are less "smart" than browns or rainbows, but because thousands of generations of selection have singled out the fish that bolt for any bit of food that appears edible.

Wet-fly fishing is such a delight to the senses that when you find a stream like this, one where you can fish wet flies nearly any time and draw strikes, it is a stream to cherish and remember.

The Wet-Fly Swing

You could spend your entire fly-fishing life just quartering a wet fly downstream, letting the current play with your fly, the fish hooking themselves by sheer effort combined with the current's tension on the line. Fly fishermen fished this way from the Middle Ages until the turn of the century, when city fishermen began to read articles in the English sporting press and turned around to face the current, fishing the new dry flies and nymphs that can be so deadly. Today you still find pockets of rural fly fishermen who cling to three wet flies on droppers, and you have to admire the simplicity of their methods. My neighbor Harry Hayden is a native Vermonter who fishes the brook trout streams that feed the Battenkill, and when I meet him on the stream I'm ashamed to be all decked out in nippers, fly floatant, six diameters of tippet, several dozen different types of leaders, and thousands of fly patterns. He's always curious about my bushy dry flies and weighted nymphs, and he asks polite questions about the newest emerger. But when I stop for sweet corn in late summer, I see his rod hanging from the rafters in his garage, still strung with the same three wet-fly patterns—probably the same *flies*—that I saw him using on the stream in April.

If you watch one of these old-timers, whether it's in Vermont or Potter County in northern Pennsylvania, or in the mountains of North Carolina, you'll see that they don't just chuck their flies at the same angle every time. They vary the angle they fish with the speed and the depth of the water. A great place to fish a wet fly quartering downstream is in a gentle riffle, as shallow as you can find that will still hold fish—two to four feet deep. Even better is a place where a shallow riffle dumps into a deeper pool or pocket, as it seems that this kind of water just makes a wet fly move at exactly the right speed, taunting the fish into striking. If you think I'm going to give you a scientific reason for this, you're mistaken. Just try a wet fly here and enjoy it.

When you find deeper water, deeper than four feet, it's better to cast your fly quartering upstream, as the farther upstream you pitch your flies, the deeper they will sink before the current pulls them from the bottom and across the current. When you start a wet-fly drift at an upstream angle, it's best to try to set your mind to leading the fly through the current, much as you would lead a strong dog circling around you while you hold a leash. Keeping the rod at a 30-degree angle above the water will help you keep in touch with the fly and keep it where it is supposed to be swinging, just as if that dog you were leading is on the other side of a short hedge. You want the fly to stay in the same downstream current as much as possible, with just enough gentle tension on the line to slide it ever so slightly toward you as it drifts downstream, so that it is only subtly contrary to the current. Mends help, particularly on casts longer than three times the length of your rod. On a long cast, as soon as you feel the belly of the fly line is getting downstream of the place your fly is drifting, flip the belly of the line upstream. Try to do it so that you only move the line on the water, not the fly. If you move too much line with a mend, the line pulls the fly up and it darts toward the surface, and although this dipping motion should look like an insect rising to the surface, it seldom draws strikes for me until the fly is at the end of the swing. Don't ask me for the scientific basis of that one, either.

Fast, deep water requires an upstream cast, with frequent mends to keep the line upstream of the fly. If you don't keep the line upstream of the fly, when the line has completely tightened below you and you run out of drift, an arc at the end of the line will snap the fly around like a bullwhip, with an appearance to the trout that must be as frightening as a bad back cast cracked a few inches in front of your face. Contrast this with a drift where the line is upstream of the fly, and as the line tightens the fly is just drawn smoothly to the surface. An underwater bug doesn't turn corners like a racing car around a pylon, nor does it look lifelike for a fly to streak downstream as if it were being yanked around by a piece of string. In water that is fast but shallow, like that in the tail of a pool, where you don't need to sink the fly more than a couple of inches, you can cast at a sharp downstream angle to lessen the snap at the

Leading a wet fly through a deep pocket.

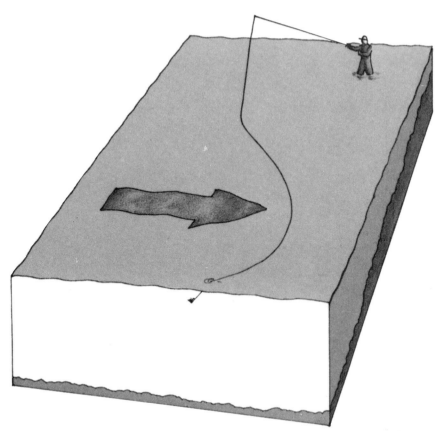

If you cast straight across the current, the line will belly and pull your fly toward the surface.

end of a drift. Here you may not get more than a few feet of drift, but better a couple of feet of fish-catching swing than having your fly career across twenty feet of good water. Try to avoid casting your fly directly across the current, unless you are fishing in slow, shallow water. Casting a wet fly perpendicular to the current gives you neither the sinking advantage of casting at an upstream angle nor the swing truncation of the downstream angle.

Position: Where you stand when you fish a wet fly is as important as with any other kind of fly. Try to pick your position so that your fly line will fall in water that is moving at the same speed as your fly. This isn't always possible, so in general, if the water at your feet is

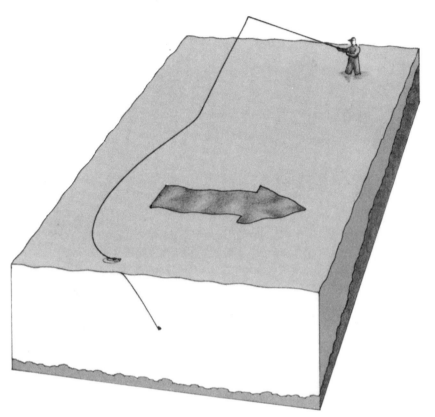

Casting upstream and placing an upstream mend in the line will keep your fly deeper and will keep it from moving too quickly.

faster than the water where your fly lands, then frequent upstream mends are required. Otherwise the fly is quickly pulled out of the productive water where fast meets slow—the seam. Holding the rod at a relatively high angle, around 30 degrees above the horizontal, will keep more of your line out of the faster water and will help to keep the current from bellying the line. If the water at your feet is slower than the water where the fly is swinging, the fly quickly arcs out of the fast water and hangs against the upstream bow in your line, so to keep it swimming you need to add a downstream mend. This keeps the fly slightly broadside to the current, so it is more visible to the fish, and keeps you in touch with the fly.

To help the fly sink when it first hits the water, it's often helpful to throw a bit of slack into the leader. This will give the fly a second or two to sink before the line starts to pull it. If you are casting into water that is slower than that at your feet, you can also throw an upstream curve into the line by using a reach cast. If you throw the curve onto the faster water closest to you, the fly will have an added chance to sink, and you will decrease the arc that the faster current will put into your line, reducing the severity of the fly's swing.

As the fly reaches the end of the swing downstream of your position, lower the rod tip to keep the fly from swinging to the surface too violently and to keep it in productive water. This adds a foot or so to the swing and thus extends your drift. It also keeps the fly slightly deeper—keeps it from skimming across the surface. You can also try to release slack line from your hand, although this technique needs a fairly fast current so that there is enough tension on the line that it is pulled smoothly from your hand. If you have to jerk on the rod to get line to feed downstream, it ruins the effect, and if you let too much line out the fly goes slack and you lose the constant tension on it that distinguishes the fly from other drifting junk. These manipulations are particularly effective when your fly is swinging right on the edge of a seam, where the trout are supposed to be, and you want to keep the fly from swinging into the less productive water directly below you.

To jiggle or not to jiggle: many books recommend that you "work" the rod tip as the flies swing around. It should make your fly appear more lifelike, if you believe aquatic insects do a lot of darting around down there. The ones I have watched don't swim very strongly, and I suspect that anything we can do with the tip of a nine-foot rod is too overt to look as though it was done by an insect that weighs a fraction of a gram. Don Owens, the best wet-fly fisherman I know, whom I'll talk about in a little more detail later, says he'll "sometimes jiggle it a little when things get slow, but usually I prefer the straight sweep." John Atherton wrote that a wet fly was "best shown to the fish as a constantly moving object." Apparently, jiggling the fly was used more in earlier days than it is today, and I've seen old movies of salmon fishermen on the Patapedia in the thirties, where every shot of fishermen shows them working the rod. When it works for me, it seems to be in slower currents.

The process I've just described is the standard way of fishing a wet fly, best in water where you suspect the trout may be uniformly distributed. Honest fishermen would describe this as water where they have absolutely no idea where the fish are holding. Standard procedure is to start out with the water at your feet, making short casts, then gradually increasing the length of your casts out to the point where you run out of water or where you can't cast any farther. Then you take a few steps downstream and repeat the process. It's a pedantic way of fishing, but it sure covers the water thoroughly. Often, though, once you get out into the water, you'll see that a lot of it is way too shallow to fish, or you'll begin to catch fish in a certain type of water, so you can narrow down the search and cast more thoughtfully. In this kind of fishing the rod should usually be held at 30 degrees, except at the end of the cast, and just as important is that you should follow the progress of the fly with the tip of your rod, except when you're mending line. If you stop following the fly's progress with the tip, you'll put almost immediate tension on the line; the fly will cross the current, moving toward you, and will rise to the surface. Which sets you up for another method.

Lifting a Wet Fly

The most effective part of a wet-fly swing, where most strikes occur, is at the point where, if your drift is right, the fly suddenly hesitates and begins to struggle against the current. If you have an idea where a trout is lying, maybe in front of a log or on the edge of a rock, a smart move is to plan your cast so that this movement occurs just as your fly reaches the spot. The problem is that most of us daydreamed through geometry class, and to plan a cast like this is more than we bargain for during a day of fishing. But there is an easier way around the problem. It's called the Leisenring Lift, developed by a famous Pennsylvania wet-fly fisherman named Jim Leisenring, and chronicled by him in his 1941 book *The Art of Tying the Wet Fly*. Rather than a lift, which is what this technique makes the fly

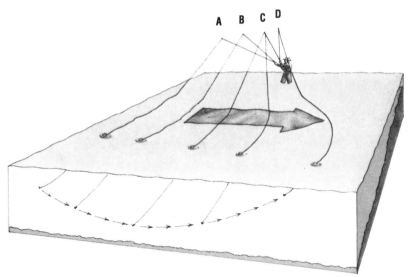

Lifting a wet fly. You cast at A, drift at B and C by following the progress of the fly with the rod tip, then stop following with the rod at D.

do, it is more appropriately described as a stop, which is what you do with the tip of the rod.

To execute the lift, cast above where you think a trout is lying, and slightly beyond the position. You'll have to judge exactly how far above by the depth of the water—deeper water calls for casting farther upstream. Keep the rod at 30 degrees, and let the fly swing under slight tension down toward the fish; follow the fly with the tip of your rod. Retrieve just enough line to keep slack from developing between your rod tip and the fly. A foot or two upstream of the place where the trout may be lying, stop moving your rod tip, letting the current increase the tension on the line. At this point the fly will stop and will rise toward the surface just in front of the fish, an almost irresistible motion to a trout at all interested in eating. When a trout takes a wet fly with this method, it will often be with a violent swirl or even a splash that appears to be a rise, leaving you no doubt as to whether there was a trout in that position. In most water it's important not to actually lift the rod when you begin the "lift," because if you do you'll combine the lifting action of the current with your own lifting motion, and the fly will rise too quickly. In slow currents you might try drawing the fly upward by using a long, smooth strip, or by lifting the rod tip, but I'd advise you to try using the current first, because it is much more subtle and lifelike to have the current move it for you.

Retrieves

At the end of the swing, no matter what kind of manipulations you employ to reduce the swing on the fly, eventually you'll run out of tricks and the fly will end up hanging directly below you. If you haven't hooked a fish yet, all is not lost. First, you can just let the fly hang below you in the current. This can often produce a strike from a fish that would not chase the fly as it was swinging, and I have often watched a trout chase a fly as it swung across the current, only to stop below the fly, watch it for a couple of seconds, then move forward and inhale it. The bad news is that a trout that takes a fly when it is hanging below you will often be a small one. Next, you can twitch the rod tip as the fly hangs in the current, letting the fly rise and move forward slightly, then dropping the rod tip to let it sink back. Again, trout that take a fly in this manner are usually small ones, I suppose because a larger trout either takes a fly when he first sees it, or ignores it if that first glimpse didn't induce him to strike. It seems that smaller trout are more susceptible to teasing than bigger ones.

If hanging the fly doesn't interest the fish, you can also retrieve it toward you, hoping that there is a trout between you and the place your fly ended its swing, one that hasn't been spooked by the fact that you are standing directly upstream of him. Because you will be standing in the place that is most visible and threatening to a trout, you'll pick up most fish on a retrieve in riffled water, where they can't see you as well, and once again they will usually be smaller ones. For a retrieve, first try stripping line six inches at a time, about a second per strip. You can also try long, slow strips, drawing two feet of line at a time. The old standby with wet-fly fishermen was the hand-twist retrieve, which gives you about the same effect as slow, steady strips, although the hand-twist eliminates the pauses between strips. Jim Lepage finds that on his Maine rivers, especially if there are any caddis on the water, short, fast strips, say two three-inch strips every second, will draw strikes, especially in deeper pools. Don Owens, who uses wets more than any other person I know, likes to hand-twist and then give every third rotation of his hand a hard twist, which gives the fly a sudden dart through the water.

It seems that the effectiveness of a retrieved wet fly is a characteristic of a given stream, and its usefulness as a nonhatch technique holds throughout the season, regardless of time of year or water conditions. When I lived in Syracuse, New York, I was teaching a Saturday morning fly-tying class, and one of my students, Les Gillett, who had fished the southern Adirondacks all his life, told me about a stream that fished well with wet flies. One Saturday I decided to try the stream, and after an hour of fishing all kinds of patterns on a standard swing, I was without a single strike. I had used my usual halfhearted retrieve, with a couple of quick strips after the swing was completed, because I had never done well stripping a wet fly. Les's voice came out of the streamside brush. "You're doing it all wrong." He got into the river below me and demonstrated his technique. He cast almost straight downstream, let his fly swing just enough to get it under the surface, then began stripping back until the fly was almost to his rod tip. I was not about to argue with local knowledge, so I began imitating his technique, and soon I began to pick up wild brook and brown trout with fair regularity—all of them about halfway through the retrieve.

Subsequent trips to the same stream produced the same results, all through the season. Why this method worked so much better than a swing, or even fishing a streamer or dead-drifted nymph, I have no idea, but I did see an unusually large population of swimming mayfly nymphs of the genus *Isonychia*, or Leadwing Coachmen as fishermen call them. Perhaps the trout were used to feeding on tiny fish as well. Since then I have always tried long retrieves when a wet-fly swing did not produce on unfamiliar rivers, and I have found a few streams where the retrieve works better than the swing.

One place in particular bears mention because it is a spring creek, as far removed from that relatively sterile Adirondack stream in both character and productivity as you'll find. This spring creek has one stretch where a riffle piles against a log cribbing. The trout barely poke their noses beyond the shaded protection of the crib-bing to feed, as the place is full of herons that crop and educate the trout population into a neurotic state. Casting a nymph straight upstream will spook the fish, but if you get above them, kneeling down so they won't see you, you can cast off to the side of the riffle, letting the current gently work your fly to the edge of the cribbing. You then line your rod tip up with the upper end of the cribbing and slowly crawl the fly back upstream with tentative strips. It requires a tiny wet fly, a size 18 Blue Quill, and a 6X or 7X tippet, and some of the brown trout are over sixteen inches long. Many break off if the strike carries any authority, and I always treat the first couple of casts as if I've spotted a fifty-dollar bill on a crowded sidewalk.

Getting the Fly Deeper

You may wonder why I haven't mentioned weighted flies or leaders or sinking lines yet. Do they have a place in wet-fly fishing? Although I use a floating line for about 98 percent of my stream trout fishing, it's usually because I want the option of going from a blind-fished streamer to a nymph with an indicator to a dry fly to a wet fly in the same pool. The only line that has this versatility is a floater, or an intermediate line that can be dressed to float. There are times, especially in deep, fast water, that having weight on the fly or a sinking line will get your fly to where the fish can see it. If you look into a run and can't see bottom, you can assume the trout lying on the bottom can't see your fly if it's swinging right under the surface, so it is time to change tactics.

The best advice I can give you on getting a fly closer to the bottom is to avoid the use of split shot on the leader, at least when swinging a wet. I use split shot all the time for fishing upstream nymphs, and it works just fine for getting a nymph quickly into a deep pocket, but let the fly swing below you and strikes will disappear as if your fly had been removed from the leader. Time and again I've tried to get some extra mileage out of a dead-drifted nymph with split shot on the leader, and as the nymph drifted even with my position I've held the rod at 45 degrees, letting the tip follow the fly through the swing. Something about split shot on the leader puts the trout off: maybe the shot swinging in the current spooks the fish, or perhaps at the end of the swing the fly swings too abruptly as it pivots around the short piece of leader between the fly and the shot, instead of the less severe pivot around your line.

Perhaps the easiest way to keep a wet fly below the surface, a way that does not require changing your line or modifying your leader, is to use a weighted fly, one that has lead added to the shank of the hook before the fly is tied. You can buy weighted nymphs in anything from a specialty fly shop to a drugstore, but have you ever seen weighted wet flies or soft hackles? I've seen them a few times in over twenty-five years of haunting fly shops for business and pleasure, but if you asked me where you could buy a weighted wet fly today, I wouldn't have a clue. Won't a weighted nymph like a Hare's Ear work just as well as a weighted fly tied specifically over a wet-fly dressing? I'm not so sure. For a fly that will be swung downstream, you'll have more success with either a fly that has a collar of hackle around its head—a concentric hackle that will activate when the current pulls on it, as on a soft hackle, a flymph, or a plain old Gray Hackle Peacock—or a fly with a wing that will stabilize it as it swings in the current, like a Blue Quill or Light Cahill. A natural fly doesn't rock back and forth when it struggles against the current (although it will wiggle along the long axis of the body), so you need either a fly that looks the same from any angle no matter how much it rolls, or a fly that won't rock in the current because of the rudder effect of its wing.

The late Charlie Brooks, famous for fishing big stonefly nymphs on the Madison with a sink-tip line and an upstream-and-across technique (really a cross between a wet-fly and a dead-drifted nymph technique), tied all his nymphs "in the round." His technique put moderate tension on the fly rather than a strict dead-drift. His patterns were tied without a wing case and with a 360-degree collared hackle so they would look the same from any angle to the trout. For the way we are viewing wet flies and nymphs, both his technique and his flies were really giant wet flies rather than nymphs.

If you tie your own flies, or if you have a friend who will custom tie some for you, try making weighted versions of your favorite patterns. I once spent a week fishing the Esopus with Terry Finger, a college friend who grew up fishing that river under the tutelage of the irascible Ray Smith. Ray was the Catskill mentor of Arnold Gingrich, among others. I don't remember too much of my audience with Smith—who was known for his beautiful wet-fly patterns, in particular the Olive Quill—other than his first words to me, at 9 in the morning. "You want a warm beer, kid?" I do remember that we spent evenings tying flies to be fished on droppers three at a time; they were always an Olive Quill, a Hare's Ear, and a Black Gnat, and there was a special order you had to use, although the priority escapes me. We weighted all of them lightly with the finest lead wire we could find, and we tied it in along the sides of the hook shank, rather than winding it around the shank, which I'm sure helps to further stabilize the fly in the current. I'm not sure that the locals knew why the weight worked better tied in along the shank, but probably someone did it once that way and it proved to be effective, just as there may have been a valid reason why the order of the flies along the leader was so important.

Putting some light weight on a March Brown wet, or a Partridge and Orange soft hackle, or a flymph will not ruin the action of the fly in the water, and it will help to break the surface tension and pull both the fly and the leader under the surface faster, as well as keep the fly from skimming on top of the water at the end of the swing. For very fast or deep water, though, you'll have to resort to more drastic (although easier to obtain) means, like putting a piece of lead-core line between your leader and line, or going to a sinking-tip line. Even when you angle your cast upstream, using a floating line and a weighted fly with a nine-foot leader, the deepest you can expect the fly to swing is about three feet. The fly will never hang vertically below the fly line, and a floating line—combined with a leader that, although nylon has neutral buoyancy, tends to float from any line dressing or oil from your hands—will keep pulling the fly toward the surface. Stretching the weight over a longer distance—using a sink-tip line or lead head attached to your leader, rather than a single-point source like split shot—will make the fly swing through a longer, less drastic arc when tension is placed on the line at the end of the swing.

The easiest way to get a wet fly to swing deeper at the end of the swing is to add a section of lead-core line between your floating line and leader. The lead core has loops on both ends so you can

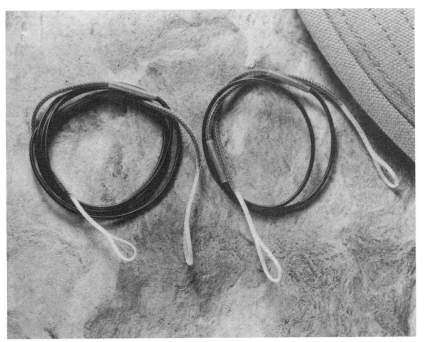

Lead heads can keep your fly swinging deep. They can be looped to the fly line or to the end of the leader.

loop one end to your fly line and the other to a short. Leaders in this case should be no longer than six feet, but even better is to just loop a tippet section, a level piece of anything from 2X to 6X, right to the lead head, since you don't need a tapered leader when fishing subsurface. If you use a tippet shorter than two feet, you place the heavy lead-head section too close to the fly, and it will pass by the trout's nose before the fly. The other option is to replace your floating line with a regular sink-tip line, which, because the sinking section can be up to eighteen feet long, will keep the fly running even deeper. The disadvantage of using a sink-tip line is that if you want to switch to a dry quickly, you have to switch spools again.

With a sink-tip line or a lead head you can reduce the speed at which your fly swings because the sinking section is lower in the water, where the current is slower, and because the resistance of a submerged piece of line is greater than that of a line floating on the surface. The most useful place for this kind of rig is in the middle of a fast, deep pool, where you want the fly to swing several feet below the surface, rather than just under the surface. Cast well upstream, so the line has a chance to pull the fly under as it sinks. Strikes usually won't occur until the fly is at least even with your position, because when the fly is upstream of you the sinking line will draw the fly downstream as it sinks, an unnatural movement. As the fly comes directly across from you, mend as much line as you can, all of the floating portion of the line that is on the surface, so the tension on the fly begins to come from upstream. Because the sinking part of the line has a lot of resistance in the water, you can also shake some loose line from your stripping hand by pointing the tip of the rod directly at the place where the line enters the water, and moving the tip of the rod gently from side to side as you release line. This movement will allow the fly to swing slower and deeper, but you may also miss strikes as you do it, so only use it if you think the fly isn't getting deep enough. Keep the rod tip at 30 degrees above the water as the fly swings below you, and try to keep as much line as possible off the water; then as the line is fully stretched below you in the current, lower the rod tip to lessen the swing just a bit. And hold on. This is where strikes usually happen with a sink-tip line. The retrieve is also usually more productive with a lead head or sink-tip line, because you can keep your fly below the surface throughout the retrieve. Sometimes fast, quick strips, a motion you can't use effectively with a floating line because it pulls the fly right to the surface, will work well, particularly if there is deep water below you.

I feel that full-sinking lines are a disadvantage in stream trout fishing, because mends are almost impossible with this kind of line, and they really seem to get the fly no deeper than a modern high-density sink tip. The effective part of a sinking line seems to be the first fifteen feet, and any more just puts an underwater bow in the line that can't be removed by mending.

Jim Lepage disagrees with me and uses full-sinking lines in deep pools on big, deep Maine rivers like the Kennebec, especially in midsummer, when he wants to crawl a wet fly back to him, keeping the fly close to the bottom throughout the retrieve. He casts directly across the river, lets the fly swing, and even feeds line into the swing to get the fly deeper. Of course this is going to work best in one of those rivers where a retrieved wet fly is effective. One place Jim uses this technique to great advantage is where you encounter a big, swirling back eddy, the kind you will find at the head of a waterfall pool or other pool where the water at the head rushes in quickly. Here trout will lie in the deep water where the outside of the back eddy meets the main current, and it's virtually impossible to fish that seam with either an upstream dead-drifted nymph or a swung wet fly because of the strong conflicting currents on the surface. Jim stands to the outside of the back eddy, at the upstream end, and casts his wet fly on full-sinking line out into the main current. He lets the fly swing and sink, and then points his rod tip along the seam between the main current and the outside of the back eddy. When he retrieves, the fly will slide in between the main current and the back eddy, staying in the relatively calm water beneath the conflicting surface currents, where it is easier for the trout to lie. He often holds his rod tip underwater to keep the fly even deeper on the retrieve.

Droppers

Fishing more than one wet fly at a time is a technique that has been used for hundreds of years, but it reached its zenith in the last century in America, when wet-fly fishermen would sometimes fish a half-dozen flies on a single leader. We often view the nineteenth-century wet-fly fisherman as always using at least three flies—the "stretcher" or farthest fly from the rod tip, the "dropper" or middle fly, and the "hand fly," uppermost on the leader. From Mary Orvis Marbury's 1892 *Favorite Flies and Their Histories*, though, it appears that the turn-of-the-century fly fisherman had the same problems with tangling we do today, despite the fact that gut is much stiffer than nylon in the same diameter. This book was a compilation of fishing methods from fishermen throughout the country, and most admitted they fished a single fly, or at the most two at a time, in which case the lower fly was called the "tail fly" and the upper one the "dropper."

I can assure you that fishing two or three wet flies at a time is not a technique reserved for backwoods fishermen who haven't been introduced to modern fly fishing techniques or indoor plumbing. It is a valuable method for anyone who does not want to be confined by the agenda of aquatic insects; it is a wonderful way to find out which fly the fish prefer, and it also has merit because the sight of two or three swinging in front of a trout may provide a bigger stimulus than just a single fly. My friend Don Owens has been a fly fisherman for almost half a century, and he has been involved in the fly fishing tackle business for most of those years, so he has had access to all of the modern flies and techniques that have been developed. Yet for nearly 90 percent of his hours on the stream, he fishes three wet flies at a time—and almost always downstream. I asked him at what times three wet flies are not effective.

"Oh, almost never," he said. "I carry a box of dry flies in case there's a really good hatch. But I fish wets all over—on the Battenkill, and in my home state of Pennsylvania, where a lot of the fishermen still fish that way. When I go out West to fish, many times I'll see guides with clients on the river, and they'll leave their clients and come over to watch me. 'I never saw anybody fish like that,' they tell me."

Don sets up his three wet flies so they are equally spaced along his leader, which keeps them from tangling and makes casting easier. He starts with a nine-foot, 4X leader, with about a twenty-inch tippet, and puts one of the flies on the tippet, the biggest one if they are of different sizes. Then he comes up to the first knot, the one that connects the tippet to the rest of the leader, and ties a three-inch section of anything from 2X to 0X to the standing part of the leader with a regular clinch knot. He then comes up the leader the distance between the first two flies, around eighteen inches, and attaches the third fly in the same manner. If you're fishing just two flies, you can also just leave the tag end of the heavier strand extra long when you attach your tippet, and tie the dropper fly to that

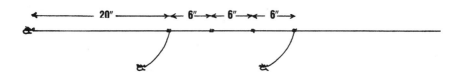

Don Owens' dropper spacing for fishing multiple wet flies.

piece. Make sure it's the heavier piece or the flies will tangle. A third way to attach a dropper is to simply thread your fly onto the last section of leader before the tippet—in other words, if you're using a nine-foot, 4X leader, the section before the tippet will usually be a six-inch strand of 2X or 3X, and you thread the fly onto the heavier strand, push the fly out of the way, and tie on the tippet. This is an almost tangle-free way of attaching a dropper fly, and the trout don't seem to be put off by the fly right next to the leader, nor do you have any hooking problems.

You can also attach droppers to a knotless leader by tying a dropper loop anyplace on the leader and then tying a piece of tippet material to the loop with a clinch knot. The dropper loop is a knot that is not commonly used these days, and I've included an illustration in case you've never seen it done.

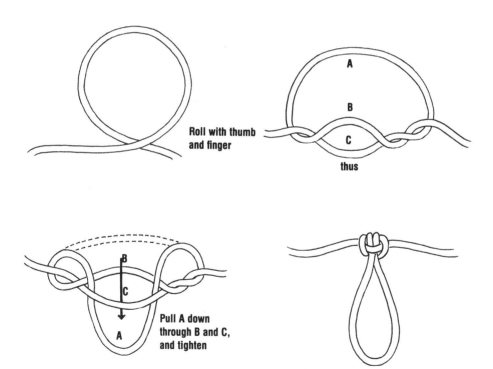

The dropper loop, for placing a dropper anywhere along a leader. Just clinch-knot a section to the loop and tie a fly onto the extra section.

Using a dropper allows you to use a technique that is larcenous on brook trout, and at times also spectacular on browns and rainbows—the skittered wet fly. It is similar to a skated dry, but not as difficult to execute. It also gives a different effect, which may look totally different from underwater—as I remember from boyhood vacations spent on the brook trout streams of New Brunswick and Nova Scotia, where brook trout were seldom interested in a dragging dry fly but would literally turn somersaults trying to catch a wet fly that was cutting a V-wake on the surface. I was never smart enough to fish a second fly in those days, or maybe my casting was so convoluted I was afraid of more than one fly on the leader, but if I were to go back I'd fish two flies. This way you can use the tail fly as an anchor, to keep the end of the leader in the water, and raise the rod tip so the dropper fly just touches the water. Then retrieve line or just let the flies hang below you. You're limited to fishing the water just downstream of your position with this method, and the distance at which you can do it is dependent on the length of your rod, but if you are surrounded by pocket water and are tired of straining to steer your fly through conflicting currents, try this one. It's a handy way to fish the slick immediately behind a rock, where you can't get a fly to swing or drift, and by anchoring the tail fly at the bottom of the slick, you can dangle and twitch your fly in the eddy until you drive the trout mad.

If you fish three flies, try combining different sizes, shapes, and colors so you can find what the trout prefer. Fishermen often go to the less traumatic single fly once they catch several fish on the same fly. (Yes, they *do* tangle, no matter how careful you are.) Try combining a cream or yellow pattern like a Light Cahill, a medium-colored fly like a Hare's Ear and a dark fly like a Black Gnat. I'm not a true believer in the magic of one color over another, so I like to combine different sizes, like a 10 on the tail fly, a 12 on the dropper, and a 14 on the second dropper. Or better yet I combine flies with different styles of tying and thus different behavior in the water: maybe a herl-bodied fly with no wings like a Gray Hackle, a standard wet with wings like a Dark Cahill, and a flymph like a Leisenring Spider or a soft hackle. Another variation might be a quill-bodied wet like the Quill Gordon, and I would definitely throw in something with bright colors in brook trout country—a Brown

Hackle with a red wool tail, a Professor, or even the gaudy Parma-chene Belle.

There is nothing unethical or unsporting about combining a small streamer or weighted nymph with a wet fly, either. I'll some-times use a large weighted nymph as the tail fly and a wet fly or emerger as the dropper. I don't expect to get many strikes on a weighted nymph when I swing it downsteam, but I use it mainly to get the wet fly deeper. It's better than a split shot. This brings up an important point, though. Your casting will be easier, and you'll spend less time picking out tangles, if you keep the biggest fly on the tail and make the droppers smaller, if you're using flies of different sizes and weights.

Choosing Sizes and Colors

If you are intimidated by small flies, take heart. In the Battenkill, where a size 16 fly is thought of by most of us as a big one, Don Owens regularly fishes size 10 and 12 wet flies and often outfishes the technical fishermen who are sweating over size 18 dries and nymphs. Don admits that he might have to go to a size 16 flymph during the summer when the water is low and clear, but he will also go to a buggy size 8 if the water is heavy or discolored.

Although a size 16 or 18 is a small wet fly, these sizes will be effective during conditions that require a much smaller dry—size 22 or smaller. Thus a wet can be an effective blind-fishing pattern during difficult midsummer conditions, not only because you can take advantage of the better hooking qualities of a larger hook, but also because it is difficult to blind-fish a tiny dry. Don has discovered this in a rather backhanded manner. He told me that he catches more trout on overcast or rainy days on a relatively dead float, when the fly is directly across from him and before the swing at the end of the drift comes into effect. He says that he catches more trout on the swing on bright days. I asked him why he thinks that is true. "I'm not sure," he said, "but I think it's because when I'm fishing directly across from the fish with a high rod, I have to get closer, but on sunny days you'll spook them if you get too close, so you catch them when the fly is further away, swinging below you." Atherton discovered the same advantage to wets, and in *The Fly and the Fish* he documented several instances where a dry fly would spook the trout, but a tiny wet swung carefully over the fish would not only not frighten them but draw more strikes.

A dry fly requires more false casting, and thus there's a greater chance for a line to be passed over the heads of the fish. Also, effective dry-fly presentation requires that at least the leader passes over a trout's head first, unless you are fishing a dry downstream. But downstream dry-fly techniques are not easy to perform in all currents, and after the fly passes over the fish's head you still have to be careful about picking up the leader. A small wet fly, presented well above the fish with a single cast, comes to the trout underwater, where it presents much less disturbance to the fish than a dry floating on the surface. If the fish doesn't take, you can retrieve the fly back to you without an obnoxious wake on the surface.

A couple of years ago I had just returned from a great fishing trip to Montana, and on my first evening on the Battenkill I was worried about reentry into the world of eight-inch brook trout and ten-inch browns after a week of fish that were twice that size. It was midsummer, I knew the fishing would be tough, and instead of knocking myself out on the risers I decided to sit on the bank, fish a wet fly swung through the current, and enjoy the lush scenery and bird life that are the drawing cards the Battenkill has over the Rockies. I tied on a size 16 Leisenring Black Gnat flymph, which consists of a few fibers of crow herl for the body and two turns of starling hackle—almost a bare hook dirtied with some wisps of feathers. I cast the fly directly across in the feeble midsummer current, mended once, and then let the fly soar over the tail of a riffle like a seagull coming in for a landing on a windy beach. The first fish was a fourteen-inch brown that tore the pool apart. Montana seemed months in the past.

Don, and most other serious wet-fly fishermen I have known, agree that not only can your subsurface flies be larger than the prevailing insect hatches, they don't need to be slavish copies of the naturals in color or shape. It seems that once you find the half-dozen patterns that will work on your river, it's seldom necessary to switch to new patterns, except maybe under extremely low and clear water. Since my episode with the Leisenring Black Gnat I've used the same fly throughout the season, and I have not found a

The Leisenring
Black Gnat.

time it doesn't work. It's just a good Battenkill fly, a good fly on many other rivers as well. When I find out I can catch trout with the same fly throughout the season—a fly often much larger than the naturals—I feel guilty at times, as if I'm playing poker with a marked deck. Or even worse—the thought that the trout might be taking my wet flies for tiny trout fry, after I've spent so much time choosing my wet flies to match the color of the Pale Morning Duns I saw hatching yesterday. Why do we view matching a minnow as so much less sporting than matching a bug?

You may find out what wet-fly patterns work in your rivers by trial and error: by fishing a single fly and changing it often, or by fishing multiple flies on droppers. It never hurts to match the insects you saw yesterday. A wet fly could look like the emerging duns that are starting to rise to the surface for a hatch that might occur hours later (and that you can't see), or drowned flies that didn't pierce the surface during this morning's hatch, or drowned spinners from last night's spinner fall. You're relying on a trout's relatively acute short-term memory for recognizing your fly as something edible.

When you're on an unfamiliar river, there are also a few guidelines to help you narrow down the process. The colors of insects that hatch throughout the season reflect an insect's cold-blooded nature: early in the season, when temperatures are cold, most of the insects are dark in color to take advantage of the light- and heat-absorbing nature of these colors. Use, for instance, early black stoneflies in March, dark gray Quill Gordons and dark olive *Baetis* mayflies in April. In May the colors reach a more neutral shade: the light gray of the Hendrickson and the pale brown of March Browns in the East, the dark olive of the Western Green Drakes in the West. Later in the season, when daytime temperatures are high and the sun is strong, an insect's main environmental problem is desiccation, so the flies are light-colored to reflect the sunlight—pale oranges, olives, and creams in the eastern Sulphurs and in the western Pale Morning Duns, and all cream in Cream Variants and Light Cahills. There are exceptions to this color scheme, but if you stick to darker flies like the Dark Cahill, Black Gnat, or Quill Gordon in the early season, medium-toned flies like the Hare's Ear or Orange Fish Hawk in the midseason, and light-colored flies like the Light Cahill or Little Marryatt in early summer, you'll be making at least an educated step in the right direction. In the dog days of midsummer often dark flies will begin to hold the edge. Once more, don't ask me for a scientific reason for that one.

I've found that when mayflies prevail on the water a standard wet fly with wings will draw more strikes, and when there are a lot of caddis around, wingless flies like soft hackles or flymphs seem to work better. A flymph or soft hackle is a wet fly tied with a body of sparse fur, floss, or feather herl like pheasant tail or crow herl, with

I've found that when mayflies are on the water a winged wet fly like the one on the left will work better. When caddisflies are hatching, try a soft hackle like the one on the right.

a collared hackle of partridge, woodcock, starling, or soft hen hackle. When Doug Swisher and Carl Richards observed insects hatching underwater for their book *Emergers*, they found that caddisflies kept their bodies straight and sculled through the water using their legs— a motion perfectly imitated by a soft hackle wet fly. This is not to be taken as gospel, though, as the best wet fly I have found during the period when Hendrickson mayflies are hatching is a flymph with a wood duck tail, mixed cream and red fur body, and collared hackle from a mourning dove. Mourning dove isn't available commercially, and if you don't hunt them or don't have any friends that do, a soft blue-dun hen hackle works just fine. One of the best all-around flymphs, a fly that seems to work whenever caddis are on the water, is a Leisenring Spider, a simple fly tied with a hare's ear fur body ribbed with gold tinsel and a Hungarian partridge hackle. I use them throughout the season, starting with a size 8 or 10 early in the season and going down to a size 16 in midsummer.

If you don't have any recent hatches to guide you, try a bigger fly—size 10 or 12—in the early season, a 12 or 14 in May and June, and a size 16 or even 18 in low, clear midsummer water. The progression of insects through the season ranges toward smaller flies as the days get longer.

Also, in heavy water a bigger fly draws more strikes, probably because it is more visible in the tumbling, foamy water. Fish in pools get a better look at a fly, so they are less likely to spot something wrong with a smaller fly. Every time I go from a riffle to a pool when fishing wet flies, I'm reminded of a vivid example of the difference fifty yards can make in the effectiveness of one fly size over another. When I was a teenager, I tied flies for a small fly shop owned by Carl Coleman, and as a bonus he would take me fishing once a year to his private club water on an upstate New York stream, rich with insect life and wild brown trout from the limestone bedrock that cradled it. The first section we ever fished, he put me into a riffle and took the pool above me. I started out with a size 10 Light Cahill wet and had my first initiation into real trout fishing—tarnished brass browns that grabbed the fly on the swing and jumped as I thought only rainbows did. After I had landed several fish, Carl yelled over the riffle for me to come up and join him. I fished above

If you fish a Light Cahill, pay attention to the size!

him in the pool for what seemed like hours, fishless, while he pulled trout from the river without taking a step. Finally he asked me what size fly I was using. I told him a 10 and he said, "Oh, no, you never fish a 10 in a *pool*. Tens are only good in the riffles."

I felt like a fool for violating this basic commandment of his private club. With blood rushing into the capillaries in my face I tied on a size 12 and the trout returned.

When choosing flies for spring creeks, throw everything I've just said aside. The insects fish eat in spring creeks remain relatively constant throughout the season, and you will find that the same wet-fly patterns and sizes should work from April to November, and beyond into the winter if the law allows winter fishing. Wet flies for spring creeks should be smaller than the ones you use for freestone streams, and they should be thinner and sparser, to reflect the swimming mayfly nymphs and midge larvae that make up the bulk of spring creek insects. I would be confident fishing wet flies in any spring creek in the world with a Blue Quill wet; a Little Marryatt; a sparse flymph with blue-dun hen hackle and tail, a thinly dubbed olive fur body, and a blue-dun hen hackle-collar; and maybe the Leisenring Black Gnat—all in sizes 14, 16, and 18.

Fishing Wets After the Hatch

The wet fly can extend your evening fishing well into darkness on any river. After a hatch, when you can't see your dry fly or any fish feeding, trout will often eat submerged flies that have been pulled under the surface without giving their feeding away. I can't count the number of times I've been disappointed during a Sulphur hatch, when the fish would not take my carefully presented dry flies, only to put on a Little Marryatt, turn around and face downstream, and catch half a dozen good trout without seeing or hearing any sign of surface activity. I've also used this technique when household obligations have prevented me from reaching the river until it's almost dark, and if I can find anyone on the river I'll yell into the darkness, asking the barely visible humps rising out of the river what has been hatching. If I haven't been interrogating a stump and get an answer, I'll try to match the insect that was hatching in size and color. For example, if Green Drakes were hatching, I'll tie on a big size 8 Light Cahill wet. I've found that soft hackles of flymphs work best if caddis have been emerging or returning to lay eggs, just as in the daytime. If mayfly duns were the major fly, a fur-bodied wet with wings seems to produce better. And if there has been a spinner

Sparse wet flies for spring creeks. Clockwise from the top: Olive Flymph, Little Marryatt, Blue Quill.

fall, a quill-bodied wet, to imitate the slim profile of the spinner, will usually catch the most fish.

It's important, in this kind of blind-fishing, to make sure your fly swings with as little swing as possible, if that doesn't sound like a foolish contradiction. You need to have some tension on the line so you can feel strikes, because you may not be able to see or hear them, but drowned insects don't swim across currents, so frequent mends, across-stream casts with initial slack thrown into them, and short casts are the rule. This kind of after-the-hatch fishing works best where a riffle flattens into a pool, or at the very tail of a pool. Don't call this night fishing. Night fishing is a specialized form of fishing, best done with a wet fly, but as my wife says about striped bass fishing you should be gearing up when everyone else is brushing their teeth for bed.

Night Fishing with Wets

There seems to be a lull after the posthatch wet-fly fishing when neither small fish nor large ones are feeding, and biologists have seen that it takes a trout about two hours to adjust to the low light levels of true night fishing. On a moonlit night, trout will often rise until eleven P.M., but these fish are still sight-feeding. True night fishing involves an entirely different cast of characters, trout that were still hiding in deep water or in snags along the bank when the smaller fish were cavorting after tiny insects. Studies of trout energetics have proven that for a trout to grow larger than fourteen inches in most rivers, it has to forage for food rather than drift feed, and much of this feeding is done after dark or on cloudy days, when a trout seems to have an advantage over smaller, more maneuverable forage fish.

Night fishing begins when days get hot and nights become humid, as proven by both radio telemetry studies and the experiences of night fishermen. In late June large trout start to exhibit feeding activity that start at sunrise and end at dawn, with peaks at midnight and just before the sun comes up. Traditionally the kind of night best for this after-dark fishing occurs when the air seems to come directly from the tropics, when moths throw themselves in front of your car on the way to the river and you can almost smell low tide in the air. Dark nights are best. I have had my best night fishing either during the new moon or when clouds or fog prevented the bright reflection of the moon from reaching the water. On a stream I haunted when I was growing up, we'd fish certain pools until the moon came up, taking fish until it peaked over the surrounding hills. Then we'd move to other pools that were protected from moonlight by rises of land, with strikes coming to an abrupt halt when the moon rose directly overhead.

It goes without saying that you need to fish a pool you know well at night. I would not muck around in a pool I was going to night-fish on the same evening, but it's a good idea to do a reconnaissance earlier in the day, from the bank if possible. Know where the slippery boulders and deep holes are. Keep your flashlight in your fishing vest if at all possible, and tie on your fly well away from the stream, because a light flashing over a river at night is certain to frighten any big trout in the area.

Predatory browns do not feed in the same deep-water refuges they use during the day. They move to where they can find the greatest amounts of forage, like shallow riffles, side channels, backwaters, and best of all, the tails of pools. Think of places you see minnows and crayfish during the day. For this fishing you want a short, stiff leader to prevent tangles and to be able to horse fish away from unseen branches. I use a level piece of ten-pound test, about four feet long, but you can also use a six-foot tapered leader. It's strictly a floating-line game, first because you don't want to bother with snagging on the bottom at night, second because your fly is more visible to the fish when it is near the surface, and third because trout hunt at night in shallow water, sometimes with their dorsal fins high and dry.

As long as you wade slowly and carefully (and you should for safety's sake as well as for stealth), casts can be kept short, under thirty feet. Wade into the river just enough to get a back cast; in fact, if you can make your first casts from the bank, you're better off, because the fish may be in inches of water right next to the bank. Casting can be done at almost any angle, but you must keep a tight line and the fly must be constantly moving, slightly contrary to the current. My favorite way to night-fish is to cover the tail of a pool by casting straight across the river and getting a good downstream hook

This is the kind of brown trout you pursue at night.

in the line, just the kind you don't want when fishing during the day. The slower the water, the more extreme the downstream mend. Don't forget, here you are trying to imitate the look not of an emerging insect, but of a minnow or crayfish bumbling around in slow water. Another way to keep in touch with the fly is to hand-twist as it comes around in the current, a favorite with friends of mine born and bred in Pennsylvania, where night fishing for large browns has been honed to perfection. Other successful night fishermen cast their flies upstream and across with a high rod, stripping line gently, just enough to feel the fly slipping back toward them. The one motion to avoid at all costs is to strip the line quickly or abruptly—a predatory trout feeding at night is not interested in burning many calories chasing a fast-moving prey.

Strikes will not be the kind of nips you feel when fishing wet flies during the day. It will feel as if you're trying to jump across a narrow creek and someone on the other side has grabbed your arm to help you across. You'll be surprised how wide awake you can be at two in the morning.

You've seen how large trout can cruise for hundreds of yards in a single evening hunting for food, so you may be in a quandary as to whether it's best to stay put—like a shad or Atlantic salmon fisherman blind-casting into a pool when he knows there is a run of fish on the move—or to move around hoping to intercept a fish in a pool. Night fishing seems to require a greater dose of persistence and luck than daylight versions of trout fishing, as you don't know for sure if you're fishing over a pool of juvenile trout that are asleep or not interested in venturing out at night, or a pool that contains a giant brown that had moved a hundred yards to search through the pool you are fishing. Rest assured that if you take one large fish from a small or medium-sized pool, it's a good idea to move on; unless your stream is exceptionally rich in forage fish or crayfish, a single pool won't support more than one large trout hunting in it at one time. The hunting grounds of the fish studied on the Au Sable in Michigan overlapped—but not in the same evening.

The Au Sable is a river that consists mainly of flat water with few barriers to movement other than gentle riffles. I would imagine that in rivers where pools are separated by fast water at the head of each pool, this nightly migration might not be as dramatic as on the Au Sable. If you work through a pool on a river like the Beaverkill, where pools are punctuated by fast runs at both the head and tail, and you don't connect with a fish, try another pool.

Jim Bashline, in his book *Night Fishing for Trout*, written mainly about night fishing in Pennsylvania streams, recommends mainly oversized (sizes 2 through 8) versions of classic wet flies like the Light Cahill, Quill Gordon, Gray Hackle, and Royal Coachman. His favorite night fly is a salmon fly, the Silver Doctor. I've found that bulky patterns work best, flies with thick heads that set up vibrations in the water and help trout find them with their lateral line system, which can pick up the commotion made by a fly with a deer hair head, like a Muddler Minnow, or a peacock herl head, like the Picket Pin. Any big wet fly that incorporates palmered hackle will also set up the same kind of vibrations. My favorite is a traditional upstate New York night pattern, and I mention it mainly because when I moved to Vermont and started night-fishing with Rick Rishell, director of the Orvis Fishing Schools, I found Rick fishing the same pattern, which he grew up using in Potter County in northern Pennsylvania. It's called the Night Caddis, and it's made from a body of orange wool palmered with brown hackle, with a heavy

The Night Caddis.

wing made out of wide slips of gray duck quill, or sometimes the wing is just a big clump of mottled black and white mallard flank feathers. In size 6, the size we use most often at night, it takes two entire mallard flank feathers to get enough bulk.

You can fish big wet flies well into the night. In fact one of the biggest peaks in feeding activity in the Michigan study was just before dawn. Once the first light begins to lighten the surrounding hills, though, the big trout return to deep-water refuges. But if you still have enough energy, something begins to happen in streams that sets up one of the most active times in the day of a drift-feeding trout. But it requires a different technique, as the next chapter on nymph fishing will describe.

NYMPHS

The Battenkill near West Arlington, Vermont, is a difficult trout stream. Some say it is the most frustrating trout stream in the world, and many days I agree with them. A medium-sized eastern stream from this point almost to the New York border, its smooth surface currents bely the speed at which its water rushes to the Hudson, but the fine gravel in its bed, drawn from two large glacial moraines at Manchester and Arlington, lets the water push through a crack in the Taconic Range without turbulence, resulting in slower currents that another stream, with typically larger rocks and boulders on the bottom, would have. Trout rise here with reluctance. Because the slower water that trout prefer to lie in, the boundary layer, is close to the bottom, it takes a hatch of major proportions to bring trout to the surface. It is just too much work for a trout to rise to the surface for single tidbits, as the fish get pushed downstream when they reach the surface, and the energy required to get back into position makes it worthwhile for them to feed on emerging insects only when there is an abundance of them. In Bob Bachman's Spruce Creek study he observed that it took brown trout only one second to intercept food items in subsurface drift, but it took six seconds for a fish to return to its position after a surface feed—and his study area was in relatively slow current! The point at which trout respond to surface food is programmed into their genes. And they are good at judging the risk.

It's obvious, then, that subsurface fishing will release the hold of those Battenkill trout from the bottom. But wait. Streamers, as on most rivers, are useful only during the early hours of the day or

147

when a rainstorm roils up the river. You can catch trout on streamers in the Battenkill on a sunny day with clear water, but you'll have to walk hundreds of yards between fish. And wet flies are useful only to those fish that are willing to chase a swung fly. Well, a dead-drifted nymph, then. After all, trout between six and fourteen inches, drift feeders, eat insects from the drift all day long, and a dead-drifted nymph is the most natural, unthreatening way to present a fly. Right again, but to know what they're doing doesn't mean you're going to sink a hook into their jaws. Unfortunately the same surface currents that make surface feeding unrewarding to a trout will also snatch your leader and fly line, not only keeping your fly away from the bottom, but even more damaging, preventing your nymph from getting a natural, unimpeded drift.

So how do you fish this miserable river?

You wait for a good hatch, or an evening spinner fall or caddis hatch; fortunately these are frequent. You fish wet flies and streamers and pick up the odd fish. And if you can find the right pocket of water, a place where a nymph can get to the fish and drift in a natural manner, you can really clean up on nymphs. In fifteen years of fishing the Battenkill I've found a half dozen of these pockets by dumb luck, trial and error, and a few educated guesses. The first one I found was below a big, flat pool, in a spot where a riffle started to become a run, an almost imperceptible increase in depth and increase in current. It was one of those dumb luck spots. I had been fishing the tail of the pool above, a rare place where trout would rise almost constantly if any insects at all were on the water, because the tail of the pool flattened out enough to spread the swift current out and made sipping from the surface film an easy matter. The trout here were easily spooked, so I would often stand in the riffle below for over an hour in the evening, watching the fish, looking for a good one, waiting for the sun to get off the water so I could approach them without the whole pool bolting at my first cast.

One evening I decided to check my leader to make sure it was straightening properly, and I made a few casts with a nymph I had been using in another local river, which was still attached to the leader. After a couple of casts I thought I saw the leader twitch, so I cast with a little more interest, tucking the end of the cast under by overpowering the forward cast, so the fly landed with some slack to

Margot in that special nymph riffle on the Battenkill.

Bob Jones in another of those nymph spots on the Battenkill. Note the gentle, uniform riffle. Margot Page photo.

help it sink. After a few casts the line twitched upstream and I set the hook into a fourteen-inch brown, who made quite a fuss in the shallow, fast water. Three more fish, all over twelve inches long, firm and healthy, took the nymph. That was ten years ago. I had never seen a fish rise there before, but you can bet in the last ten years I've looked the place over carefully—in the evening when dimples covered the pool above, during a heavy Hendrickson hatch when *every* fish in the river *seemed* to be rising, and every other chance I could get. I have never seen a rise there. I have never seen a fish flash there. Yet I can catch at least two trout there, with a nymph, any time I want.

After that first episode I thought I had the Battenkill figured out. I had the fly. I had the method. I was going to make angling history. It didn't work out that way, but I've found a few more places like this by trying to discover pockets with the same depth and current speed as the first one. But only with the confidence that nymphs worked *some* places was I able to find these other places.

Luckily most rivers are more easily fished with a nymph than the Battenkill. I genuinely like to fish nymphs, and I take perverse pleasure in telling people so, because most fishermen are intimidated by true dead-drift nymph fishing. It is the most difficult way to catch trout, and the magazine articles make it out to be some voodoo art, practiced by a few fishermen who are systematically cleaning out our trout streams before our very eyes. Over the past twenty years new flies, stronger tippet material that allows you to fish finer diameters, new ways of presenting the cast, and most of all, a dozen different kinds of strike indicators have reduced nymph fishing to just one of the many ways you can hook trout when they aren't feeding on the surface.

Want to see how easy dead-drift nymphing can be? Take a float with my friend Jim McFadyean on the Bighorn, any month of the year. Ask him if you can fish what he calls "junk." He'll attach a San Juan Worm (an imitation of an aquatic worm or a big midge larva) or a Bighorn Scud (an orange-colored freshwater shrimp imitation) to the end of your leader, crimp a couple of split shot twelve to eighteen inches above the fly, and slide a large cork strike indicator (or a small bobber if you're a bluegill fisherman) onto the butt of your leader, just below where the leader joins the fly line.

Jim McFadyean
and a fat Bighorn
rainbow taken on
a nymph with a
strike indicator.

Then he'll drift the boat into a rolling, thigh-deep run with cobbles
on the bottom and tell you to cast the rig quartering downstream,
about thirty feet from the boat. You can sit or stand in the bow of
the boat, watch the scenery, eat your lunch, smoke your pipe. No
need to mend line as long as the boat is in current that is moving at
the same speed as the place your fly is drifting—Jim will keep the
boat drifting at a speed that will allow the fly to drift drag-free
through fifty yards of water, until the current speed changes. When
the bobber dips under or hesitates, you set the hook. It is about as
demanding as ice fishing with an experienced man like Jim at the

oars, and it is the way guides get their clients into trout when nothing else works. On the Bighorn, and in many other rivers, you can take someone who has never cast a fly and get him into an eighteen-inch rainbow in short order, even if the wind is blowing at gale force and there isn't a sign of rising fish.

How Important Are Nymphs?

If you took everything you read in the outdoor press as gospel, you would be fishing nymphs all the time and not even bother with any other kind of fly or presentation. "Trout do 90 percent of their feeding underwater," the hook-and-bullet sages proclaim, "and the fisherman who fishes nymphs will be far more productive than any other." I have a problem with that statement. First, who did the research? It seems that the research behind this axiom was done by cribbing old magazine articles and by reading the ads for weighted nymph selections. Hard scientific data do not support the statement that trout do most of their feeding underwater—at least not in the Spruce Creek pool that Bob Bachman studied, at the time of year he could observe the fish. Bob observed the tail of a pool during the late spring, summer, and early fall months in a rich stream and found that his trout fed with equal frequency from subsurface drift and from the surface. But in all fairness the place he watched was perfect for surface feeding, in the tail of a pool where it was energetically feasible, and just as easy for a trout to feed from the surface as from underwater. Also because it was a rich stream, there was always some food on the surface.

My observations over twenty-five years of looking at trout streams do support the fact that trout feed mostly underwater, if you look at riffles, pocket water, runs, and pools together. But I still wouldn't throw all my other flies away, even discounting the enjoyment factor of seeing a trout rise to a dry fly. A trout can see your dry fly from much farther away, because a piece of food drifting at his level is only visible from a few feet away. So when you're fishing a nymph, you have to be better at reading the water and estimating where the trout will be lying than you do when fishing a dry. Also, not only do you have to be in just the right groove as far as current lanes are concerned, you have to make sure that your fly is deep enough, and that it is drifting drag-free. Trout feeding on drift are nearly as suspicious as trout feeding on the surface, unless some insects are hatching and rising toward the surface, and you can't see underwater drag; you have to guess. It is much harder to get a drag-free drift underwater than on the surface, because not only do horizontal currents drag your fly sideways, but vertical differences in current speed are always working against you. It literally adds a new dimension to problems of presentation.

Nymph fishing can be easy and productive. Just don't get the idea that all you have to do is fish a sunken fly casually to take advantage of that 90 percent probability.

Luckily it's not essential to get your nymph right on the bottom to be effective. We'll explore this matter in detail when we get into presentation later in the chapter, but I feel that the contortions that we go through to get a nymph closer to the bottom are much more effective in reducing underwater drag then they are in getting a fly deeper. Bachman found that his trout spent 86 percent of their time in a sit-and-wait attitude, watching for food items in the drift, yet they obtained less than 15 percent of their food directly off the bottom.

Behavioral Drift and How It Affects Your Fishing

Understanding drift will make you a better nymph fisherman; it will also increase your understanding of what goes on under the surface of a trout stream. Entomologists have pigeonholed drift into three categories: catastrophic, constant, and behavioral. Catastrophic drift happens during floods, when anchor ice scours a stream, or when high water temperatures or pollution forces insects to migrate away from danger. As I've discussed in the chapter on wet flies, once a river gets to the point of discoloring, a swung wet fly is a better choice than a nymph, but when the water first starts rising and nymphs are dislodged, but before it gets dirty enough where you have to turn to streamers and wet flies, a nymph can be deadly.

Constant drift is what you see when you watch a trout in the middle of the day, out in the open, sampling food from the current. Aquatic insects and crustaceans just screw up—they make mistakes and get washed away. Other than swimming mayfly nymphs like those of the genus *Isonychia* or *Siphlonurus*, if an insect larva loses its hold on the substrate, it's going to take a ride.

Emerging insects also fall into the constant drift category, and at any given time there will be some type of insect preparing for emergence, sometimes drifting a hundred yards in the current, rising to the surface, and then returning to the bottom before they finally emerge.

Behavioral drift is the presence of invertebrates drifting in the current that can't be explained by hatching, floods, or mistakes. If you put a drift net across the current of your favorite trout stream and checked it hourly, you'd find the usual assortment of insects from the evening hatch just before dark—but surprise! As the night goes on, you'd find even greater concentrations of insects, species that are not hatching during this time of year. Just before dawn you'd probably find a greater volume of invertebrates in the net than at any other time in a twenty-four-hour period. This is behavioral drift, and it is most often thought of as being a mechanism that invertebrates use in response to overpopulation—as a means of recolonization. Behavioral drift is triggered by darkness, but it is related to photoperiod and not just the absence of light. During cloudy periods or eclipses it does not increase, and in the constant light of summer in streams near the Arctic Circle, it does not happen. Moonlight also depresses drift, and artificially lighting a section of stream will stop it entirely. Because drift-feeding trout feed by sight, they are not always able to take advantage of drift, except in the early morning, when they can catch the end of the drift period just as it gets light enough for them to see the drifting food. On cloudy mornings behavioral drift lasts longer.

Behavioral drift is also seasonal: it is heaviest in late spring, decreasing through the summer, and is lowest in the winter. This does not mean that nymph fishing, however, will be the least successful method in the winter. In winter subsurface insects may be the only food trout will see; they just see less of them. In late spring they see more of all kinds of food.

Insects drift at night because their predators, including fish, carnivorous beetle, dobsonfly, fishfly, dragonfly, and stonefly larvae feed during the daylight hours. Large trout do feed at night, but a drifting insect is not large enough to trigger a reading on a trout's lateral line system. At dawn, as soon as light hits the water, drifting insects plunge to the bottom, but many of them are still drifting when it is light enough for trout to spot them.

When I first switched over from being a worm fisherman to being a fly fisherman, I forgot many of the lessons I had learned about trout behavior. I got so engrossed in hatches that I planned my fishing schedule around the activity period of bugs rather than the behavior patterns of fish. My first trout ever were caught in a tiny spring-fed stream that wound its way through eskers, drumlins, and moraines just a few miles south of Lake Ontario. It held a healthy population of wild brook trout, spared from suburban development by a park and golf course that took advantage of the rugged beauty of the glacial plains. It was a half-hour walk from my house, through abandoned terraced hills that once held plum, apple, and peach trees, and when I was a teenager they were filled with the hoarse calling of pheasants at dawn. I found through trial

A drift sample from a trout stream. The forceps are pointing at a midge pupa, and there are some mayfly and caddisfly larvae as well.

and error that I could catch trout from the tangles of alders and undercut banks on worms. Later, as a fly fisherman, I'd dap on a Yellow Marabou Streamer into hubcap-sized holes in the logjams— but since I had to crimp a split shot right at the head, it was more like a jig than a fly. As soon as the light came up strikes were spotty. I thought the trout were just afraid to feed out in the open during the day until I found a place where they would feed on tiny midges right out in the open all day long.

Watching those trout for hours, unable to interest them in worms or jigs and spooking them anyway, I decided to become a fly fisherman, and part of the lesson I learned, unlike most of those we learn as young bait fishermen, was a misguided one. I stopped fishing at dawn.

Most of my early fly fishing education came from books, and my head was filled with ideas from Art Flick and Ernest Schweibert. I fished dry flies and caught a few small trout. When I was fourteen, I began to tie flies for Carl Coleman, who owned a small fly shop in Greece, New York, and after I had tied for him for a year, he awarded me with a fishing trip. It was my first fishing trip with a real expert, and he picked me up before dawn in a yellow Karmann Ghia, driving an hour to the best trout stream in the area. The reason for his insistence on getting to the river at dawn became apparent when he pulled three large brown trout from a tiny pocket on a big, heavily weighted March Brown nymph, then turned the pocket over to me and watched over my shoulder as I caught my first big trout from the same spot. We both caught more nice trout and were done fishing by ten in the morning. We never saw a rise and I couldn't have been happier. Carl is the finest nymph fisherman I have ever seen, and he practically ignored dry flies and hatches entirely, as he liked to catch only large trout and had found during his teenage years that he could catch more and bigger trout by fishing in the morning with nymphs. He wasn't aware of the drift phenomenon, but he had fished at all hours of the day with all kinds of flies until he found the combination that worked best.

He did understand that to be most effective a nymph must be fished without the slightest hint of drag, but unlike most nymph fishermen today he used neither strike indicators nor split shot, and instead of a high rod to keep slack off the water, he fished directly upstream with a heavily weighted nymph and a low rod. Like most experienced nymph fishermen, he used only a few patterns on this river and relied on presentation rather than fly switching. I'll detail his method later in this chapter.

Crustaceans like sow bugs and scuds also show up in behavioral drift, and the first time I fished the famous Letort Spring Run in Pennsylvania, I was able to see the importance of drift on a practical basis. The late Tony Skilton and I had taken a trip to his hometown, Boiling Springs, where he had grown up under the wing of famous Letort regulars like Charley Fox, Vince Marinaro, Ross Trimmer, and Gene Utech. It was March, not a great time to go trout fishing in the Northern Hemisphere, but our work schedule at the time didn't give us much time for traveling during the trout season, as Tony was the director of the Orvis Fishing Schools and I was working for him. Tony said we had to get up at dawn to get the best nymph fishing, not a pleasant prospect on a rainy day in March, but I was willing to give his vast knowledge of the area the benefit of the doubt, even though I had never bothered to venture out early in the day during March and April, as early season hatches never occur until midday.

We parked just upstream of Charley Fox's house and stumbled down to the river in near darkness, with rain that was just a few degrees shy of snow trickling down our necks. As it got light enough to see into the water, Tony showed me how to look into the water for long, dark shapes that looked out of place, how to look for a slight movement of a trout moving for food or grabbing a hunk of watercress and shaking it to dislodge the freshwater shrimp, or the wink of white in front that showed a big brown opening his mouth to inhale a sow bug. How to tell the difference between a brown trout and a stick in the fuzzy light of dawn. We saw trout, lots of them, and spooked most of them, but I remember catching a few around a foot long, and Tony exhibiting one of his rare losses of composure when he stuck a fish that had to be two feet long and the hook pulled loose. As soon as it got light enough to really spot the fish, they melted into the weeds and feeding stopped. At the time I thought their disappearing act was a negative reaction to an increase in light, but now, years later, after seeing trout in similar spring creeks showing activity in the brightest sunlight if there was enough food around, and knowing what I do about drift, I think those fish had just run out of food. Studies of trout taking advantage of drift have shown that experience with drift feeding in a site is important to feeding efficiency, and when the food supply becomes insufficient the trout move—and if the food supply stops, their activity rate decreases dramatically.

Through my twenties and thirties I again got lulled into the hatch-meeting routine, and prospecting with nymphs almost got stuck back into the corner of my brain where algebraic theorems hibernate. But when my daughter was born, I soon found that a liberated husband does not get to run off to meet the evening hatch, especially when his wife likes to fish as well. The only time I found to fish hard and concentrate on technique was early in the morning, for a few hours before work. The Battenkill is known as a lousy early morning stream, probably because it doesn't offer many morning hatches, except for an occasional sparse caddis hatch and the Tricos in August. I fished one entire summer—probably two or three mornings a week, from six to seven thirty—and saw exactly four rises. Yet I averaged a half-dozen trout each time, and most of them were larger than ones I would have caught in the evening. It was an eminently satisfying experience, compounded by the fact that I never saw another fisherman.

Although the early morning is both an underutilized and effective time for nymphing, you can catch trout on nymphs throughout the day. There is always some kind of insect hatching on most trout streams, and most of these are too sparse to create concentrated surface feeding, but they do provide drift-feeding trout with a constant buffet line of food. In addition there are two types of insects that have been found to show peaks in behavioral drift during the middle of the day, and they are biggies—caddis larvae and pupae, and *Baetis* mayfly larvae, commonly known as Blue-Winged Olive nymphs. These insects are two of the most abundant invertebrates in trout streams throughout the world, and they are favorites of trout as well. In the research I've done on behavioral drift, *Baetis* nymphs of various species were mentioned in every single study, and that includes drift samples from many streams in this country as well as rivers in Scotland, Ireland, England, and Finland. *Baetis* nymphs are swimming, crawling nymphs that spend their time darting between

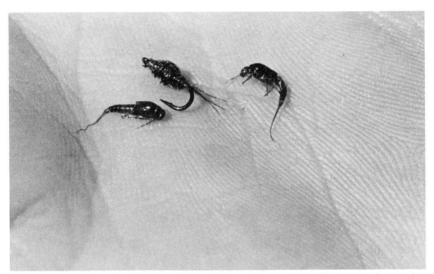

The *Baetis* nymph is one of the most common mayfly nymphs in the world. A couple of naturals are shown here with the most common imitation, the Pheasant Tail nymph.

the dead-water spaces among gravel and weedy bottoms, and they are far more likely to be drifting free than nymphs of flattened, clinging nymphs that possess hold-fast mechanisms, suckerlike spots on their legs that keep time attached to the underside of rocks. Examples of nymphs that possess these hold-fast mechanisms include such common species as the March Brown and Gray Fox genus (*Stenonema*), and the Quill Gordon (*Epeorus*). The Pheasant Tail nymph is one of the finest and most popular nymphs in the world, and it's no accident that this fly has the shape and color of a *Baetis* nymph.

Although trout seem to like to eat *Baetis* nymphs, you have to recognize that if a certain insect is the most abundant one in the drift, it may not be the one chosen most often by the trout. Trout prefer certain invertebrates over others. In a study done on a wild trout stream in Wisconsin, the ratio of the volume of an item in the drift was compared with the item's abundance in autopsied trout stomachs in the same stretch of river. In other words, if an insect comprised 20 percent of the drift and also made up 20 percent of the items in a trout's stomach, its ratio would be 1. Caddisfly larvae had a ratio of 2.1, as opposed to around 0.5 for mayflies. Tiny midge larvae showed a ratio of 6.4! Food preferences of trout will vary greatly from river to river, so I wouldn't throw away all my mayfly nymph imitations. Although midge larvae seemed to be of great significance in this study, other studies have shown that trout select the largest recognizable food item from the drift. The midges may have been drifting more during the day, when the trout could see them. Another study done on a New York stream in the thirties found that caddisfly larvae and pupae were the first choice of trout every month except May, August, and December, when mayfly nymphs were the first choice.

How to Pick the Right Nymph

I think the only conclusions we can make as fishermen from this information is that trout prefer certain foods in certain streams, and that their choices may not always relate to a food's abundance. This is why I'd advise you to choose your flies, if you can, by your own empirical evidence gained from trial-and-error fishing or by using a fly that the local experts prefer, using stream samples only as a rough guideline.

I'll give you an example of how stream samples can mislead you. I once fished the South Platte in Colorado with Rick Wollum, whose job as a guide includes a daily "commute" of two and a half hours from Denver to the river. This piece of river is crowded with both fishermen and fat rainbows and browns twelve months a year. It is shallow, clear, and full of food, and the fish are bothered little by the thrashings of fishermen, as you'll see. When I got to the river, I lifted some weed from the bottom and found it crawling with scuds and *Baetis* nymphs, so the first time I saw a big rainbow swaying in the current in the shallow water in front of me, I pitched a scud to him. And they were good casts, if I may allow myself to brag. The fish never showed a hint of movement for my fly, so I decided to try another fish rather than switch flies, an impatient strategy I often use when there are a lot of fish to cast to. Three trout told me the scud was not a good choice, so I switched to a size 18 Pheasant Tail nymph, which I consider almost cheating in a rich tailwater like the South Platte. I expected to see the white glint of a trout opening his

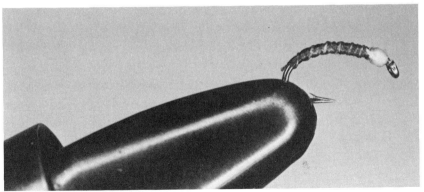

Rick Wollum's thread fly.

mouth on the first cast, but after about thirty casts I was dumb-founded that the infallible had failed miserably.

I forgot to tell you a couple of things. First is that after I had stood in the river for a while, I happened to turn around and found six or eight rainbows in the eddy behind my waders, eating like a swarm of chickadees at a feeder. I could see them swaying in the current, jockeying for position, and when I moved sideways the whole pod of them followed me. Below my position I could see another couple of fish moving up, following the rich line of food that I had been kicking up as I stood in the river. The fish were so close I should have been able to see what they were eating, but it looked as if they were grazing on invisible morsels. If I moved my foot to try to kick them out of the way, they backed off but would then return in seconds. Then I remembered that Rick had given me a couple of tiny, size 22 bright green midge larvae imitations, little more than green thread on a hook, a pattern he had developed. I could have tried to dunk the pattern in the eddy below me, but this is known as shuffling and is considered highly unethical, as when you do it on purpose it damages the stream bottom.

I used the midge pattern on the fish above me, who were probably feeding on a plume from the next fisherman upstream, and started to pick up fish. A little later I'll tell you how Rick fishes these tiny nymphs. So although those midge larvae weren't the biggest food item in the river, they were probably the most common item in the drift, because the scuds and *Baetis* nymphs were able to swim back into the weeds after being dislodged. The midges were so small and were such weak swimmers that they probably drifted for hundreds of yards after being kicked up. It pays to listen to the locals.

When you're fishing blind, without any hatches to guide you, and if you don't have a guide handy, how can you choose the right nymph pattern? It's always best to start with a popular pattern, as a best-seller list for flies can be as reliable a guideline as one for good books. The Hare's Ear, Pheasant Tail, and Zug Bug are the three best-selling nymphs of all time. What do they have in common? First you have to look at why a trout takes a nymph.

Trout are constantly trying to pick food items out of all the inedible junk that floats down a river, and as with dry flies, size, shape, and color are important. But when fish are feeding on nymphs, they seldom feed as selectively as they do on the surface, and another factor gets entered in the equation: movement. Studies by behavioral scientists have shown that a fish distinguishes its subsurface food by movement in its prey, as pieces of weed and stick do not move as they drift. It appears to be the movement of the tiny gills along the abdomen of a mayfly nymph, or under the thorax of a stonefly, or the paddling of tiny legs that helps trigger a strike.

A buggy Hare's Ear nymph gives the impression of movement in the water.

Rick Wollum with the result of fishing his thread fly.

Look at the three nymphs just mentioned. The Hare's Ear is tied with rough fur from the face of a rabbit, with many tiny hairs sticking out all over that can move in the current or at least give the impression of movement. Pheasant tail fibers also have tiny flues that sway in the current, as does the peacock herl of the Zug Bug. Flash is also important, as caddis pupae and many mayfly nymphs are reported to develop gas bubbles inside their skins as they emerge, which act like a tiny mirror inside the body of the insect. The recent development of the Flashback-type nymph, which uses a sparkling piece of synthetic material like Flashabou or Krystal Flash or Lureflash, has been a great development in nymph design, and I believe that a nymph with some flash in it can draw a trout's eye from a long distance, as most debris in the water doesn't sparkle.

The recent development of Antron yarn as a material in nymph bodies, especially by Gary LaFontaine in his Deep Pupa patterns, also relies on a material that makes a fly sparkle in the water. There is debate among fishermen as to whether most or even any emerg-

Gary LaFontaine's Deep Pupa, tied with Antron yarn.

ing nymphs develop a gas bubble inside their skin to buoy them to the surface, but I can say with total confidence that Antron, regardless of the reason, makes a nymph sparkle because the trilobal fibers of the yarn hold air bubbles to the fly, and the Deep Pupa has become one of my most reliable patterns for prospecting with nymphs.

Choosing Nymphs by Water Type

But a good fly in the wrong place won't get you very far. You can choose the right nymph by water type, without ever turning over a rock to see what's living on the bottom. A river that is lined with large, flat rocks will host many large, flat nymphs, like the March Brown, Quill Gordon, and all kinds of stoneflies. Here you should try beefy nymphs that give the impression of flatness—you don't have to worry about actually using a nymph with a flat body, as a trout only sees your nymph from one side, so as long as the fly has

A beefy March Brown nymph and Coleman's March Brown imitation.

a bulky profile, it will look flat. In addition flies like the Hare's Ear, with fuzzy bodies, appear flat when they get wet because the fuzz lines up along the side of the fly in the current.

In a river with a fine gravel bottom, on the other hand, like the Battenkill or the Au Sable in Michigan, a big flattened nymph has no place to hide, no flat rock to protect it and to keep it from getting washed away in the current. The insects living here will be rounder, less robust, and generally smaller, so they can clamber around in the dead-water interstices between the gravel. Here, a big, robust nymph may look out of place. Nymphs like the Zug Bug, and most of the standard mayfly nymph imitations like the Hendrickson nymph or Pale Morning Dun nymph, are more likely to be found here. Of course you can also find these smaller, rounder nymphs living in the gravel between the boulders in pocket water, but since trout generally choose the largest edible piece of subsurface food, they are more likely to go for the fatter stuff in bouldery water. Caddis pupae and larvae are found in both types of water, so a Sparkle Pupa, one of the finest searching nymphs I have found, will work almost everywhere.

Spring creeks and weedy tailwater present a different set of

A smaller, rounder crawling mayfly nymph and its imitation.

In a gravelly riffle like this, round, crawling mayfly nymphs may be most common, and your imitations should reflect that shape. Margot Page photo.

conditions, and fishing a fat stonefly nymph in a spring creek is often a futile gesture. Nymphs in weedy, silty waters have few stones to hide under, so they will be the smaller swimming varieties that are adapted to living under these conditions. Midge larvae are also abundant in these waters, as they thrive in the silt-laden areas typical of streams with slow currents. Insect larvae that live in weedy or silty waters are skinny and have legs that are much finer than those of flattened nymphs, and when they drift or swim they tuck their legs under their bodies, making them insignificant to a trout. The Pheasant Tail, tied English-style without legs and very thin, is as perfect a spring creek nymph as I have found, and the addition of a flashy wing case, turning it into a Flashback Pheasant Tail, seems to make it even better. Many Americans tie their Pheasant Tails with a robust thorax of peacock herl and thick legs, and unfortunately many commercial versions are tied the same way because they look

Water like this is best tried first with a robust nymph imitation. Margot Page photo.

Caddis larvae can be found in almost any type of water.

Spring creek nymphs and their imitations are slimmer and sparser.

Here is the kind of water you'll want to fish with skinny nymphs.

prettier on the counter of a tackle shop. It's a good fly for rockier waters, but an anemic rendition of the Pheasant Tail is a far better fly for the richer spring creeks and tailwaters. Worm flies tied with floss, thread, or tinsel (no fuzzy materials) such as the San Juan Worm or other worm-type flies, make excellent midge larvae and pupae imitations in the smaller sizes, and they also imitate an aquatic annelid that is common in silty waters.

The one kind of fuzzy fly that can be successfully fished in spring creeks and tailwaters is a scud or sow bug imitation like the Flashback Scud, Otter nymph, or Pennsylvania Cress Bug, because the fuzzy profile imitates both the flattened shape of these crustaceans and their relatively robust (and plentiful!) legs.

Commodity Flies

Blind-fishing with a nymph requires less deliberation on fly selection than with any other type of fly—once you find the correct pattern or patterns. Every stream seems to have its commodity nymph, one that shows a recognizable search pattern to the fish, and some fiddling with size and methods of presentation can free you from poking through your fly box, turning over rocks, or studying the hatch charts. Carl Coleman was nearly oblivious to hatches in the stream he fished, as he was only interested in catching big trout; he had found the method and had found the fly pattern, so he could concentrate on reading water, approach, and fishing the right time of day. Carl's pattern, one he developed himself, was the March Brown nymph, made with a fat, lacquered brown floss body ribbed with white floss, a peacock herl thorax ribbed with brown hackle, and a wing case made from black duck primary fibers. His stream was strewn with flat rocks, so it had a dense population of March Brown and similar flat-bodied nymphs of the genus *Stenonema*. He started with a size 10 in the early season and went to a size 12 when the water got lower, but throughout the summer he continued to fish the same fly, long after the flattened mayflies had vacated the river for the season.

He confessed to me once that when he was young and had killed a lot of fish, the large trout always had crayfish in their stomachs, and they seemed to prefer the small crayfish. He felt that

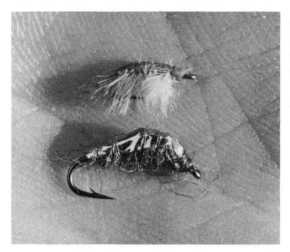

A couple of small scud imitations. The bottom one is tied "Flashback" style.

his fly was close enough to both the mayfly nymphs and the crayfish to pass for either.

In every spring creek I've ever fished, the Pheasant Tail nymph was the commodity fly, as it is a wonderful imitation of *Baetis* nymphs. These mayflies are found in all rich, weedy streams as well as gravel riffles, and they seem to be present year-round. I've often seen it written in fishing books that *Baetis* are multibrooded through any given season, but I suspect this may be one of those self-perpetuating myths that become fact through countless repetitions, as I have never seen this presented as fact in an entomology book. Because no one has ever followed a single generation of *Baetis* through a season, it might be that there are different races of the same species that hatch at different times throughout the year. In spring creeks you need to throw in a scud or sow bug imitation as well, because these crustaceans are true commodity flies, present all year long because, like crayfish, they never hatch out of the water.

In many of our bigger western rivers, from the Madison in Montana to the Deschutes in Oregon, the commodity fly is a large black stonefly. These nymphs have a two-year aquatic period, unlike most aquatic insects that grow, hatch, mate, reproduce, and die in a single season, so there is an overlap of generations that keeps some nymphs in the river at all times. Notice that, in all cases, the commodity fly is one of the largest food forms in the river that is favored by the trout; this is consistent with the theory that trout select the largest recognizable food form when feeding underwater. Yes, even though *Baetis* are barely a size 16 or 18, they are often the largest abundant mayfly nymph in a spring creek.

Try Oddball Sizes

When you get really stuck for the right fly pattern, when you can't seem to find the right combination, it's often a smart idea to try a fly that is much larger or smaller than you think is reasonable. My experience on the South Platte was an example of how a fly that seems to be too small to use for prospecting can change your day. This end of the spectrum often works in spring creeks, in tailwaters, and in slower pools on freestone rivers. You can also lean the other way. When I was a teenager, I fished a spring creek with an older gentleman named Jim who would sometimes allude to a nymph he had found that would take fish every time he used it. He was afraid of using the fly, was ashamed to use it because he felt it would ruin his fishing, and refused to show it to me, because he sensed that my fishing philosophy had not reached the maturity to see the danger in discovering this fly. He was right. Once in a moment of weakness he gave me a glimpse of the fly, his hands sweating and his voice shaking, and I craned my neck and tried to force my brain to burn an image of the fly into my memory so I could rush home and tie one. The average size nymph we fished in this stream was a size 22, and the fly he showed me was a monstrous concoction of muskrat fur that was at least a size 6. Of course I did try to imitate the fly, and my versions of it never moved a single fish—in fact they ran from it. I'll never know if Jim just happened to catch the trout in a weird mood the day he tried the fly, or if my imitation was not quite right.

The upper Connecticut River, on the northern part of the border between New Hampshire and Vermont, is a brawling water with boulders of Precambrian granite, a Madison in three-quarter size. Most of the flies we fish on this river are typical eastern freestone size, dries in sizes 14 through 22 and nymphs in sizes 12, 14, and 16. One day, when there was absolutely nothing happening, I decided to fish western-style with a huge, size 4 black stonefly nymph in a deep cut in the center of the river, with three large split shot attached to the leader. I pulled larger-than-average rainbows out of that run until I must have almost cleaned it out. If the river you are fishing can support big stoneflies and helgrammites, if it has the rocky character conducive to these monstrous flies, don't be afraid to try an oversized nymph, even if no one ever fishes flies this big.

How to Make Sure Your Fly Drifts Properly

Prospecting with a nymph, for trout that may be actively feeding but are not following flies to the surface and thus not showing themselves, requires more than just knowing where they are by studying currents, rocks, and other features in a river that may attract trout. You must put your fly at a level at which the fish can see it, and I believe that in most instances the fly should be moving just as fast as the current. Both of these requirements make it essential that you reduce drag, or the influence of surface currents on your line. Water in a stream is always moving faster at the surface than where your fly is drifting, and you are constantly fighting the tendency of surface currents to move your fly unnaturally and to pull it toward the surface. Most nymph-fishing experts talk about the importance of getting your fly "right on the bottom," but as we've seen, trout eat most of their subsurface food above the bottom, either at their level or a few feet above their level. It is nearly impossible to fish your fly right on the bottom, because if you do, it gets hung up halfway through most of your drifts, and a fly that is drifting very close to the bottom is difficult for the trout to see. But by striving to fish right on the bottom, we end up getting down to a level where the fish can see our flies, and we reduce drag. I've found that if anything is true in nymph fishing it is that the fly is always drifting shallower than you think it is. The only way to really fish on the bottom in most currents is to fish straight monofilament without a fly line and add a bunch of huge split shot to your leader, as midwestern steelhead fishermen do when they fish egg flies. By eliminating the water resistance of the fly line, the monofilament cuts right through the water, but it also eliminates the means to cast the fly in the normal sense.

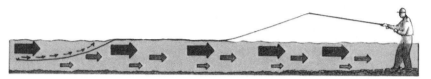

Without a tuck cast, weight on the leader, or a weighted fly, the faster currents at the surface will pull your fly back toward the surface.

As you'll see as we progress, I am not a purist in my fly fishing. I use and wholeheartedly endorse the use of split shot and indicators. But eliminating the fly line is where I start to turn up my nose, at least in trout fishing. I will fish the mono method for steelhead and Pacific salmon, but only because the size of the fish and the appeal of an all-out battle with a big fish outweigh the repulsiveness of plunking a volley of split shot over my head.

Simple Direct Upstream Nymphing

In looking at nymph presentation, let's start with the most uncomplicated in terms of the kind of adjustments you need to make to your leader, and then progress to techniques that require additions such as split shot and indicators to your tackle. The simplest rig is the kind used by Carl Coleman, which requires that you merely substitute a weighted nymph on your leader for a dry or wet fly. This is the way we fished nymphs up until the 1970s, when indicators began to get popular—and made nymph fishing easier, even for the novice fisherman. When nymphs first became an accepted way of fishing in North America, back in the 1930s, by all accounts they were just more realistic imitations fished the same way we had always fished wet flies, swung on a tight line. Occasionally a fisherman would cast his nymph in an upstream direction, but not with the fanaticism of Carl Coleman. Never one to mince his words, Carl often said that "downstream fishing is for jerks," and by his reckoning, a nymph should be always fished directly upstream, in order to sink the nymph as quickly as possible and reduce the drag. He stressed how important it was to be standing in the same current you were fishing, and you can see yourself how just 10 degrees to either side of directly upstream hinders the dead-drift of

Direct upstream nymphing. Note the line and rod are pointed as close to directly upstream as possible. Margot Page photo.

your nymph, as the line will quickly develop a belly, preventing a nymph from drifting naturally.

To try this method, find a riffle or run that is in the main current of a river—the head of a pool where a riffle dumps in is one of the best places, because the current in a place like this is relatively uniform from top to bottom. Here, the nymph sinks quickly and is not pulled back to the surface, as it would be in the tail of a pool, where the current at the surface is much faster than it is at the top. Waist- to knee-deep water is perfect. Choose the biggest fly you think is acceptable; in most rivers a size 12 is a good starting point, something like a heavily weighted Hare's Ear, stonefly nymph, Zug Bug, or whatever the local favorite is. Your floating line should be cleaned and dressed so it floats high, and your leader should be free of grease or line dressing by cleaning it with soap, alcohol, or one of the commercial leader preparations like Mud. Carefully wade into the pool and try to determine where the fish might be lying by using your stream reading skills, and position yourself so you are twenty to forty feet directly behind the spot.

Now cast straight upstream, about ten or fifteen feet above the place where you think the fish is lying, and retrieve line just as fast as the current brings it back to you. The line should remain tight and straight, and you should glue your eyes to the place where the leader joins the line. If the line jumps forward, stops, or does anything that looks like movement not made by the current, strike quickly and decisively by raising the rod straight upward. Trout hooked by this method will have the fly firmly placed in the upper jaw, as they would be hooked if you were using a dry flat, and they will seldom shake loose. Learning when to strike is an acquired skill, but after dozens of takes you'll soon be striking by instinct, just as you duck your head when an object comes into your peripheral vision. It is not as hard to detect strikes by this method as you might think, despite what has been written about upstream nymphing, especially if you learn on faster water. When you are fishing straight upstream in a swift current and your line is tight, think about what is happening underwater. In order for a trout to take your fly he must rise up and grab the nymph, stopping its relatively swift downstream progress. This motion cannot help but be reflected in the motion of your fly line.

With this method you effectively cover an area about two feet wide by about ten feet long, as the first ten feet of your cast are needed to get the fly to sink, and under the area close to you, you've spooked any trout that may be lying under the line, unless the water is so heavily riffled that your approach is disguised. And we know from our discussions of trout behavior that a fish will move about two feet to either side to intercept a drifting nymph. How many casts do you give one spot? I have watched trout ignore a dozen casts when I've been able to watch them react to a dead-drifted nymph, only to have them take cast number thirteen. On the other hand the first couple of casts are usually the best, and subsequent drifts in the same spot reduce the possibility of a strike. Remember that each cast will drift a little differently, though, as no cast is a carbon copy of the previous one, so fifteen casts to the same spot is not unreasonable. In general the colder the water, the more thoroughly you'll have to cover the water, as when the temperature is 55 to 65 degrees trout are more active and move farther for their food. At 50 degrees they do not move very far for a fly, nor do they react as quickly.

After I've covered one spot, with the Coleman method I usually move straight upstream, following a main current line, and if the current line moves sideways I'll move over to one side to make sure I'm fishing directly upstream. If you come to a place where a riffle dumps into a pool and are faced with a wide area of what looks like prime water, it's better to move sideways below the riffle. As soon as you start trying to cast across the current, you're going to reduce the amount of strikes you get because of the water's effect on your drifts.

How do you know if you're fishing deep enough? A good rule is that if you hang up on the bottom every fifth or sixth cast, you're fishing deep enough, although this rule applies mainly to water temperatures below 55 degrees. When water is in the optimum temperature range, 55 to 65 degrees, I have had days when I never touched bottom yet picked up fish regularly. If you don't think you are getting deep enough, or drag is setting in too early, there are a number of manipulations that can correct the situation. One is to lengthen your tippet, as the more fine-diameter tippet you have up front, the less resistance to sinking your fly will have. A longer tippet also allows your leader to fall in a pile of slack, yet your line stays straight so you can detect strikes. The slack tippet lets the fly sink unimpeded, until the slack is taken up and the line starts to pull on the fly. Carl Coleman weights his flies heavily, which not only gets the fly down quicker but also makes the fly tuck underneath the leader, driving it into the water straight down rather than just lying out straight. Joe Humphreys popularized a cast called the tuck cast,

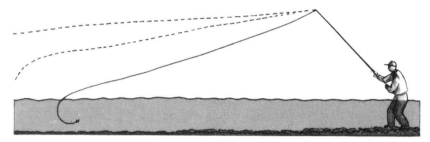

The tuck cast drives your fly and leader under the line and gets them to the bottom quicker.

which gives you the same effect without having to use a heavily weighted fly, and I highly recommend this cast, which is easy to learn and does not require any modification of your tackle.

The Deadly Tuck Cast

To make a tuck cast, start your back cast as usual; then as you feel the weighted nymph pull on the line behind you, start the forward cast and stop the rod sharply at about the ten o'clock position, pulling back with the last two fingers of your casting hand and driving the thumb forward, then pulling the thumb back and up slightly. Your elbow tucks back under your arm when you finish the cast. The earlier in your forward stroke you start the tuck, the more forceful the action of your fly, so you can modify the cast depending on the depth and the speed of the water. The tuck cast, with some practice, will let you drive just the nymph into the water, without slamming the line down and spooking the fish. Your fly will land below and downstream of the leader as well, giving it added slack that complements the sinking action it gets from being slammed into the water. In shallow water, with a properly executed tuck cast, your nymph becomes effective much earlier in the drift, because it has gotten to the proper depth much quicker.

The Coleman method and the tuck cast have the advantage of working straight upstream, so you are always approaching a trout from its blind spot. They also have disadvantages, the obvious one being that your line may be passing right over the fish. In situations where the trout may be spooky, in low or clear water, you may have

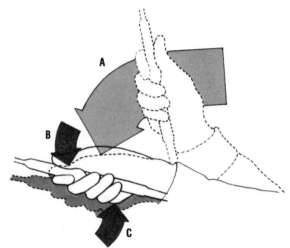

Close-up of the casting motion. A is at the completion of power on the casting stroke; B and C are done at the same time and effect a quick flip of the wrist.

to switch to another method that allows you to cast upstream and across so your line will not fall right over their heads. Also, in swirly currents, as in pocket water or in the whirlpool at the head of the pool, it's difficult to detect strikes because your line is being pulled all over the place. But in riffles and runs with uniform currents, in the heads of tiny pockets in small streams, or in bouldery pocket water, they are deadly.

Techniques for High and Cold Water

There are many times and places when you want a nymph to fish faster and deeper than with the Coleman method, particularly when you are fishing deep, swirly pockets that keep trying to push your fly back to the surface. Or you often find yourself in a position where you cannot fish directly upstream. In these situations you'll need to add some kind of weight to your leader. A couple of years ago I was fishing in mid-April on a local river, in a deep slot in a riffle that always holds a half-dozen nice rainbows. It's one of those spots where you know the fish are there, and you just keep changing tactics until you hook a fish. The water was barely 48 degrees, so I knew the fish would be staying close to the bottom. I started out fishing directly upstream to them without any weight on the leader, but with a weighted nymph and the tuck cast, and after a couple of dozen casts I knew that a change was in order. I put two small split shot on my leader to get the fly deeper, but still no fish. I moved up closer to the slot, so that I stood almost opposite the place I thought the fish would be lying, waded about ten feet to the side of the slot, added two more split shot, and cast five or six feet above the slot, keeping my rod high so that most of the line would be off the water. I followed the fly through the slot, with almost a straight, tight line to the fly, fishing the fly almost under the rod tip. I could feel the shot ticking on the rocks. Steering the fly through the slot required intense concentration, but on casts where no bow developed in the line and the fly was drifting totally dead-drift, I would pick up a fat eleven-inch rainbow. Every time the current would catch the line and move it downstream of the rod tip or sideways, I would not see

A regular cast across the current will put a bow in your line, and your fly will never get deep enough—and it will not drift at the same speed as the current. Margot Page photo.

the line tighten with a fish, and only every fourth or fifth cast would be right on.

This is the best way to fish nymphs in fast, deep, or cold water, and it is known as high sticking because of the attitude of the rod. It's really bait fishing with a fly, and it is based on the method the most successful worm fishermen use. It's important to note that the farther you get from the fish, the less successful the technique, because you need to keep as much line as possible off the water. This is why, in those little game plans we carry around in our heads, I look at the straight upstream method, with a weighted fly but without any split shot or indicators, as my long-line nymphing option, and when I put shot and/or an indicator on the leader, I'm in my short-line nymphing mode. Not only can't you cast as well and as far with added junk on the leader, you really need to be right on top of the action to produce the best results.

Raising the tip of your rod will keep your nymph on a deep and natural drift. Margot Page photo.

Rick Wollum high-sticking on the South Platte in extremely cold water in February.

Why do you hold the rod at a relatively low angle with the Coleman method and at a high angle with the high-sticking method? When you raise the rod tip to keep your line off conflicting currents, you also draw the line back toward you, because gravity makes the line droop between the rod tip and the water. This makes the fly drag back downstream, pulling your fly away from the bottom and making it move faster than the current. When you're fishing straight upstream, you don't need to worry about crosscurrents, so why raise the rod and move the fly toward you? When high-sticking across currents, you generally utilize a weighted-fly-and-weight-on-the-leader combination that provides some resistance against the fly pulling back toward you, so you neutralize the effect of the line pulling back toward the rod tip.

When using the high-sticking method, you can also get further reduction in drag and get your fly deeper by throwing a quick upstream mend just after the fly hits the water, or use a reach cast to make the mend just before it hits the water. The tuck cast can also be used here as well, as long as you don't have too much lead on your leader.

Weighting the Leader

Adding weight to your leader can be done in any number of ways, but before we talk about lead on the leader we need to talk about the necessity for weight added to the fly. Yes. Always. If you have some nymphs tied without weight, fish them like wet flies on a

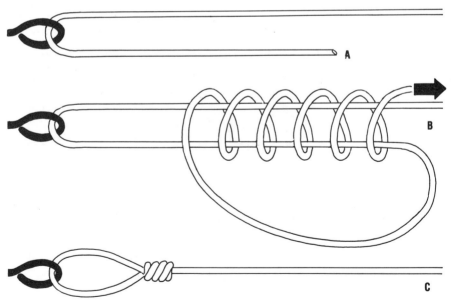

A

B

C

The Duncan loop can give your nymph a lifelike connection to your tippet.

downstream swing, or grease them up and use them as emergers during the hatch. When you're fishing dead-drift nymphs, prospecting for trout, I can't think of a single reason not to have lead on the fly, and a couple of strong reasons in favor. It's been said that a nymph tied without lead is more realistic in the water, that it will appear more lifelike. I don't agree, because I feel the single biggest deterrent to obtaining a lifelike drift is the effect of a piece of nylon attached to the fly. The heavier your fly in relation to the tippet, the less it will be yanked around by the leader, and a weighted fly will have a much greater tendency to drift unimpeded. When I fished with Carl Coleman, he used a 3X tippet with a size 12 fly, because if we went any lighter we'd break off most of the fish on the strike. This was back in the days when 3X tested about three pounds, and now that we can get 5X material that tests at almost five pounds, I would never think of fishing a tippet as heavy as 3X with a size 12 nymph, and the last I checked in with Carl he had gone the same route.

You can go one step further in getting your nymph to drift in a more natural manner by attaching the fly to the tippet with a Duncan loop or uni-knot rather than a standard clinch knot. This loop knot is as strong as or stronger than a clinch, particularly when you're using a big weighted fly with a light tippet, and the loop in front of the eye goes one step further in helping the fly to swing free in the current. When you hook a fish, the knot tightens right up to the eye, but you can slide it open after you unhook the fish.

Weight can be added to your tippet in a number of ways, and I carry all kinds of lead in my vest and use all of them depending on the situation. The most common type of lead is split shot, crimped to the leader in one or several spots. It's wise to carry both the heavier variety that has the little wings on the side, so it can be removed easily, and the traditional round type that must be removed by replacing the tippet—I'd use only the removable type, but often you want less weight than you can get with the removable style, and the tiny sizes favored by fly fishermen don't come in a removable style. The first shot to attach is best placed about eight to twenty-four inches above the fly on the tippet, and you should start with the smallest size you think will do the job. Especially when using the smaller, nonremovable jobs, you can always add another shot, but it is difficult to remove it without damaging the tippet, as sliding a shot off the tippet will at the very least put a pigtail in your tippet and will often weaken it. The clearer the water and the smaller the fly, the farther you want the shot from the tippet, as the longer the length of tippet between the fly and the weight, the more naturally the fly will drift. With a big fly in deep or discolored water you can put the shot closer to the fly to get it quickly near the bottom.

If the fly seems to be drifting too fast—if it comes back to you without seeming to strain the leader in an upstream direction—you'll need to add more weight. Remember, you don't always have to find that the fly touches bottom, but you've got to slow it down. I was fishing a deep, fast run on the Cheeseman Canyon of the South Platte in Colorado early one morning with a size 18 Pheasant Tail nymph—admittedly a small nymph to be blind-fishing, but I knew from reading about this stream that the average size fly the locals fish in midsummer is smaller than a 20, and the water was higher than normal, so I thought I could get away with an 18. One shot seemed not to make a difference at all in the way the fly was coming back to me, so I added two more shot. The leader seemed to drag behind the line at the surface, exactly what I wanted to do, and even though the water was four feet deep and I was only getting halfway to the bottom, the fly was moving at about the same speed as the subsurface currents, and trout started banging the fly at a satisfyingly regular pace. I wrote in my fishing log that the brown trout in this river seemed hotter than any I had hooked in a long time, and one huge fish jerked my rod tip out into the main current and made a vicious upstream run, so fast that the stripping line at my feet flew into the guides in a knot and the fish popped the tippet.

Often you'll be fishing a stretch of water that has varying depths, and in this case you may want to use a kind of weight that you can easily remove or add as the depth changes. Here it's handy to use strip lead, which you twist around the leader, as you can remove sections of it easily without damaging the tippet or add small pieces until you get the right depth. Equally handy is soft lead putty, which you roll into a torpedo shape around the tippet at any point you want. Soft lead will come off the leader if you cast too hard, so you have to lob your casts, but it is useful in places where you frequently hang up on the bottom, because if it catches on the bottom it will slide off the tippet, so you only lose your weight and not the fly and the tippet. It's also easy to add and remove weight with soft lead.

When the fish seem to be striking short, when you see the line jump forward but can't seem to connect, or if you are fishing a small nymph and need to get as lifelike a presentation as possible, you can also add lead or copper sleeves to the leader. These are threaded onto the last section of leader, before you tie on your tippet, and they will slide freely on the leader, as they are trapped between the knot before the tippet and the next knot up on the leader. If you are using a knotless leader, just cut off the knotless tippet and add a new one with a barrel or surgeon's knot. You can keep adding sleeves to the leader until you get enough weight, and because they present a slim profile they are less likely to hang up, and they cast better because they are less air-resistant.

You can also add weight to a nymph rig by adding a second nymph as a dropper. This gives you a number of advantages: the second nymph adds as much weight as a small split shot, it lets you test two patterns at once, and it may also excite the trout by letting them see two flies drifting by at the same time. I'll often use an outrageously big nymph as the lower fly and a more reasonable imitation of prevailing stream life as the upper fly. I think that often the trout will move to the bigger fly just to investigate, but they end up taking the smaller nymph. A good combination for me has been a big stonefly nymph, say a size 10 in the East and as big as a size 4 in the West, and a Sparkle Caddis Pupa in size 14 or 16 as the upper fly. Other good combinations include a size 10 or 12 Hare's Ear nymph as the lower fly with a size 16 Pheasant Tail nymph as the upper fly, or a size 10 or 12 Zug Bug as the lower fly and a small flymph or soft hackle as the upper fly. If you feel you aren't getting deep enough, or you go for a while without a strike, add a small shot or two to the tippet halfway between the lower fly and the dropper.

You can attach the upper nymph to your leader by adding a dropper as you would a wet fly; by leaving the heavy end of your last barrel knot long, or by attaching a new piece of leader material above the last knot with a clinch knot. An easier, tangle-free way to

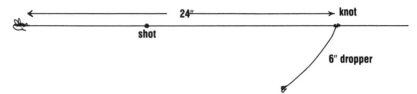

A two-fly nymph rig with one fly on a dropper and a shot in between.

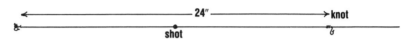

Two flies with shot in between; top fly threaded right onto the leader.

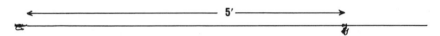

No lead on leader, lower fly bigger and heavier, upper fly threaded onto leader.

attach a second fly is to thread the smaller nymph right onto the leader above the last knot. I had always felt this would hinder the action or hooking ability of the upper fly until Rick Wollum showed me the method he uses on the South Platte. The day he showed me how effective tiny midge larvae can be, the rig we used was simple and completely free of snarls, even in the wind. To the end of a twelve-foot 5X leader Rick threaded a size 22 midge larva onto the 5X tippet, then attached a foot-long piece of 6X. He tied another midge larva to the end of the 6X and put one tiny microshot in the middle of the 6X. We hooked trout on the upper fly and the lower fly with equal regularity, and even the tiny size 22 threaded on the leader had no trouble sinking itself into the jaws of the trout.

Strike Indicators Make It an Easy Game

The strike indicator has put nymphing within the reach of even the beginning fly fisherman; it has also created a controversy among fly fishermen regarding the ethics and aesthetics of what some consider merely a bobber. I have no quarrel with those who choose not to use a strike indicator. But I resent their self-righteous condemnation of those who do, especially when novice fly fishermen are exposed to turmoil over a silly attachment to a leader when the fly fishing community should be devoting its energies toward habitat protection and stricter limits. I use strike indicators and have never felt a tinge of guilt when I do, even though I consider myself a rabid purist when it comes to fly fishing. I don't use a spinning rod, even in the roaring surf off our northeast coast when it seems futile to throw a fly for striped bass or bluefish, but I don't care if you do, nor do I even care if you tip your nymph with a piece of worm when fishing gets tough—an absolutely deadly technique, by the way.

One way of detecting strikes is to grease up the butt section of your leader, either a braided leader or a solid monofilament leader. If you see the floating part of the leader twitch or hesitate, strike. You can also run your thumbnail across the butt section of a solid monofilament leader to make a curl in the leader that sticks up above the water; if it straightens or twitches, it may mean a trout has grabbed your nymph. Some fishermen take a piece of orange fly line, remove the braided core, and slide the piece of fly line onto the leader. It gives you a point to watch, and it casts easier than other kinds of strike indicators, but it doesn't give you some advantages that other kinds of strike indicators offer.

True strike indicators, though, in tricky currents do much more than tell you when a trout takes your nymph. They are equally important as drag indicators and drag reducers. When currents swirl around your line or leader at all points of the compass—when the water you want to fish does not have a nice steady, uniform downstream progression—it's time to add some kind of indicator to your leader. If currents push your fly downstream of the leader or put a lot of slack into your leader, it is nearly impossible to tell if you have a strike because the connection between fly and leader is not tight enough to register the strike, and if you try to get the slack out of your line, you end up pulling the fly toward you and toward the surface of the stream. In addition, just as you can see when drag makes your dry fly wake across the surface of a river, an indicator can tell you if your fly is making drag-free progress as it comes back to you: if the indicator is bobbing happily downstream, just as fast as the current, you can assume that your fly is making the same progress underwater. If the indicator starts to streak downstream with a wake behind it, or if it lags in an upstream direction and a tiny eddy forms behind it, it is an indication that your next cast should be either a slack line cast or a curve cast to ensure it doesn't happen again. Be careful of mending line with an indicator, as I usually find that trying to mend line with an indicator makes it gurgle across the surface, with a good chance of spooking the fish. There is always the next cast, and if you don't rip your line off the water, a dragging indicator is just a temporary missed opportunity, not a blown one.

A strike indicator can also help to reduce drag because of its resistance to minor current changes. Drag on the leader has to move the strike indicator before it moves the fly, and it takes a lot more force to move an indicator than it does to slide a leader through the water.

One of the oldest and simplest indicators is a dry fly on a dropper above a nymph. Ed Schroeder has modified this technique into an extremely deadly and simple method he calls two-level fishing, and it is worth examining exactly how he rigs his two-level system because it is tangle-free. Rather than attaching a dropper to his leader, Ed threads a high-floating dry fly in size 12 or 14 to the last intermediate section of his leader. He uses a Parachute Hare's Ear because it floats like a cork and the white wing is highly visible, but you can also use a heavily winged Elk Hair Caddis, a Wulff, or a Bivisible—anything that floats well and that you can follow on the water. Below the fly he ties on no less than five feet of 5X or 6X and attaches his nymph to the end of the tippet. This arrangement is not easy to cast, especially if you're casting over forty feet, as the combination of the air-resistant fly and the long tippet does not turn over well. But the dry-fly indicator is more sensitive than any cork or plastic indicator, registering the slightest pause in your fly's progress, and the long tippet lets you fish deep and drag-free without having to add shot to the leader. And you'd be surprised at the number of times you'll hook a trout on the indicator, something you can't do with a plastic indicator.

Schroeder feels that often trout will rise up to take a look at the big dry fly bobbing along, and as they do they notice the nymph and inhale it, as a dry fly is visible from a longer distance away than a nymph drifting below the surface. So the indicator serves as an attractor as well.

A dry-fly indicator does not show up as well in heavily riffled water, or in places where the glare of the water makes it nearly impossible to see even the high-floating dry fly with its white wings. A piece of orange, red, or chartreuse yarn, plastic, or painted cork is hard to miss, and these materials will float all day long without your having to redress them as you would a dry. These indicators are also visible even if the weighted fly and/or shot pull them underwater.

The easiest indicator to attach to your leader is a foam tab that has a sticky backing. You just bend the back of the tab around your leader and continue fishing. This kind of indicator is fine if you will be fishing the same depth of water for a long time, but it cannot be moved on the leader, so when you need to raise or lower the indicator on your leader, you have to remove the indicator from the leader, sometimes a messy process, and attach another one some-where along the leader. Generally it's best to place the indicator up from the fly twice the depth of the water you are fishing, because unless you are precise enough with your tuck casts and get the fly to land under the indicator every time, the fly rides back behind the indicator at about 45 degrees—so if you want your fly near the bottom in three-foot water, you need to place the indicator six feet above the fly.

Cork or plastic indicators have a hole in the middle so you can thread the tippet through the indicator and jam it in place with a piece of twig or a toothpick. You can move this kind of indicator anyplace along the leader you want, so it's an obvious choice if you are moving from riffles to pools often. This kind of indicator is also reusable, and you can usually buy them in a package of two or three different sizes in a couple of colors, so you can change to a bigger indicator if you add a couple of shot and the indicator repeatedly sinks. My experience with them has been that the red or orange colors are best in the middle of the day when the light is strong, or if glare is intense, and the chartreuse color shows up best in early morning, in the evening, and on drizzly days.

Many nymph fishermen use fluorescent yarn, greased up with silicone line dressing or dry-fly paste, as an indicator. The yarn can be tied in an overhand knot around the leader or placed inside the loops of a barrel knot before you tighten the knot. You then tease the yarn into a pair of upright wings and trim it with scissors until it is about a half inch long. Then rub silicone paste into it. The yarn sticks up above the water higher than a low-floating indicator, and it casts easier because it weighs less. The disadvantage of yarn is that it won't float as long as cork or plastic without redressing; I use white sodium silicate crystals to keep it floating after it gets waterlogged, the same stuff you use to redress a dry fly. Yarn also won't counter the weight of split shot, so it's best used when you're fishing a heavily weighted nymph without added weight on the leader.

Yarn has uses, though, that make it superior for nymphing under tough conditions. Plastic and cork indicators can spook fish. On flat water, or in shallow water when anything plunking to the surface sends the trout bolting for cover, a piece of yarn lands with about as much force as a cottonwood fuzzball, and you can get away with casts over trout in spring creeks and flat pools with yarn that you could not with a standard indicator.

Yarn is also an essential ingredient to what is called the right-

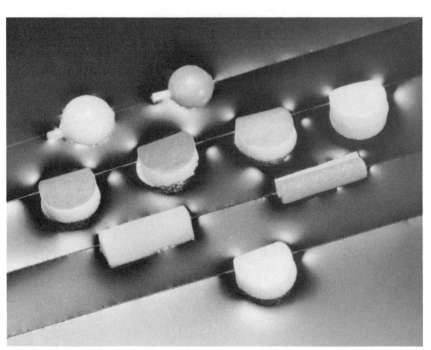

Various kinds of indicators.

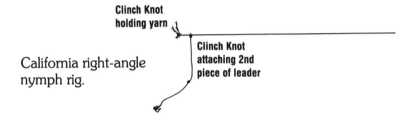

Clinch Knot
holding yarn

Clinch Knot
attaching 2nd
piece of leader

California right-angle
nymph rig.

angle nymph rig, which originated in California and was developed for fishing nymphs in water a foot to three feet deep. Here, you need to get the nymph to the bottom quickly but don't want to add shot, either because the water is slow and shot will impede the natural drift of the nymph, or because the fish are spooky. To make a right-angle nymph rig, cut off your tippet and attach a piece of yarn, an inch or two, to the end of the leader with a regular clinch knot. Now tie on a tippet, anywhere from two to five feet long depending on the depth of the water, to the leader above the yarn with another clinch knot. Pull the yarn together and trim until you have around a half-inch piece left—you could merely tie in a half-inch piece, but it's easier to tie the leader to the yarn if you start with a longer piece. Tie a nymph to the end of the tippet and the rig is complete. The big advantage to this rig is that when it lands on the water the right angle between the tippet and the rest of the leader forces the fly and tippet down, right under the leader, so you get a deeper, more drag-free float for a longer distance. It serves the same purpose as a tuck cast—in fact it is almost like an automatic tuck cast.

Using Strike Indicators in Tricky Spots

An indicator can be used in some places to get a drag-free float where you would not be able to follow your fly's progress any other way and would not be able to detect many strikes. One such place is where you want to fish directly across from your position or even downstream of the spot in which you are standing, especially if you have to cast across a couple of different currents. Here you can cast upstream and across, using a reach cast or a quick mend just after the fly lands to get your fly line upstream of the indicator and fly.

The fly will sink below the indicator, and because the fly line and leader are upstream of the fly and indicator, the fly will sink naturally below the indicator and will be suspended beneath the indicator as it drifts downstream. The indicator keeps the fly protected from minor drag, and it lets you know when drag sets in as well. Drag will invariably set in because the fly line is floating on the faster surface currents, and you can try to mend your line without moving the indicator and the fly: lift the fly line until only a foot or so closest to the indicator is on the water, then roll the line upstream again, trying not to move the indicator. If you move the indicator, it will pull the fly toward the surface, which may prompt a take—but I have better luck trying not to move the indicator at all.

One of the most clever ways of avoiding drag is to use two or even three strike indicators on a leader. I first saw this method used on the South Platte by innovative guides like Monroe Coleman, Kevin Gregory, and Jim Cannon. When they have a client who is having trouble reading surface currents, they put one strike indicator just below where the fly line attaches to the leader, and another one twelve to eighteen inches closer to the fly. By asking the client to keep both indicators in line with the rod tip, they can assure a drag-free float regardless of whether the fisherman is casting directly upstream, across-stream, or downstream. As soon as the line hits the water, they direct the fisherman to mend line either upstream or down to keep everything in line. Although it is not the most pleasant arrangement to cast, I can assure you it is deadly for the experienced as well as the novice nymph fisherman.

You can also get a dead-drift for a short distance downstream by using a parachute or other type of slack line cast, combined with a quick mend after the fly hits the water. The fly will float drag-free until the indicator starts to pull upstream because of the fly line. This is an especially useful technique in the tail of the pool, as if you try to fish upstream in the tail of a fast pool, the line will almost immediately start to drag the indicator and the fly, no matter how severe the upstream mend. When you're fishing downstream with this arrangement, once the indicator starts to drag, any kind of mend will do little to get you out of trouble, as the fly and indicator will start to drag again almost immediately. And no matter what angle you start at, when the indicator and fly begin to swing below you,

Tricky water like this calls for two strike indicators. Margot Page photo.

it's all over. I have seldom had a trout take a nymph fished with an indicator once the indicator started to drag, so don't try to turn your dead-drift into a wet-fly swing. The wake of a swinging indicator may put them off.

An indicator is also nearly essential if you are fishing pocket water, at least in the swirly slicks behind rocks. When you're fishing this kind of water, your first step should be to get as close to your target as possible; otherwise you can be casting over three or four different currents, jerking your fly line all over the place, preventing your nymph from getting anywhere near the bottom, ruining any chance of a drag-free float, and not giving you any indication of a strike. In places like this, where you need to get close to the fish, using a straight upstream approach with the Coleman method is difficult because you don't get a long enough cast and don't have enough line on the water to give the nymph a chance to sink. Here it is difficult to get your line straight enough to detect a strike. But by using an indicator and casting so that little line is on the water, you can get a decent drift by using a tuck cast or a right-angle rig to get the fly down quickly into the pocket behind the rock. I'll often get close enough and cast so that only the leader below the indicator is on the water; all the fly line and some of the leader butt are held in the air to keep them from getting snatched by the conflicting

Once the fly swings around to this position, your effective drift is usually over. Margot Page photo.

currents. You can get close to trout in pocket water because the foamy water hides you from the fish, so you can use this approach from directly downstream, from across, or even from directly upstream.

Sometimes you'll want to fish in water behind a large rock that is nearly devoid of current. In this case I get close, cast in behind the rock, and just let the fly sink and hang motionless below the indicator. Often the trout will take the nymph as it's sinking; if your indicator has hung there motionless for ten seconds and nothing happens, try nudging the indicator slowly toward you for six inches, making the fly rise toward the surface, then drop your rod tip and let it sink again. And hold on.

Strikes when you're using an indicator are apparent almost immediately after the fly hits the water. You don't have to wait until the initial slack is taken out of the leader, as you would with the Coleman method, so I often use this method in small streams. In many of the tiny pools you fish in small streams, when you're using just a floating line directly upstream, by the time your nymph gets to the proper level and the line gets straightened out to the point where you can detect a strike, the fly has already drifted out of the pool.

The Brooks Method

So far all the methods I've described have used a floating line and have stressed a completely dead-drift approach. During nonhatch periods, when you are prospecting, the food a trout will be eating is not rising to the surface, nor is it moving against the surface current. If a few flies are on the surface and you see sporadic rises, you are better off using a wet fly and the techniques we saw in the chapter on wet flies. There is one nymph method, though, that uses a sink-tip line and is really a crossbreed of some of the wet-fly and nymph techniques I've talked about—the Brooks method. Developed by the late Charlie Brooks for fishing big stonefly nymphs in the water around Yellowstone Park, it is a method I have used more effectively in Alaska for Pacific salmon, char, Dolly Varden, and Alaskan rainbows, and even though I feel one of the floating-line techniques will take trout more often than this method in most cases, I include it here because it is considered a nymph-fishing technique.

In the Brooks method, you use a large, size 4 to 10, weighted stonefly or other big nymph with a short, stout leader, no more than six feet in length, and a sink-tip line. Cast up and across about fifteen feet, and as the fly comes back to you, raise the rod tip to take up the slack. Strip in a little line to keep in touch with the fly. As the fly drifts below you, pivot so you are following the fly with the rod tip, and lower the rod tip to give the fly more slack. Strikes usually come when the fly is below you and rising to the surface, so it is really more of a wet-fly technique, as the fly is always under some tension from the line and never is allowed to drift totally free. Nevertheless it uses a nymph imitation and has caught many nice fish, especially in big water.

Fishing to Visible Fish

Fishing a nymph to a visible fish, while not truly prospecting, is a nonhatch diversion that is every bit as exciting and satisfying as pitching to a rising fish. I think it's more challenging because it is more difficult—first because you have the added dimension of depth, as it is difficult to tell if your size 16 nymph is at a trout's level from thirty feet away. Second, you don't know exactly when and if a trout takes your fly, so unlike with dry-fly fishing, when you sense a trout has taken your nymph there is the half second when you involuntarily inhale, as if you hope the fish will mirror your actions. By definition visible nymphing requires a fish in shallow, clear water, but it is not limited to English-like spring creeks, as many fishermen think. Trout in shallow water are spooky, and most fishermen scare them before they even see them; yet most of our freestone rivers and especially tailwaters offer superb visible nymphing in the second half of the season, or anytime the water is low and clear.

Look for them in tails of pools, on the shallow edges of deep riffles, on top of weedbeds, and in the gravel pockets between weed patches in spring creeks. (Careful! In spring creeks and tailwaters they can be found in almost any kind of shallow water—remember what you've learned about richness.) I've also found visible trout I could pitch a nymph to on top of bedrock outcrops that loom out of the depths of dark pools with invisible bottoms. When you find a trout that is lying on or near the bottom, only half the battle is solved. Often you'll find a trout that is either uninterested in feeding or spooked, especially if you find one in deeper water. In one of our local rivers I can often see "fright huddles" of rainbows in the deepest part of a pool, where they think they are secure from predators because they are in the deepest water they can find. These fish will appear nervous, and you can watch them tremble and jockey for positions, but this movement is totally unlike the movement of a fish that is eating or on the lookout for food. On the other hand, when you find a trout in water that is only a foot deep, and there is deeper water or cover nearby, you can safely assume that this fish is not spooked and is ready to feed.

When you find a trout that appears to be eating, the best strategy is to sit or kneel right away and watch the fish for a few minutes. A trout interested in food will sway in the current, moving to the unseen rhythms of the subsurface currents, trying to stay in a comfortable position. You'll then see the fish tip up or sideways, and many of these motions will be feints, where the trout is initially interested in a piece of drift, but as he moves to get a closer look he

This rainbow took a size 18 Pheasant Tail nymph in a shallow riffle. Shortly after this jump it broke off in the bushes. Margot Page photo.

turns away and starts looking for something else. Watch which side the trout favors. Often the food will be concentrated on the main current to one side of the fish, and that is the side to which you should pitch your nymph. It's a wise idea to position yourself so you can cast to the near side of the fish. Imagine yourself just below a trout that keeps plucking food from the drift, always moving to his right side. Of course you want to place your fly on his right side, but before you cast right over his head, move carefully sideways, maybe just a couple of feet, so that when you place your nymph to his right side, you are never placing the leader or line over his head. In the same light, if you approach a fish from his side—as you can sometimes do either in streams where the trout are so intent on feeding that you don't spook them, or in streams that host so much fishing pressure that the trout get used to fishermen in close prox-imity—don't try to cast your nymph to his far side. If he favors the far side, either pitch your nymph to the near side and hope for the

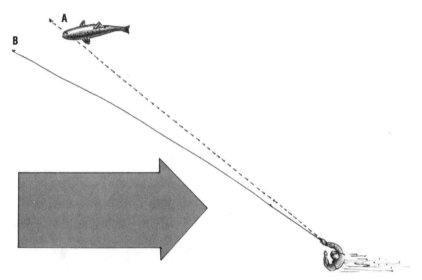

Casting a nymph to a visible fish. Try his near side first, B, rather than take the chance of spooking him by casting to A.

best, or cross the river well behind him and approach him from the other side.

I always try to find more than one fish feeding in one place, because I've always found it to be easier to take a trout when there is competition for food. Margot and I were fishing a small spring creek that feeds into the Beaverhead in Montana with guide Bob Butler one summer, and we came to a pool that held some respectable brown trout. Bob and I crouched on the bank above the fish, where we could spot for Margot as she fished to them with a small nymph. The fish were milling around, not spooked but constantly pushing each other into different positions. I noticed that when she fished to a lone trout it would visibly flinch as the leader landed on the water, but after a flurry of activity, when two or three fish were in sight of each other, one of them would always move for the nymph. It probably has to do both with competition for food and with the safety that trout feel when surrounded by other fish.

If the sun is bright and you are at an angle where you can see every move a trout makes, it's best to leave the strike indicators off your leader, and if you need any shot to get the fly down, use only one or two microshot. Because you'll be doing this work in shallow water, you seldom need much weight other than a weighted nymph to get the fly to the fish anyway. How do you tell if the trout takes your fly? I try to watch both my fly and my leader at the same time, which is difficult to do, and I usually end up staring at the fish, but trying to keep my peripheral vision on the leader. Sometimes your cast is so accurate that the move the fish makes for the fly goes unnoticed, and you can't tell he has taken the fly until the leader starts to tighten, and you start to wonder why that silly fish has started to shake his head as though he's trying to get something out of his—*oh, damn, missed the strike.*

If you can see every move the fish is making, strike if he has moved toward the place your fly is drifting, just at the moment he starts to return to his original position. At that point either he has the fly in his mouth or he has refused the fly and is not looking at it anymore. It's a good idea to try to strike not with the rod tip, but with a quick strip of the line. A foot-long strike is plenty of motion to set the hook in a short cast with a tight line, but is not violent enough to spook the fish if he has refused the fly, because instead of ripping the line off the water with your rod tip, you are merely sliding the line through the water. I manage to resist my reflex to strike with the rod tip about half the time if I concentrate hard enough; maybe you can control yourself better than I can. Other clues to watch are the white flash of a trout's mouth as he takes the fly, visible only if you are across or upstream from the fish, or the head-shaking motion as a fish tries to eject the inedible fly but finds that it has lodged itself in the corner of his mouth as the current pulls the fly downstream. Take them cheap if you can!

If the light is bad, if the sun is blocked by clouds periodically, or if the wind is riffling the surface of the water, you may only see the fish part of the time, visible as a shadow or dark spot that moves from time to time. In this case you may either want to grease the butt section of your leader or else use a yarn indicator to help you detect strikes. Keep the indicator well up toward the butt of your leader in this case, as an indicator that is too big, or one that lands too close to a trout, will spook him when he is in such shallow water.

Edward Hewitt, the famous Catskill fisherman and writer, wrote in the 1930s that a good nymph fisherman could strip a stream of its trout population in short order. After fishing over a visible trout for a half hour, having made a dozen fly changes without hooking the fish, you'll see how wrong he was. It will also be an education you can't get from books, videos, or any other kind of fishing. What can you do if a trout continues to feed but will not take your fly? Changing the pattern you're using is often the first move, and usually a reasonable one. I've had my best luck moving to a nymph of a completely different shape, and a smaller size as well. If you're casting a Pheasant Tail, with its mayfly shape, and the fish refuses to move for it, try a midge larva, with its slim body and head. Try a scud or shrimp imitation, with its bulky shape and fuzzy legs streaming from the underside of the fly. A smaller fly will often produce because we often start fishing with a fly that is too big, as we tend to have more confidence in the hooking qualities and visibility of a larger fly. Trout can see items in the drift that are smaller than anything you can tie, and they seem to be less suspicious of smaller flies: I've had them take nymphs as small as a size 26 when they would refuse a 22.

But you don't always have to change your fly to get results. Try putting on a longer tippet—maybe you're getting small amounts of drag that you can't see. Especially with the smaller nymphs it doesn't take much of a pull on your leader to make the fly drag, and it may be almost invisible to you. Try a tuck cast of a small split shot on your leader, as it's important to remember that your fly will usually be drifting shallower than you think. Often a change in position, even a couple of feet to the right or left, will make your drifts more drag-free or will get the fly deeper. Sometimes a curve or reach cast will help, although for visible nymphing these casts are not as handy as in other situations, because you will be fishing so close to the trout that one false move will send him running for cover. I prefer the more accurate and dependable straight line cast when I'm so close to the fish.

When dead-drifts fail, you have other options that may either spook the fish or draw them to your fly as if they hadn't seen it for the past two dozen casts. One is the plop, which is merely casting your fly about six inches to the near side of the trout so it lands with an audible (to the trout) splat. Trout are often on the lookout for things falling into the water, and their reaction to this is a reflex, as they will take the fly without really seeing what it looks like. You can

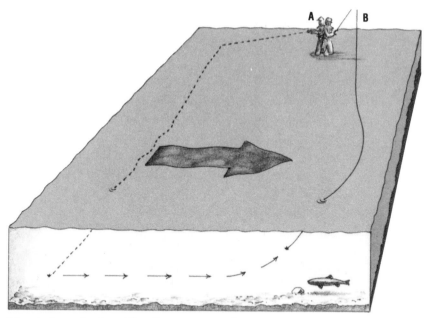

The induced take. The fly is cast well upstream of the fish at A and lifted gently at B, just upstream of the fish.

get the fly to plop by overpowering your forward cast slightly, or by pointing the tip of your rod down at the water than toward the horizon as you normally would. Don't overdo it, and if a plop doesn't work to one side, try doing the same thing behind the fish so he has to whirl around and grab the fly.

Another technique, developed by Frank Sawyer, the legendary English riverkeeper who developed the Pheasant Tail nymph, is called the induced take. Here you cast well above the fish so the fly is almost to his level as it drifts toward him, and when you think the fly is about a foot ahead of the fish, draw it to the surface by raising your rod tip a few inches. This can be done if you're directly behind the fish, but that motion often makes the fly move right toward the fish, which may frighten him, so it's better if you are off to one side of the fish. The very best motion is if you can cast an upstream curve into your line and leader, so when the fly moves it rises up and away from the fish. When performed subtly, the induced take can be deadly, as the motion of a fly moving toward the surface, as if it were hatching, can at times be an irresistible motion to a fish.

Dry Flies

You might think that when you're trying to catch trout when there is no hatch, the least likely fly to produce would be the dry fly. Nothing could be further from the truth. In fact, under certain conditions, particularly in shallow water during the summer, I am confident that I can catch more trout, and often bigger ones, than I can on any bait, lure, or fly—including worms, Rapalas, Mepps spinners, or nymphs.

During a hatch we assume that trout take our dry flies because they are fooled into thinking an imitation is the same bug they are eating, although even this point is sometimes debatable, especially when a fish that is sipping tiny duns with barely a ripple suddenly takes your Adams with an ardent splash. Other times, within hours after a hatch or spinner fall, trout will take a reasonable imitation of the fly they have just been eating because their short-term memory seems to be fairly acute. They also may be able to anticipate a hatch to come, if the hatch has been consistent and predictable for a few days, as I have seen trout slide out from cover along the banks to intercept a spinner fall an hour before the flies have touched the water. But there are times when trout will rise to artificial dry flies when there has been no hatch for days, or when there has been a hatch but the fish have not responded to surface food. A dry fly can be as effective a lure as anything the Norwegians can carve out of balsa wood or factories in the Midwest can fashion from bent wire, beads, and polished metal.

A couple of seasons ago we had extremely low water in April, water that looked more like late July than opening day. On my local rivers I am fortunate to be able to live close enough to trout water to sneak away from the office for five minutes and check the hatches, or walk across the street from my house on a weekend and check the water for insect life. These investigations become compulsive during the New England mud season, somehow a pleasant alternative to the delights of early spring yard cleanup. Our Vermont rivers host few early season hatches, and that spring I had not seen anything except a sparse hatch of black stoneflies in late March and a few midges in the middle of the day. I had not seen a trout rise since October. Three days into the season I was fishing a pair of nymphs on droppers with a strike indicator, and although the water was barely 50 degrees four different fish came up and tried to inhale a red plastic strike indicator. The water was so cold that they didn't move very fast, and the brook trout that came to the dropper reminded me of an old man without his dentures trying to gum an ear of corn. Now later in the season I might have theorized that the trout were taking the round indicator because they thought it was a beetle, but it would be a month before any beetles would be falling into this stream. And I was reasonably certain these fish had not yet been exposed to a hatch this season.

I have no idea what those trout thought the indicator was, but I do feel that they took it because the water was so thin that taking food on the surface was no greater effort than eating something subsurface. Another foot of water in the brook and they would have ignored (or not even seen) the indicator. Case number one for the dry fly as a lure.

Case number two takes place throughout the season in a tumbling brown trout stream that falls through a deep notch in the Vermont mountains. It's a true escape, especially in midsummer, as the air in the canyon is a full 10 degrees cooler than the ridges above, the music of the river fills your head better than the best pair of stereo headphones, and the light that barely filters through the trees forces you to squint after you finally leave the river. I have seen about a dozen rises in this stream over the past fifteen years, yet I have caught thousands of trout on dry flies here. During a heavy March Brown or stonefly hatch I have stared at places I know hold trout for half an hour without seeing a rise, yet the first cast into one of the pockets will hook a fish. But nine trips out of ten there are no insects hatching, and the trout are just as eager to eat an Ausable Wulff or Humpy. I know the fish eat insects here, and I am equally certain they respond to hatches, but for some reason they seldom feed on the surface. The flies that work best are bulky ones that penetrate the surface film, so I think the fish are probably taking my dries as nymphs, and the fact that part of the fly is riding above the water is irrelevant.

Although I often start to prospect with a dry fly on an unfamiliar river, there are a number of conditions that should be met before you start to pound away with a surface pattern. First is a combination of depth and surface velocity.

For a trout to rise to the surface to pluck an insect from the top requires more energy than any other kind of feeding, except for chasing a minnow streaking through the shallows. You can see this phenomenon by watching how trout respond to the hatches in your favorite river. The Hendrickson mayfly is the first major hatch of the season in most of the rivers I fish, and if the water is high and fast at the beginning of the hatch, even if it is not muddy, the trout will ignore the delicate duns twitching on the surface, even if the hatch is heavy and covers the surface of the water. If you go to the river every day as the water drops, one afternoon you'll start to find fish feeding in the slower water, next to the bank and in the eddies behind large rocks. In a few days they will be feeding all over the river, in the riffles and runs, and in all but the fastest water. You might think it takes a few days for the fish to get the idea that Hendricksons can be captured easily on top of the water, but if we have an unusually dry spring and the water is low at the start of the hatch, trout will be rising to duns on the first day of the hatch.

In the East we also have a number of smaller, less significant hatches—like size 18 black stoneflies, midges, and Blue-Winged Olives—that hatch before the Hendricksons. If the water is high, they will be ignored and the Hendricksons will be the first flies that bring the fish to the surface in force, but again, if the water is low in March or April these minor hatches can be amazingly productive, even if water temperatures are in the low 40s. One steady rain and it's all over, though.

Later in the season, when the velocity has slowed to a yearly minimum, trout seem to respond to nearly any surface food except water striders, which can skate unmolested through a pod of trout all season long. (Pick up a water strider and try to crush it in your fingers sometime, and you'll see why trout never bother with them— they're as hard as pebbles). Midges, tiny ants and beetles, small spinners—anything that gets trapped in the surface film is eaten, stuff that would have been ignored in April or May.

Dries—When and Where

In prospecting with dries, I've found that depth and velocity are much more important than clarity or temperature. Don't ignore the temperature, because blind-fishing a dry is far more effective at 60 degrees than it is at 50, but trout feed more often, period, as the water gets warmer and nymph fishing is light-years more productive at 60 degrees, too. Although you don't often get dirty water without a corresponding increase in velocity, I have seen times when road construction has clouded the water without measurably decreasing the effectiveness of dries. As long as the water is shallow, trout can see flies on the surface much better than you suspect.

How shallow is shallow enough to try a dry? When is the water too fast? You have to juxtapose the two variables—and then guess a lot. If you could predict exactly when to blind-fish a dry, it would be mathematics and not fishing. Reasonable depth is anything from the minimum depth for trout survival to where you can just barely see bottom. From midcalf- to waist-deep is another way of looking at it. Velocity is tougher to pin down, because although it is one of the most important factors in trout fishing, we have no easy way to measure the speed of a trout stream. If you look at the surface of a stream and it looks like one smooth sheet of water, and it is moving faster than you can walk, chances are your dry-fly fishing will be only in the eddies and backwaters along the bank. If, however, the surface is made up of many different speeds of current, and if you toss a stick into the water and can stay even with it while walking along the bank, you have my permission to try a dry fly.

Trout will swim up through deep, fast water for a dry fly if something they have been eating in the past couple of weeks makes them watch the surface. The first time I fished the New Fork in Wyoming was in early July, and because the ranches on its head-waters had not started to draw off large volumes of irrigation water,

Craig Matthews took this brown trout, and many like it, prospecting with a small caddis imitation just inches from the bank in the Madison. Note that his knees haven't even gotten wet.

the river was still plump with runoff from the Wind River range. My friend Mark Bressler was running a cattle ranch on the upper New Fork, and although the river was running too fast to wade in many places, we walked the banks looking for rises, seeing more sage grouse and pronghorns than trout. I had tied up some monstrous adult stonefly imitations called K-Butt stoneflies, horrible things to tie that involve cutting and cleaning the inside of a peacock feather stem and lashing it to the hook, along with mallard feathers dipped in Pliobond and rubber legs tied in knots. It's the kind of fly that makes commercial fly tyers wake up in cold sweats in the middle of the night.

Mark was poking through my fly box and found a couple of these adult stonefly imitations, his eyes taking on the same look they had the morning I saw him breakfast on ouzo and a chocolate doughnut. "Try this thing, buddy. It oughta rile 'em up. We had some of these big stoneflies hatching a few weeks ago." Standing

Great depth and velocity for prospecting with a dry.

on the bank, beside a pool that was too deep and too fast to wade, I saw brown trout from sixteen to twenty-two inches come up from five feet below the surface to nail that fly. It was like fishing with a bass bug, and on a 5-weight rod the casting wasn't much fun—but the strike and the fight were worth the trouble.

This incident makes a couple of valuable points about blind-fishing a dry fly. First, the deeper and faster the water, the bigger the fly. You have to make it worth a trout's effort to go all the way to the surface, and even though trout don't weigh decisions as we do, selection has given them some amazing powers of calculating the energetics of a situation in a split second. Second, when you're blind-fishing a dry fly, the best pattern you can use is one that reminds the fish of something they have eaten recently, although I like to go a size larger than the most recent hatch, using a fly that is more or less a caricature of the fly that has been hatching. For example, if you know March Browns have been hatching for the past couple of days, or you see them on the water, but the trout don't seem to be responding to them, it doesn't mean you should forsake a dry. Often, when I have seen size 12 March Browns around, I can pound fish up with a size 10 Ausable Wulff; when Light Hendricksons in size 14 have been hatching, a size 12 Irresistible with dun hackle will make them eat; or if Pale Morning Duns in

When a mayfly dun like this has been hatching, try a dry fly slightly larger for prospecting.

size 16 hatched yesterday but haven't shown today, a size 14 Yellow Humpy will work.

How long does this memory last? Neil Ringler, in his laboratory experiments with wild trout, found that trout "remembered" a specific food for about three weeks but forgot about it completely after three months. This may explain why even five-year-old trout, who have fed on juicy size 8 Green Drake duns for several seasons in the past, will let the duns float by for several days before they start feeding on them—the last time they saw the duns was twelve months ago.

Last summer I was floating the Madison with guide Mark Innis during the late June Salmon Fly hatch, which lasts for less than a week in any given stretch of the river. Thinking how much a Salmon Fly imitation resembles a grasshopper fly, I asked Mark if he thought trout took hopper imitations so well in August because they resembled the Salmon Fly.

"No, I don't think so," he said. "There's a long period in between Salmon Flies and hoppers when a big fly like this"—he pointed to the Macrame Hopper on my hook keeper—"won't draw a single rise. They won't start eating the big flies again until hoppers start falling into the water."

Less obvious but even more interesting is the fact that trout seem to be able to anticipate a hatch on a daily basis once it has begun to establish a daily pattern. I found this out by dumb luck once during the Hendrickson spinner fall on the Battenkill, fishing a size 12 Dun Variant a good hour before the spinners were to fall. Not a trout was rising anyplace I could see, and I was trying out the big, bushy dries merely because I had just bought a new blue-dun cape and wanted to see how the hackles floated a fly in the larger sizes. Trout came one after the other to the fly and solidly hooked up—much more so than usually happens with a variant, as trout coming to these flies usually strike short five times out of ten. It was not a fluke, and since that day I have extended the time I can catch fish on dries during the spinner falls an additional couple of hours, instead of sitting on the bank, waiting for the trout to rise. The same trick has worked on the Beaverkill and the Ausable with a White Wulff before a Coffin Fly spinner fall, and I would expect it to work whenever your river gets a steady, consistent fall of mayfly spinners.

Dry-Fly Patterns for Prospecting

In most trout streams caddisflies are more abundant and hatch throughout a longer period than mayflies. A caddis imitation fished blind will often draw more rises than a traditional mayfly imitation with upright wings, so this important reminder of a familiar food is a favorite searching pattern with some of the best fishermen I know. The Elk Hair Caddis is a special favorite with many of them, because it floats well, is durable, is easy to tie, and is highly visible on the riffled water that prospecting relies so heavily upon. I also feel the Elk Hair Caddis is much more than just a reminder of caddisflies. It could also be mistaken for an emerging mayfly, with its wings tucked along the body. So what if it doesn't have a tail? I doubt the trout notice. It also is a great imitation of a small grasshopper, especially the little ones that fall into the water in the early summer. Of course it has a perfect profile of a small stonefly, and it could be mistaken for a beetle as well, because not all beetles fall into the water with their wings tucked in nice and smooth to their bodies. Beetles fly as well as other insects, and often when they fall into the water their wings are still in the flight stage, splayed alongside their bodies, not as in the neat profile we try to imitate with our smooth, round foam and deer hair beetles. And the Elk Hair Caddis is a fine imitation of a moth, an insect I never thought trout bothered with much until I fished the Big Hole one summer and found hundreds of spruce budworms drawn to the river as though it was a shimmering candle, where they would fall to the river like mayfly spinners. The trout ate our size 12 cream Elk Hair Caddis as though they were designed to be budworm imitations.

This book is supposed to free you from swooping around with a butterfly net identifying insects, yet I seem to be spending an inordinate amount of time on bugs. Of course you're never really free from the influence of hatches, because insects are what drift-feeding trout eat all day long, but you can also choose your prospecting flies with more utilitarian purposes in mind. For the past five years I have relied on one dry-fly pattern for blind-fishing more than any other. It is mottled gray and brown, yet it catches trout in the early season in the afternoon when light gray and olive flies are hatching, in late spring when most of the flies are light cream or

The Dun Variant will produce before the Hendrickson spinner fall.

The Elk Hair Caddis is a great prospecting fly, and it imitates many different aquatic and terrestrial insects.

brown, and throughout the late season when tiny flies of all colors are around. It has an upright wing yet pounds fish up when most of the natural insects are caddisflies or terrestrials. The fly is the Parachute Hare's Ear.

Part of the reason it works so well for me, of course, is that I fish it more than any other fly—with confidence. Two of the most popular flies of all the times, the Royal Wulff and the Wooly Worm, are flies that I can't buy a fish on, but sometime early in my fishing career I must have used them and not done very well. As a result I never use them. But nevertheless I have switched back and forth from the Parachute Hare's Ear to another fly many days and always drummed up more fish on the Parachute Hare's Ear. It works for me in the Catskills, in Montana and Idaho, in California, and in Pennsylvania.

But the Parachute Hare's Ear is just a good lure. It is as near a perfect dry for blind-fishing as any fly I've seen. First, it's highly visible. It has an upright wing of white calf body hair, and it is tied with parachute hackle, which does not obscure the visibility of the wing as traditional hackle does. I have tried wings dyed orange and bright yellow, but for most water conditions white still reflects more visible light than any other color, so you can pick it up better. A visible fly is vastly more important when you're blind-fishing than when you're fishing to rising fish, which I'll go into more detail about when I discuss technique later in this chapter.

Second, it has more bulk than standard dry flies, and you need bulk when you're trying to catch the attention of a trout that may not be staring at the surface looking for floating insects. The deer hair tail of this fly, combined with a fat body of hare's ear fur, makes sure it's noticed. The parachute hackle allows the fly to lie in or below the surface film, helping to catch a trout's attention from a greater distance than a fly that floats on its hackle tips, as a well-tied standard dry fly does. Trout can't see objects above the water well, especially in riffled water, but they can easily spot objects in the surface film. This may also be a reason why dry flies outperform nymphs when you're blind-fishing: a nymph drifting down at a trout's level is camouflaged against the bottom of the stream and against all the water upstream, whereas a dry is silhouetted against the sky, where it is far more visible.

The Parachute Hare's Ear from above.

An often overlooked point is that both the grizzly hackle, speck-led black and white after it is wound, and the hare's ear fur, made from many tiny fibers that range from white to black to brown, suggest movement without really moving. They make it look as though the fly is alive, like something fluttering and trying to get away, without the unnatural drag that happens when you try to twitch a fly. Atlantic salmon fishermen feel that hairwing flies that use squirrel tail, and traditional flies that feature speckled bronze mallard, bustard, turkey, and peacock tail fibers, excite the salmon because the barring on these feathers and hairs suggests movement.

Other flies are great for blind-fishing, and patterns that have worked for me and fishermen whose opinions I value include the Royal Wulff (hey, some people swear by it), Humpy, Double Humpy (an incredibly nasty fly to tie, as even a single Humpy is not one you'd want to crank out for a living. The theory here is that if one Humpy will bring them up in fast water, two on the same hook should work twice as well), Irresistible, Renegade, Wright's Royal, Ausable Wulff, Madame X, Haystack, and Goddard Caddis. Most of these flies are standard patterns and can be found in your favorite catalog or fly shop, and if you tie your own the pattern descriptions are in any one of many pattern books. They all have visibility, floatability, and bulk, and for blind-fishing you should try to stay away from standard hatch-matching patterns, especially those with no hackle, because they do not suggest movement very well, nor

The Parachute Hare's Ear from below.

can they be seen easily by the trout or by fishermen. Lastly, there is no substitute for local knowledge, and some flies just seem to work better on certain streams than others. Stop in at the closest fly shop to your destination and ask what they use for a dry when nothing is hatching.

Change Your Fly Selection with the Season

When you are choosing your flies for blind-fishing, it's wise to follow a seasonal diminution that parallels the hatches. In most rivers the early season hatches are larger than those that hatch in late spring and summer, and the water in summer is lower and clearer than that in the spring, so the subtlety of your offering should increase. In May and June on eastern streams I'll depend on a size 10 or 12 fly for most of my fishing—I've found that the fish will often take a size 16, too, but the bigger fly is easier for me to see and will draw more strikes, especially from the bigger fish. But along toward mid-June I'll start to have days where a size 12 will only bring short strikes, or splashy rises that don't connect. Then it's time to go to a size 14, 16, or even 18, although I have found few streams where a fly smaller than a 16 was necessary, even when the morning or evening hatches were a size 20 or smaller. And then around late July the trout start to come to bigger flies again. Why?

When biologists studied a brook trout population in Archuleta Creek in California, they compared the biomass of the aquatic insect population with the biomass of top carnivores (the brook trout) and found that the amount of brook trout in the stream far exceeded the amount of food in the stream required to support them. No trout were stocked, and they were not fed pellets. A stomach analysis showed that fully 45 percent of their summer diet was terrestrial insects. Paul Needham, the famous aquatic biologist who was responsible for many of the landmark studies on trout management in the 1930s, also tracked the diet of a trout population in a stream in New York State from April through November and found terrestrial insects to be most common in August (52 percent of their diet), September (64 percent), and October (63 percent).

By July most of the larger aquatic insects have hatched out of the river, and the nymphs that have recently hatched out from their eggs are too small to interest trout—but most of the trout are still drift feeding. Terrestrial insects are bigger and more abundant at this time, so eating terrestrials is an essential switch in food supply, not just an opportunistic grab at the occasional ant or grasshopper. And it's to the dry-fly fisherman's benefit. The trout start looking to the surface more and more for their food, so you don't have to worry about catching their attention; they become less selective about the sizes and shapes they are looking for because terrestrials come in a

Seasonal diminution with an Irresistible.

much greater variety than aquatic insects, and they will not be suspicious of a larger fly. Hoppers range from a size 4 to a size 14, and the average size of a beetle is size 14.

Fishing Terrestrials

When you fish dry flies to rising trout during the summer, it is mostly a dawn and dusk game, but the opposite is true of blind-fishing when the trout are eating terrestrials more than anything else. At high summer I'll fish dries right through the middle of the day, as long as water temperatures in the stream don't get above 72 degrees, and I find that I'll catch more and larger trout blind-fishing dries at noon than I will in early morning or evening, or by fishing nymphs during the day. Just as with spinner falls trout seem to be able to anticipate the daily accidents that befall terrestrial insects. You see this phenomenon most often with hoppers, but only because they are more visible and obvious than beetles and ants. I've risen at the crack of dawn and fished a hopper on the Madison or Missouri, with a few halfhearted rises for hours, until the sun hit the water, the wind pushed my leader around, and the dusty gray hoppers begin clacking in streamside grasses. Suddenly the trout showed a much greater interest in my fly.

There have been a number of myths perpetuated by fly fishing books and articles about terrestrial-eating trout. One is that only trout lying next to the bank are interested in eating terrestrials, and the sages of fly fishing throw their delicate ant imitations with a perfect seventy-foot cast to within three millimeters of the far bank, and then follow the entire thirty-foot drag-free float until the fly is taken by a twenty-one-and-a-half-inch brown. I'll agree that big trout, especially browns, do like to hug the banks, and sometimes you need to pitch your fly to within inches of the bank to get a rise. I'd also wager that those trout eat just as many caddisflies and mayfly duns and spinners as the trout out in the middle of the river, and that the trout in the center eat as many beetles, ants, and grasshoppers as the fish along the banks. Just because your beetle imitation is working on fish along the bank, don't go to the trouble of changing flies. As I mentioned, anything that falls into the water gets drawn to the center of the river quickly.

Along the same lines is the theory that you don't put on a hopper or beetle until you get to the place where the river flows through a meadow. The next time you're fishing a river where a hopper is really killing them, move to a woodland stretch of the same stream. I'll bet you do just as well. Hoppers and beetles *do* live in the woods, too, and they fall into the water from meadows above wooded places. One of my best flies for small stream brook trout in the late summer and fall is a size 10 LeTort Hopper, and I fish it in acid, upland streams that seep through granite boulders that take a good handhold and foothold to get around, hundreds of feet above the nearest meadow. Streamside foliage consists of thickets of scrubby little black spruce and yellow birch, with the occasional towering hemlock that makes sure there is no understory. Maybe the trout take it for a stonefly. Maybe these fish have migrated from meadow water below and remember the shape of the hopper. Maybe the LeTort Hopper is just a good lure. Just don't get caught up in all the rhetoric that tells you to fish a hopper only along the banks near a meadow. To be completely honest with you, I don't fish "official" terrestrial imitations like those pretty ants, beetles, and hoppers that are so much fun to tie. One favorite stream has a bountfiul head of wild rainbows and a monstrous attack of Japanese beetles in late July. About the time I hear my wife cursing into her rosebushes, I start wringing my hands with glee, plotting to grab a couple of afternoons yanking rainbows out one after another. You don't have to be a trout scientist to figure out what they're eating, as *every* one you release has a stomach that feels bumpier than a grouse's crop. For a couple of years I fashioned the neatest beetle imitations from deer hair, peacock herl, hackle, and crow feathers— just the right color, shape, and size. They worked, too, but even with a spot of orange paint on top, I had trouble following them in the shady, overgrown pools. I watched a couple of beetles fall into the water and noticed that often they would open and spread their wings upon hitting the water, a natural thing for a fellow who falls from a tree to do when he realizes at the last minute he has wings. Hardly the neat package my fly was imitating.

Then I discovered that a size 14 Irresistible would catch just as many of these beetle-eaters—probably more, because I was able to see where the fly was at all times. When you think about it, most of the terrestrials that fall into the water have wings, and a regular old buggy dry fly like a Humpy—and yes, I suppose the Royal Wulff— make as effective a terrestrial imitation as you need, at least in fast to moderately riffled water. The visibility advantage of a higher-floating fly with an upright wing is tremendous, and I have found that trout keyed in to eating terrestrials will inhale even a size 8 hopper with a rise so subtle as to be almost missed, even if you're looking right at the fly. I know, all the books tell you they take hoppers with a violent swirl, but I've fished hoppers from Vermont to Montana, and 90 percent take them like a timid diner inhaling a strand of errant spaghetti. You can imagine how subtle a rise to a size 16 ant is!

The Importance of Visible Flies

The issue of visibility is important with all types of dry flies when you're fishing blind, not just terrestrials. When you're casting to a rising trout, you know exactly where the fish is, and if you can't see your fly on the water, you just cast somewhere above the fish and keep your eyes on the spot where the fish rose last. When blind-fishing, on the other hand, you can never tell exactly where the trout will take your fly, and if you lose sight of the fly you may miss a subtle rise. I have caught many nice trout by picking up my line to cast, only to find some heavy resistance at the other end. It makes me wonder how many fish I have missed, especially when the fly gets to my feet and I find it has been mysteriously drowned.

Trout are just as suspicious of drag when you are blind-fishing, maybe even more so because they aren't caught up in a feeding frenzy. Unless you are moving the fly by design, a technique we'll get into later, you must be able to see the fly, because just looking at a piece of water cannot tell you if the fly will drag when it drifts through. In one small brown trout stream I fish regularly, about five o'clock in the afternoon the light hits the water so that you can see the fish coming for the fly, trout that are ordinarily invisible against the mottled green, brown, and gray slate bottom. These are trout that seldom see a fly, as I have never seen another fisherman of any type in this piece of stream. But browns will be browns, and they are as suspicious of drag as any chalk stream fish. One afternoon I watched as one fish after another came for the fly, flashed, and then settled back to the bottom. A second cast to the same spot would not even draw a look, and changing flies would get no better response. Those fish had been turned off by just a single cast with a dragging fly, and only when I stopped looking for the fish and started watching my fly did I realize that the tricky pocket water had been snatching my leader almost immediately, jerking the fly across the currents. If I had been watching my fly, I still would have blown the first fish, but I might have been able to correct the drag for the rest of the trout farther upstream.

And had the light not been perfect, I would have assumed either that my fly was wrong, or that this stretch of water was barren.

One way to make sure you keep your fly in sight is to choose a fly with upright wings, with a lot of hackle like a variant, or flies that have white parachute wings. Ed Schroeder, of Fresno, California, who developed my favorite Parachute Hare's Ear, has carried the visibility concept even further. Two flies that are tough to see on riffled water are hoppers and caddisflies, which by their profile float low in the water and thus are difficult to see. Ed's Parachute Hopper and Parachute Caddis incorporate standard caddis and hopper imitations with white upright wings of calf body hair. Natural caddis-flies or hoppers don't have white wings that stick straight up in the air, but the fish don't seem to mind—and these flies are sure easier on the fisherman's eyes. The LeTort Hopper, another one of my favorite blind-fishing flies, is a low floater with a collar of rough deer hair. Before I fish this fly, I'll grab the top part of the collar and force it upward, giving me a beacon that sticks above the riffles.

Beetle imitations, deadly flies when the trout aren't rising, are notoriously hard to see. Fly tyers have devised two ways to keep track of them: One is to paint the back of the fly with a spot of bright red paint, and the other is to tie in a small tuft of red or white yarn at the head. The orange spot is fine for following your fly through the flat water of a pool, but I've found the yarn idea to be much more practical in riffled water, because the visible part sticks above the water.

Essential for blind-fishing a dry is a bottle of white drying powder, consisting mostly of finely ground sodium silicate desiccant. The stuff is like magic, and it will perk up a fly that has absorbed water and make it more visible than when you first tied it on. Most fishermen use this powder only after a trout has slimed their fly, but I'd advise you to use it liberally. I'm regularly amazed at the number of good fishermen I meet who have never used the stuff—I couldn't fish without it. As soon as you have trouble seeing your fly, pour out a small amount and grind your fly gently into your palm.

When the light is tough, try moving your position a few feet to one side or the other, or bend down to catch the outline of your fly. I've often found, in certain light conditions, that removing your polarized sunglasses can help you pick out your surface fly better, as sometimes your fly provides a stronger outline when there is a glare on the water.

Avoiding Drag Is Critical

There are two ways of approaching a piece of water when blind-fishing a dry. One is to carefully analyze the water before you ever make a cast, decide exactly where the trout should be, and make precise casts, with short floats and then a careful pickup of the line to avoid drag and to avoid spooking the fish. This technique works best in pocket water, where you can predict with fair certainty where the trout will be, and where drag will set in almost immediately because of all the conflicting currents. It's also a good idea to use this technique in slower pools—where random casting all over the place will end up just spooking all the fish—or in places where there is slow water against a bank but fast water between you and your target, where you know you will only get a short drag-free float. Tails of pools especially demand that you make short, precise casts. In general, any water that offers visible structures in the stream that smell like trout responds well to this approach.

On the other hand, often you will be fishing wide expanses of riffles, or fifty-yard seams, or long runs at the heads of pools, where it's not practical, and would be exhausting, to make pinpoint casts to every square inch of the attractive water. Here you want to get as long a drag-free float as possible, with a minimum of casts, because you don't have a clue as to where the trout might be. Fishing directly upstream is usually the best approach. When fishing to a specific location, you can cast from the side or even from upstream to make

In pocket water, short, precise casts are best. Margot Page photo.

your fly float drag-free through a narrow lane where you suspect a trout is lying, but when you are covering a large piece of water, you cannot get long, economical casts any other way than standing in the same current lane your fly is drifting in and casting directly upstream. This is best done in riffled water or deeper water, because you are going to drop the line or at least the leader over the head of every fish you catch. They don't seem to be as intolerant of this in riffles, and to help alleviate lining the trout to a frightening degree, use as long a leader as possible. Braided leaders are a big advantage here, with their ability to turn over longer tippets than standard knotted or knotless nylon leaders. I like to start with a basic twelve-foot braided leader, one tippet size larger than what I intend to use for my final tippet, and add five to seven feet of tippet. You then end up with something around eighteen feet of leader that straightens fairly well but still lands in those soft curves that help to avoid drag. The only time these become a problem is with a strong upstream wind, or with a big wind-resistant fly on a light tippet. If you run into problems, cut your tippet back until it starts to behave.

In researching this book, I talked to the best fishermen I know, asking them about any special tricks they use for blind-fishing dries. I'm sorry that I don't have any blinding revelations for you, but as with asking a writer the secret of publishing a first novel, or a businessman how he built his company into a multimillion-dollar corporation, the answer, always, was: hard work. Hard work avoiding drag. From Doug Gibson, with a quarter century of guiding on Idaho streams like the Henry's Fork, the Teton, the Fall, and the South Fork of the Snake, came the succinct answer: "The more dead-drifts you get, the more fish you will catch." Ed Schroeder was a touch more specific. "When I used to guide on the Madison,

Margot was making long upstream casts into a riffle on the Madison when she hooked a frisky rainbow.

we would see fish in shallow water that would look at every fly you put over them, but they would just move almost imperceptibly for the fly and would not follow through with a take. We found that if we worked very hard on drag, changing nothing else, we could catch them. We'd change the angle we were casting to them or go to a longer tippet, always watching for the slightest hint of drag and correcting the next cast accordingly. When we finally got a perfectly drag-free float, we could take them."

Leaders, Rods, and Casts

For much of the dry-fly fishing you'll do, you won't be able to cast directly upstream, because the current lane you want to fish will be too fast, or too deep, or the water will be so shallow and clear that you worry about lining the trout. So you'll sacrifice a long drag-free float by casting upstream and across, or directly across-stream. The first step you should make in alleviating the problems that currents will cause, pulling your fly line and leader downstream faster than the fly, is to increase the length of your tippet. The amount of drag you get is directly proportional to the diameter of the stuff attached to your fly. A heavier tippet or fly line gets pulled downstream faster than a lighter one, so decreasing the diameter of your tippet as well as lengthening it will also help. Going from a twenty-inch 4X tippet to a three-foot 5X tippet will give you an extra couple of feet of drag-free float, even under the worst of conditions. And over the course of twenty-five casts, that lets you cover an extra fifty feet of water with effective presentation.

In these days of high-modulus graphite rods, with their added power and line speed, you can use a fly line of much smaller diameter than was commonly recommended even a few years ago. Unfortunately most of the recommended line sizes given to people through books and articles date back to the days of fiberglass or bamboo, when you needed a 6-weight line to propel a size 14 fly with any kind of authority. The "standard" trout rod recommended by many authorities is still an eight- or eight-and-a-half-foot 6-weight rod, yet for most trout fishing situations, especially when dry-fly fishing, this outfit is far heavier than you need. I now reserve even my 5-weight rods for only the biggest dry flies in my box, when I will be float fishing with a big stonefly dry, and I fish most often with a 2-, 3-, or 4-weight rod for all other dry-fly situations—and if I want to switch to a size 6 weighted streamer or a weighted nymph with a strike indicator, any 4-weight I own will handle the task. These high-line-speed rods work quite well in the wind also, because the thinner diameter lines can cut through the wind. I've usually found that complaints of lighter-line rods not handling a windy day are more a function of a tippet that needs to be cut back a foot or so than a line that is too light.

There are casts you can use to cut down on drag, most of which have been given fancy names that only confuse the issue and make a novice fisherman believe he has to carry a VCR with him on the stream to keep track of the various permutations and combinations. All are simply variations of the basic overhead casts and require just a small amount of common sense to get the line to do what you want it to. Although curve casts are useful in fishing to a rising trout, I don't think they're much use in prospecting, unless you are trying to place your fly in front of a midstream rock in a place where you can't move off to the side to get a better angle. Curve casts are made either by chopping your wrist off to the left or right at the end of the power snap, or by making a sidearm cast and stopping the forward stroke abruptly so the curve of your horizontal loop is carried forward onto the water. They are not easy to perform consistently.

Much more useful is the aerial mend, which will not only direct a curve upstream or downstream or to one side, but also let you throw in some added slack. This cast ought to be called the Beaverkill cast, as it is this touchy river that I associate with tricky currents and drag-shy fish more than any other river I've fished. Most often the best fish are on the other side of the river from you, against steep, rocky banks that break the flow of the river so that the water between you and the fish is much faster than the water where the trout are lying. As a result you need to cast your fly with a long upstream loop that must get turned inside out before hackle-wrenching drag sets in. Long before the loop gets completely inverted, though, the heavier part of the leader will start to drag the fly as well, so you should not only add some slack to the cast, but also lengthen your tippet. Art Lee, who spends hundreds of days on

Rick Wollum making an aerial mend on the South Platte.

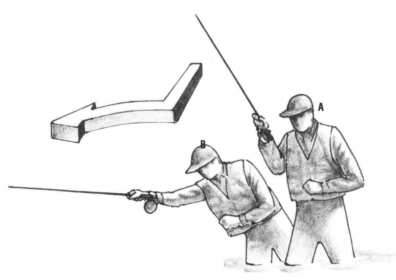

Close-up of the aerial mend.

the Beaverkill every year, uses tippets as long as ten or fifteen feet to risers. I don't think you have to go nearly that long for blind-fishing, but five feet is too short.

To make an aerial mend, simply make a normal back cast, then right before you begin your final wrist snap on the forward cast, reach up and out with your wrist and forearm in an upstream direction, as if you were tipping your hat to the fish. Point the tip of the rod where you want the upstream end of the loop to be. Then finish off the cast by bringing the rod straight out in front of you, as you would in a normal cast. It also helps to hold some slack line in reserve in your line hand, letting the upstream curve pull some of the line out as it forms. By overpowering the cast and aiming three feet higher than you usually would, then mending in the air as the line snaps back, you can also add some slack to the presentation. This is also called the reach cast.

In especially nasty water, like the tails of pools or glassy slicks where your fly seems to motorboat as soon as it touches down, you can try the parachute cast, although I usually call it the tail-of-the-pool cast, because it is the only cast that works well consistently in this tricky spot. With this cast, add about 30 percent to the length you think you'll need to reach your target, make a normal back cast, and as you come forward, instead of snapping your wrist over and pointing your thumb at where you want the fly to go, point the knuckle of your little finger at where you want the fly to go, and drop your elbow straight down. When you finish the cast, the tip of your rod, instead of pointing horizontally over the water, is sticking about 45 degrees above the horizontal. Once you master this one, you can throw one mess of slack into your cast, and it can be surprisingly accurate despite the entropy between your rod tip and the fly.

In riffles and broken runs, where you don't need to worry about too tricky an angle and are usually fishing straight upstream or quartering upstream, use just a plain old slack line cast, where you either overpower the cast and aim high so it snaps back toward you in loose piles. You can also underpower a cast, which gives you the same effect except that it isn't as good on casts over thirty feet and on windy days. Either method may be all you'll need to avoid drag. These methods give you the longest drag-free floats for your efforts,

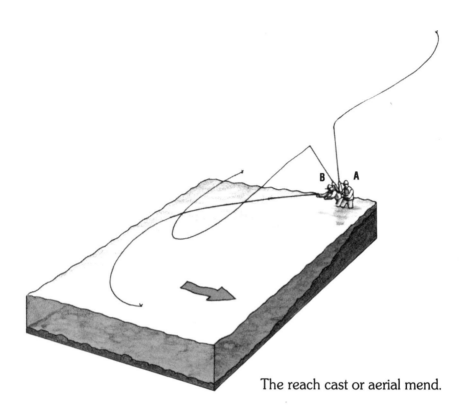

The reach cast or aerial mend.

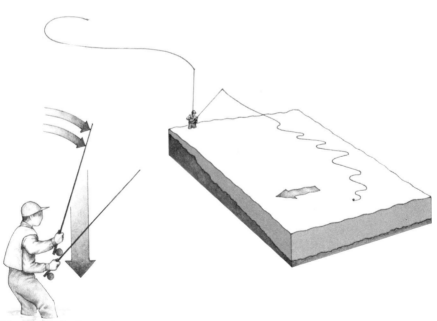

The parachute cast.

important when you need to cover a lot of water, not just the cone above a rising trout's head. Just remember to add about 20 percent to the cast's length to account for the slack you'll be putting into the line.

Tricky Water and Special Techniques

Pocket water, where coils of smooth water with frothy margins lull you into thinking *Those fish will never notice a little drag in this confused mess* can be deceiving. Look carefully at the smooth water—it's every bit as glassy as the tail of a pool, and drag will show up easily to the trout below. To be honest, these glassy places, where you find the most trout in pocket water, are not too large, so I pitch my fly to the kind and gentle riffles on either side of the glassy water first, hoping to find a trout that is generous enough to slide over and inhale my fly. After giving enough attention to the easy spots, I take a deep breath and attack the slicks. If you can approach the trout to within two rod's lengths without spooking them, the best way to fish these slicks with a dry fly is to keep your rod tip high, so all your fly line stays off the water and only the leader and fly get wet. This approach can backfire, though; with a spot that is more than fifteen feet away, the line you are trying to hold off the water after your cast does not form a straight line to your fly—rather the line becomes a saucer that gravity quickly turns into a bowl, pulling your fly downstream. I prefer to keep some line off the water, hold the rod at a lower angle—say 30 degrees above the horizontal—use a long tippet, and throw slack into the line. And I grease the daylights out of my leader. The whole thing, right down to the fly.

I originally started greasing my leader with silicone dry-fly paste because I had trouble following my fly in a pocket water stream that never seemed to see the sun. I found I could trace the fly better by looking for the shine of the leader on the water, and it didn't bother the trout at all. Using a greasy leader in other streams because I was too lazy to change leaders or rub mud onto the fly to remove the silicone, I started noticing that drag wasn't as much of a problem—I was getting longer floats. Switching back to a nontreated leader, I could see what was happening: The floating leader was far less

Fishing pocket water with a high rod and a greased leader.

affected by currents because it was riding half above the water instead of fully immersed in it. Would you fish a dry fly with a sinking line?

I still like to keep my leader sinking in smooth water, especially the last five feet, because a leader's shadow can disturb a nervous trout. But in riffled water, and in the smooth windows in pocket water where the trout don't see much of your leader, it pays to keep the whole thing floating.

I prefer to use slack-line casts combined with a leader that has a long tippet, rather than rely on special leaders that are designed to put loose curves in the entire leader. Why? Leaders designed not to straighten on purpose are fine if you always fish tricky pocket water. But five minutes after fishing a draggy stretch of water, you may creep up directly behind a sipper, where you need a dead-accurate cast with a few inches margin of error. I find that I can't get that kind of accuracy with a leader that is designed to fall in piles all the time. If you want to put slack in your presentation, add length to your tippet and control the amount of slack with your casts. The *you* will be in control of the fly, not your leader.

One of the most useful aspects of a dry fly, particularly in small or brushy streams where you may not get more than two feet of drift before your fly gets in danger of becoming a tree ornament, is that a dry is effective the moment it hits the water—sometimes even before it hits the water. Although a trout can see your fly on its way down, rarely will one take advantage of the fact, and it's almost always a small one. But if you're fishing a nymph in a small pocket behind a log, you have to cast above the spot where you think the trout is in order for the fly to sink a bit—plus until the fly sinks and takes most of the slack out of the leader, you won't be able to detect a strike even if a trout does inhale it immediately. Fishing a streamer to the same spot, you have to gather slack and begin stripping to give your fly movement, and sometimes by the time you get the fly up to speed, it has already drifted behind the trout, where it won't be spotted. And what if a trout is sitting right behind the log, where you can't get *any* drift above him?

In this situation a dry is definitely your best bet, but maybe not the visible, bushy types I've been touting so far. For a trout that is impossible to present a fly to from above, or for a place where you think a trout is but you can't get a drift above him, a useful trick is to plop a dry off to one side of the fish, about a foot away, where he does not have the advantage of binocular vision. This way he isn't able to scrutinize your fly, and he has to make a quick decision, because the fly is already almost out of range and he'll have to make a fairly substantial commitment to whirling around and taking the fly on a downstream slide. They don't often lose interest when they take a fly this way. Here you might stay away from air-resistant, high-floating Wulffs, Humpies, or Parachutes and instead pick something without any hackle: a Haystack or Comparadun, a beetle or hopper, a Goddard Caddis. These flies, without the benefit of hackle, land harder on the water, giving a satisfying splat, especially if you magnify the effect by aiming your rod tip slightly below the horizontal as you follow through on the forward cast, rather than keeping the rod parallel to the horizon. Trout can hear this splat in their lateral line system, and so they may turn around for a fly that would have been impossible for them to see.

In fact you may want to use this technique even in places that aren't so brushy, in deep or fast water where you feel the trout may

In a tight spot like this a dry fly may be the only answer.

not be paying enough attention to the surface. But use it like chili peppers. I like to reserve this technique for places where either I can see trout in the water, or I have an idea of exactly where they are, though, because it can backfire for you if you try to cover an entire pool by slamming a fly into the water. If you plop a fly right in front of a trout, particularly in his binocular vision, you are likely to spook him.

When Drag Is Desirable

Imparting movement to a dry fly is one of the most effective and exciting ways to fish dry flies, but it must be done under the right circumstances with special techniques that distinguish movement given to the fly by the fisherman from ordinary drag. Insects on the surface of the water move, no question, but when insects move they do it without creating a V-shaped wake that drag usually creates. When you purposely give movement to a fly, it should look like a skater gliding across the surface rather than a swimmer doing the crawl. If this is done properly, a skated fly will draw trout from six feet away, fish that might not be induced to take any other fly. It's more an active technique that you should use like a streamer fly to provoke strikes than a passive technique where you pitch a fly to a trout's suspected position and wait for him to inhale your fly.

Sometimes you need to add just a simple twitch to a dry fly to catch a trout's attention. In our Vermont streams in the fall the same debris that causes a migration of people from hundreds of miles away for a few short, frantic weeks while it is still on the trees is quickly shed with the first autumn cold fronts, littering the surface of our rivers with the flames of red maples, pumpkin oranges of sugar maples, burnished gold of beeches and aspens, and at the end of the season, rich brown of oaks. As soon as the first leaves hit the water, trout that would move two feet for a dead-drifted Ausable Wulff seem to lose interest. I suspect this is because during the summer, when there is little vegetable matter falling into the river, there is a good chance that something floating on the surface of the water is food, and it is worth it for a trout to inspect most items in the drift. In the fall the trout have so many false alarms, rising to the surface and either turning away or inhaling a piece of inedible plant matter, that it is difficult to catch their interest. Unlike the spring and summer, where two casts to the same spot will be all that is needed to rise a trout, in the fall you might cast ten times to the same spot without results, then twitch the fly gently, then try another cast with a twitch, and finally twitch the fly steadily as soon as it lands and keep twitching almost to your feet. You need to distinguish your fly from all the inedible junk on the surface.

Aquatic insects invariably move upstream when they twitch, so you need to position yourself where you can move the fly upstream, which usually means working downstream or at least getting across from the place you want to cast, so that when you move the fly it moves upstream. When casting downstream, cast with an upstream curve using the reach cast, and then raise your rod tip enough to move the fly an inch or so upstream; then quickly drop the rod tip so the fly drifts back downstream without drag. This is the simple but deadly Sudden Inch technique first described by Len Wright in his book *Fishing the Dry Fly as a Living Insect*. When casting across-stream to a position, try to throw an upstream hook using a curve cast or an upstream aerial mend, so that when you pull on the line,

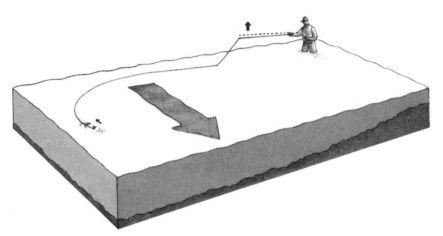

The Sudden Inch technique.

the fly moves upstream. You can also try to mend upstream after the line hits the water, letting the mending process move the fly, but I usually find that moving the rod and line enough to get a decent upstream mend makes the fly move too far, or it seems to pull the fly under the surface rather than skating it along the top.

The one exception to moving the fly upstream is when you are fishing with a hopper, as the trout are used to seeing a hopper move in almost any direction. If you get into a place where you think a twitched fly might work, but you can only cast upstream because of an obstruction, or in shallow water where you suspect you'll spook the fish by getting upstream of them, try a hopper.

Other than hoppers the flies you use with an active dry-fly presentation should be those that will skate across the surface without throwing a wake or splashing, and this means a fly with stiff, long hackles, or trimmed hackle, and also a pattern that keeps the point and bend of the hook above the surface. If your hook penetrates the surface film, the fly will resist the skating action, the hook digging into the water like an anchor, and the fly will hesitate and jerk, throwing tiny plumes of spray, rather than slipping across the top of the water like an insect. Trimming the hackle flat on the underside of a long-hackled fly like a Wulff or variant is one way to create a good skater. Trimming the hackle creates a wide base of blunt, stiff fibers that keep the fly above the surface film. I know this idea is repulsive to fly tyers, who spend their winters haunting the fly-tying materials sections of fly shops for expensive hackle capes with a combination of stiff, long fibers and just the right color, but even the best-tied dry fly, made from the finest hackles, will have a variation in fiber length underneath the fly, with some of the fibers resting on the surface but others penetrating the surface film. Take a heavily dressed fly like an Ausable Wulff, one with hackle that is twice the hook gap in length, and with a sharp pair of scissors trim the hackle flat across the bottom. Make sure that the cut you make leaves enough hackle to extend beyond the point of the hook—you should be left with hackle that is about one and a half times the gap.

Other good skating flies are ones that are palmer-hackled, mainly caddis imitations like an Elk Hair Caddis or a Henryville Special. If the palmer hackle is stiff, is uniform in length, and extends beyond the gap, you can often get away without trimming the hackle flat across the bottom, but if the fibers show some variation in length, or if you see that the fly does not skate without making some commotion on the water, get out the scissors. One of the deadliest skating flies is also the simplest, and the dressing calls for tying in a full hackle of brown and grizzly and trimming the hackle. Called the Vermont Hare's Ear, it is simply a body of rough hare's ear dubbing tied down around the bend, with a clipped collar of hackle. Gary LaFontaine, in his incredibly thorough book *Caddisflies*, introduced a fly that is one of the premier skating flies. The Dancing Caddis, an appropriate name, features a wing of elk hair that is tied upside down, so that not only does the wing cradle the point and bend of the hook to keep them out of the water, but also, because of the wing position, the fly lands with the hook pointed up every time. To add to the fly's skating properties, the hackle is also trimmed flat on the opposite side of the wing.

To keep your fly on top of the water, make sure that every part of your terminal tackle floats high on the water. If you don't pay attention to this, you'll make the fly dive underwater, ruining the effect. First, clean your fly line and apply a good line dressing. This is something I don't pay much attention to under most conditions, because with modern floating fly lines you don't have to dress them more than every dozen or so trips to the river for acceptable performance. But when skating a dry fly, you need every edge you

The Vermont Hare's Ear is a top skating fly.

can get. Next, dress your entire leader with either a paste fly floatant or line dressing, so the leader skims on top of the water as well. Don't worry about leader shadow spooking the fish, because trout will be chasing your moving fly and won't be bothered in the slightest by the shadow of a leader.

Conditions for Moving a Dry

There are two conditions that make skating a dry fly most effective: big mayfly duns or caddis hatching within the past week or so. Both of these kinds of insects skate and flutter across the surface of the water, and a trout's memory of seeing this seems to last for at least a week. Luckily there are few weeks during the regular trout season from April through September that you can't find at least one of these kinds of insects hatching. On the Battenkill, a river that resists the best efforts of a blind-fished dry fly with conventional approaches, I had poor luck for years blind-fishing a dry until one day in June, during a sporadic March Brown hatch that was not bringing the fish to the surface. My Ausable Wulff started to drag at the tail of a big pool on the lower river near Shushan, New York. As the fly started to swing, a large brown trout pounced on the fly by whirling around, clearing the water, and taking the fly in a downstream dive. I had not seen a trout rise all day. Of course I hauled back on the rod so hard that I immediately popped the tippet.

Over the next couple of seasons I refined my technique so that as soon as I saw the first March Browns hatching in the spring, I would clip a bunch of Ausable Wulffs or Gray Fox Variants flat on the bottom and would fish a skated fly from sunrise to dark, not caring if there were any flies on the water during any given hour or day. The trout would respond to the big skated flies as long as the March Brown hatch lasted, and then a week or so after I stopped seeing March Browns hatching, the fun would be over. And it is fun to see big trout fall all over themselves trying to catch a bushy dry fly careening across the surface. I have had similar success on New York's Ausable with either a White Wulff or a Gray Fox Variant when the Green Drakes were on, and on western rivers during the times Western Green Drakes were hatching—again, regardless if I actually saw flies hatching. This technique seems to work best if the water is a little above normal and slightly colored, as I suspect it spooks the trout when the water is low and clear.

Skating a Caddis

About the same time I was playing with skating the big Wulffs and variants, my friend John Harder was refining a technique that he feels is his most effective for catching trout on a dry fly when nothing is rising—the skating caddis. John has used this method on the Battenkill, on the Beaverkill, on Rhode Island's rivers like the Wood, throughout the Yellowstone area, and even on coastal cutthroat rivers near his home in Seattle. He can work magic with it, and as long as there have been caddis hatching recently, he can make a river that looks barren of trout come alive, as if the fish have been waiting for him to skitter his flies across the tail of a pool all day. John relies heavily on a Vermont Hare's Ear for this kind of fishing, but he has also been known to use a Henryville or Elk Hair Caddis if he has given away all his Vermont Hare's Ears.

It's important to note that the skating dry fly does not work in all kinds of water. Luckily, though, this method works best in water types that are difficult to blind-fish in a normal dead-drift manner—

tails of pools and other places where you find fast, slick water. Because smooth, fast water gives you such fits when trying to get a drag-free float, the skating technique rounds out your bag of tricks for prospecting with a dry. I've tried to skate dries on riffled water, and I feel that if you could get the right presentation in the riffles, it would work—but when you try to skate a fly through the riffles, the fly spits water into the air as it moves through the tiny hills and valleys. In order to fool the fish, a skated fly must slide over the surface without any added commotion.

Skating a dry fly, as opposed to just making it flutter an inch or two here and there, is a much more active, aggressive technique that you can use to cover a lot of water in just a few casts. Because

This smooth, difficult tail of a pool is the best water for skating a caddis. Margot Page photo.

you might be skating the fly twenty feet or more, then letting it dead-drift another ten, and then maybe skating it again, you can see why it is more useful on water that does not have any obvious places for trout, like the smooth tail of a hundred-foot-wide pool. In John Harder's skating technique you cast across and downstream, preferably with a rod not under nine feet long, matched with a light fly line—5-weight or lighter. As soon as the fly hits the water, begin to raise the rod tip smoothly while pulling on your line hand, almost as if you were going to single-haul. Twitch with both the rod tip and your line hand, so the fly dances across the surface, always moving upstream. When your rod almost reaches the vertical, drop the rod tip quickly to the water, throwing slack into the line; let the fly drift for a couple of feet, then try another skate. You can usually get two or three skates before the fly gets too close to you. The difference between this technique and the Sudden Inch is that with the Sudden Inch you use a small twitch in between long dead-drift floats, and with a skating fly you fish relatively long, broad twitches in between short dead-drift floats.

With a skated fly, it seems as though the less chance you give the fish of seeing your fly the better your chances of connecting. If, for any reason, the fly starts to dive underwater as it skates, and especially if it throws any water, it's poison. You might as well pick up the cast and try somewhere else. Once the fish have seen this

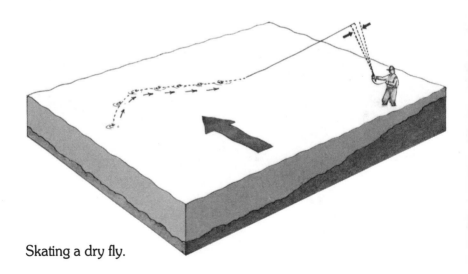

Skating a dry fly.

business, they get wise to you instantly. Also you seldom rise a trout on the tenth cast to the same spot when using this skating technique. I have seen trout respond to the Sudden Inch after a dozen casts, but the Sudden Inch is subtle, where the skated fly is nothing short of obnoxious. My friend Jim Lepage uses a skated Elk Hair Caddis on Maine rivers like the Penobscot, Kennebago, and Kennebec, and he has found that he can get a fish that has made a pass at a skated fly but not connected to rise again if he changes the color of the fly. Everything else that Jim has discovered about skating a caddis agrees with what we have found out in other parts of the country— it's best in the tails of pools, greasing the leader, the same skittering upstream motion—so I don't doubt it will work wherever trout are found.

Skating Spiders

Before there were fluttering caddis imitations, back in the thirties and forties, fishermen like Edward Hewitt and George LaBranche were skating spider flies on Catskill rivers with great success, particularly for large brown trout that would not respond to any other fly. Skating spiders are tied with stiff, oversized hackles, usually spade hackles, and have no bodies, wings, or tails. I know of no place where they can be purchased commercially today, but they are deadly flies. If you have hackle capes with stiff spade hackles along the side of the neck, regardless of color, tie some up by starting at the middle of the shank of a short-shanked size 16 hook, tying in two hackles with the dull, concave sides pointing forward, and finishing off with two more hackles with concave sides pointing to the rear, so that the tips of all the hackles meet at a point. Try to choose the hackles so that all the fibers are the same length. The diameter of the hackle should be around one and a half to two inches.

I have seen rare movie footage of Hewitt and LaBranche, fishing side by side on the Neversink, casting these oversized flies to the base of one of Hewitt's famous log cribbing dams, retrieving these flies like a modern streamer, with steady, fast pulls, the fly skimming over the water high on its tiptoes, with tremendous rises that shatter the surface. John Atherton, the famous commercial and fine artist who lived on the Battenkill in the forties and early fifties before his untimely death on a salmon river once spent an entire season fishing nothing but variants and spiders. In *The Fly and the Fish*, his only book, he wrote that although it was an experiment he would not like to repeat, he caught as many fish that season as in any other season, and most of the larger trout that took the spiders cleared the water after chasing the fly across the pool. Atherton also noticed, as I have, that these flies most often land flat, the bend of the hook pointing down into the water, and the most deadly point is just after the fisherman begins to put tension on the line, as this makes the fly lift onto the tips of his hackles. There are few manipulations a fly fisherman can do that are as lifelike as this moment.

When fishing a skating spider, get upstream and across from where you think a trout might be, and cast just upstream and to the

Skating a fly in a slick behind a boulder. Margot Page photo.

far side of the spot. As the fly drifts even with the spot, lift your rod tip enough to raise the fly onto its hackles, and let it drift over the trout's head. If you aren't rewarded with a smashing rise, draw the fly back to you, keeping as much line as you can off the water, never stopping its motion until you're ready to pick up for another cast. Trout don't have the ability to stop and start easily once they begin to chase a fly like this, and stopping and starting the fly usually isn't as effective. If, at this point, you're still not convinced that a dry fly can be as much a lure as a streamer, wait until you see a large brown trout streak across a pool chasing a spider—something you'll almost never see a trout do after a natural insect.

Another approach with a spider, or for that matter any other skating fly, is to let the fly hang below you on a tight line in one spot, as you would a wet fly. It doesn't work as often as skating the fly, but it sometimes is effective in getting into tight spots you couldn't fish any other way, like just above an impenetrable deadfall.

A spider is another skating fly that will produce savage rises.

Creating a hatch is a topic I introduce with reluctance, because although I don't believe in the technique, some fishermen I know, experienced ones at that, believe you can make a trout think there is a hatch occurring by repeatedly throwing a fly with perfect drag-free floats to the same spot. Hewitt believed it could be done, and he wrote about it frequently. I have tried this technique time and again, in places where I was certain there was a trout, and I've seldom been able to rise a trout after two dozen casts in the exact same spot. If a trout doesn't take on the first cast or the fifth but rises to the sixth, I prefer to think that he just wasn't looking up on the first few casts, or that he was chewing on a mouthful of nymphs, or that the first five casts had some microscopic drag that I couldn't see but the trout could. I have such poor luck blind-fishing by being persistent in a single spot that I prefer to spend my limited time on the water fishing over fresh places that haven't been spoiled by my thrashing and splashing. I think trout can be alerted by our presence even if they don't stop feeding, and the old saying about your first cast being the most important is nowhere more important than in prospecting.

And a Couple of Weird Techniques

As a parting shot in our discussion on dry flies, I offer a couple of crazy techniques that have worked for me a few times in my life but are a lot of fun to talk about with your fishing buddies in the bar. One is a poacher's technique that Leonard Wright wrote about in *Fishing the Dry Fly as a Living Insect*. When ovipositing caddis are over the water, often trout, mainly smaller ones, will only rise to a fly that is suspended over the water. Dapping will work, but often the fish are in the center of the river and cannot be reached by dapping. So you get a friend to cross the river, you cast to him, and he hooks your flies together at the bend. He then lets out line and you reel in until the flies are over the center of the river, and both of you put tension on the line until the flies are suspended over the trout. By raising and lowering your rod tips, you can make the flies just barely touch the water, then hover over the trout, until the trout can't stand the teasing and clear the water to take the flies. The same technique can be used when the trout aren't rising, as this dancing motion is almost irresistible to a trout that is at all interested in surface food. Once a trout is hooked, sometimes on both points at once, the only question is: Who gets to land the fish?

The other technique is also an unfair teasing of dumb trout, and it involves a fish that you can see in the water, quite close to you. I used to use this technique in an upstate New York spring creek that I grew up fishing on, where a large dry fly was a size 22. You fished one stretch of this stream by standing on a dike built up along one bank, and the trout were quite used to seeing people, so you could get close to a fish visible in the water without spooking it. Although these fish would almost never take a fly as large as a size 16 Adams, they would sometimes move to one in curiosity. I would cast the Adams just ahead of the trout, and just as I saw the trout tipping up to take a look, I would lift the fly off the water, leaving the trout looking around as if he were saying "Huh?" Then I'd cast to the same spot and again pull the fly away before the trout could get a close look at it. After three or four times I would then leave the fly on the water, and usually the fish would get a close look and ignore the fly.

But every once in a while a trout would do more than look.

APPROACH

Approach, in this chapter, will be considered in a broad sense, and we'll talk about not only how to approach unseen fish, but the overall philosophy in how you approach a day of prospecting for trout—how this philosophy is different from fishing to trout visibly feeding on a hatch of insects. Bear in mind that there is never a single right answer, that a trout in a riffle might grab a nymph, wet, or dry at a given instant, and that one of many hundreds of patterns may also work on a single fish. And if I start to sound dogmatic about a situation, you can be sure that you or I may go out tomorrow and find a trout that breaks every rule we've learned. Herbert Hoover may not be a major source of pithy quotes for twentieth-century life, but he did say that all men are equal before fish.

Pool Fish Are Different Animals

One of the most important aspects of approach is that trout in pools behave differently from trout in faster riffles and runs. Trout in pools seem to move around more than fish in faster water, they seem to have more lulls in their feeding activity, and they are tougher to approach. Given a choice, when prospecting for trout, I far prefer riffles and runs to pools. The surface of a slow pool is perfect for telegraphing your every movement, and a trout's visibility above the surface is greatly enhanced. Because most of the food in a trout stream is produced in riffles, trout in pools are more likely to wait for food to become abundant at the time of a heavy hatch, and in

244

between these times the fish are wary because they are not preoccupied with feeding.

One incident sticks in my mind as illustrating both the movement
of fish in pools and the difference between trout in a rich stream
and trout in a less productive stream. I was fishing the South Platte
in the Deckers stretch, below Cheeseman Canyon, with Rick Wollum. Rick was fishing below me in a large pool, and he began to
whistle and gesture for me to join him. As I walked downstream, I
could see him catching and releasing fish to the point where his rod
was bent more often in playing a fish than it was in casting. "They're
really in here thick," he said. "I think this low water has really
concentrated the fish in the deeper pools." We both had the same
size 20 midge pupa, the same size tippet and shot, and an indicator
on our leaders. Yet when I slid carefully above him, I went fishless
for fifteen minutes, and I even spent some time as his shadow,

Pool fish are different animals, as Rick Wollum showed me on the
South Platte.

mimicking his casts and drifts exactly. Rick moved upstream twenty feet, and then I began to hook fish on every cast, while he went fishless, as if some magic charm had passed from him to me. Later, as the sun got higher, we could see what had been happening: The trout were packed into one huge school, typical of rainbows in a rich stream, and in response to being spooked by a bad cast or by one of us moving, the entire school would whirl around and move either upstream or down, take a minute to settle down, and begin feeding in a different place in the pool.

In most streams that aren't overflowing with food, particularly in pools with faster water, once you spook a trout you're done for at least an hour, and if the fish move in response to your clumsiness, you can bet they won't be feeding. But in streams where you find a combination of abundant food, slow currents, and trout that are found in schools or pods, two fishermen can actually squeeze a school of trout between them until the fish sense they can't move either upstream or down, so they stay put and continue feeding. I've seen this happen on tailwaters like the Bighorn and Missouri, and in many spring creeks, and have heard reports of the same behavior from similar rich streams.

When I was studying fisheries science in college, I remember discussions of altruistic behavior in animals, the classic example being the flock of birds sitting on a telephone wire where one bird sounds the alarm, saving the rest of the flock from danger but calling attention to itself in the process. In a paper on trout behavior I had made a parallel observation that trout feeding close together in a group seemed to be less spooky and easier to approach, as if they felt safer in a group because there were more eyes to look out for danger. My ichthyology professor mildly ridiculed the idea, and as a result my paper didn't get an outstanding grade. But I have never changed my theory that trout in groups are easier to approach, and after leaving college I read Thomas Jenkins' paper on the Owens River, where he observed that isolated fish were more easily disturbed. If trout are visible in the water, I'll still concentrate on fish that are close together, as I feel confident that I can fish over them much longer and make more mistakes without spooking them.

Where Do You Start?

When deciding where to start fishing when prospecting for trout, you should almost always begin in places you would not look at first when fishing a hatch. Pools and slower water are usually the first places trout start to rise, and the first places we notice them, but because fish in pools may not be looking for food all the time, and because they are tougher to approach, I would start in a riffle or run, or at the head of a pool, when prospecting. It's easier to predict where the fish will be lying in a riffle, a run, or pocket water because the fish will be more limited in places they can live—in faster water you can immediately eliminate half the water as being too fast, without the breaks from the current that trout need. This, of course, has to be tempered by seasonal variations in temperature and water level. For instance, early in the season when water is below 50 degrees, and when anchor ice has recently left some of the shallower riffles, trout may be concentrated in pools for survival. High water as a result of a recent rainstorm at any time of the year can make many of the faster places in a stream unapproachable—the trout may be there, but your ability to get a nymph down to them, or to interest them in coming to the surface for a dry, may be limited. At these times trout in pools are both easier to approach and easier to fool, especially in the shallow margins at the edge of the pool.

I'm not suggesting that you glue yourself to faster water and ignore the pools, but it's more productive to start out in easier water first, until you find a fly that works and how to present it. I've also found that once you find a fly that works and a technique for presenting it, when you move from a riffle to a pool it's best to reduce the size of the fly. And don't get cocky about getting too close to the fish. If you can get within twenty feet of the trout in a riffle without spooking them, assume forty feet as a minimum when you move to a pool.

Before you enter a stream, don't ever assume there are no trout in the shallows without watching the stream for a few minutes. Look for gentle rises (and if you see them you can forget about prospecting for a while). Look for subtle ripples in the water that indicate a trout feeding on nymphs in water barely deep enough to cover its back. Look for the shadow of a trout on the bottom, which can often betray a trout's position even if you can't see the fish. This is particularly important in rich streams: spring creeks or tailwaters like the Bighorn or Madison, where fish prefer the easier living and eating in the shallows to fighting the heavier currents out in the center of the river.

Which Fly First?

Which kind of fly should you start with? If there is absolutely nothing going on—no insects on the water, cold, high water, or very dirty water—I'd start with a streamer. The advantage of a streamer is that you can invariably at least move a fish to the fly, so it gives you an idea of where the fish are lying. The disadvantage of a streamer is that slapping one around and stripping it through a piece of water generally ruin the water for another kind of fly, because the fish that

Studying the water before you cast on rich streams like this is vitally important.

don't take it can be spooked by both the fly and your manipulations of it. You also have to play the percentages with a streamer, because only a small portion of the population in any given part of a stream will move to this kind of fly.

If the water is at a normal level and the water temperature is above 50 degrees, you have a choice of nearly any kind of fly. If the water is shallow and not overly rich, I'll choose a dry fly over any other type because I can cover a lot of water quickly, without spooking the entire pool or run. Remember, the thinner the water, the more likely a blind-fished dry fly will produce. And a few insects on the water, or the promise of a hatch later in the day, will ensure that some of the fish are looking toward the surface. If you see a few sporadic rises, or if caddisflies are on the water but the trout aren't responding to them, you might try either a skated dry fly in the tails of pools or a swung wet fly.

The richer the water, the greater the chance that a nymph will be your best fly for a first choice. Start out in a gentle riffle if you

A Humpy dry fly is a great fly to start with in a riffle.

have the choice, and if conditions are such that you can't see any trout in the water. A nymph is also a wise choice for a second type of fly in less fertile streams, as the trout sometimes look at only one place in the water column at a time—especially if the water is just a little too chilly or fast for coming up to the surface. In small streams, where I feel confident of rising fish to a dry fly, especially when water temperatures are near optimum, I'll often find a deep pool where repeated casts with a dry won't produce a rise. Throwing a weighted nymph into a deeper pool may catch a trout that didn't come up for the dry.

How fast do you move when prospecting a stream? You move at a different pace because you're not fishing to an individual trout you see feeding, and often fishermen move too slowly—by this I don't mean wading too slowly, as fish that are not preoccupied with feeding are spookier, but many fishermen spend too much time flogging the water in one place. You may skip a lot of trout-filled water when prospecting, leaving the tails of pools and the slower middle of larger pools for hatch times, or at times when you don't pick up any fish in the faster water. With a streamer, of course, you move the quickest, with one good cast to each likely place. Wet flies call for a slower pace, and in the tail of a pool thirty feet wide, I might spend three or four casts in the same place, hoping that if the first cast didn't catch their interest subsequent casts might drift in a slightly different manner. Here you can hedge your bets by making the first cast a straight swing across the current, casting upstream on the second cast to get the fly deeper, and then making a downstream mend on another cast, hoping the fish may prefer a fly with a faster swing.

Dries, especially in infertile streams where trout will grab at the first edible morsel that drifts by, can sometimes be fished fairly quickly, with one or two casts to each attractive spot. In a small pool, fifteen feet long by five feet wide, I might make ten to fifteen casts before moving up to the next pool, depending on how much interesting water the pool contained. If there is tricky water in the pool or run you are fishing, where you suspect drag is influencing your fly, it might be necessary to make a half-dozen casts to the same spot, as with each succeeding cast you learn a little more

Browns, even little ones, can be sneaky about rising to your fly's first pass over their heads.

about the currents in that spot, and you can correct by throwing slack line or curve casts to improve your drift.

With dries it also makes a difference what species of trout are in a stream. Rainbows, cutthroats, and brookies are more likely to take a dry on the first decent cast, where browns, for some reason known only to them, may hold back and wait for over a dozen seemingly perfect casts. Many of the small Vermont mountain streams often contain a mixture of species, with brooks and browns or browns and rainbows the most common assortments. When I fish one of these mongrel streams with a friend, where one person fishes at a time and the other hangs back with good-humored lampooning, picking your flies out of the shrubbery, we'll often come to a place that reeks of a good fish. If the first few casts don't draw a fish to the surface, it's the duty of the watcher to say, "Uh-oh. Brown trout." When fishing a stream with browns, spend more time at each pocket. Another rule when prospecting for browns with a dry is that if you miss a brown, of if he rises short and you fail to hook him, you seldom have another chance. I have counted the times a brown trout over ten inches long has come back to a dry fly—twice in my lifetime. On the other hand I've kept track of the number of times I could get a brook trout to come back for a fly after missing or refusing it, and my record stands at six rises on six consecutive casts.

Nymphs require a slower pace, especially if you are certain there are trout in a spot and you feel confident you haven't spooked them. Your first cast with a nymph should still be your best, because you will most likely be fishing over a trout that isn't spooked, as each subsequent cast has the potential to frighten the fish. But trout may often ignore a nymph until it drifts right in front of them, particularly if the stream offers a heavy food supply. A smart plan is to keep adding weight to your leader, or to use a tuck cast, to get the fly deeper if your first dozen casts don't produce a strike. Keep adding weight until you start hanging bottom.

How long do you go before changing flies? If I could answer that question with complete confidence, I'd be playing the stock market and spending the rest of my time fishing instead of writing about it, but I do have a few educated suggestions to offer. Richness plays a big part in the question. The richer the stream, the more likely the fish will have developed a search image for a particular size and shape, because they can afford to be fussy and not starve, and in the same light a trout in an infertile stream may grab any fly that looks remotely edible. If you don't get any strikes in an infertile stream with a fly that you feel has a reasonable chance of producing strikes, you can assume that you have spooked the fish, that you have not read the stream properly and you aren't fishing over any trout, or that they can't see your fly.

I'll always give one fly pattern a complete run through a pool in a small stream, or maybe half a riffle in a larger river. If I catch any trout at all, I'll likely stay with the same fly, or if the trout I catch are all small I might try a similar fly in a larger or smaller size, usually smaller. For instance, if I start in a riffle with a size 12 Royal Wulff and only manage to hook a seven-inch brown in fifty casts, I could assume that the trout are at least mildly interested in surface food but I'm missing the larger ones. I'd then try a fly with a different profile and size, maybe something like a size 14 Elk Hair Caddis. If I got the same results with the caddis, then I would almost always try a nymph, figuring the larger trout were not interested in surface food right now. You'll often find this situation—smaller fish coming to the surface but the lazier, more efficient, more careful adult fish more reluctant to come to the top for their food.

If a nymph in an average size, say size 12 or 14 in a freestone stream and size 16 or 18 in a tailwater or spring creek, doesn't offer encouragement, then I'll try a nymph that is on the wild side, two sizes larger or two sizes smaller. If a nymph does not draw any strikes, I will almost never switch to a wet fly, as a trout that will come to a wet will almost always come easier to a properly fished nymph. I reserve wet flies for four circumstances: when the water is murky and fish may be seeing much debris in the water; when currents are swirly and tricky and I feel I won't be able to get consistent dead-drifts with a nymph; when there are hatching insects on the water, particularly caddisflies; or when the river is an intimidating size and I just don't feel like working hard.

When the River Seems Dead

You *will* have days when no trout come to your flies, no matter what pattern and techniques you try. One reason can be that the water temperature is too low, under 50 degrees, or too high, over 70 degrees. Water at either end of the temperature scale makes trout feed erratically, and they may just not be feeding at the instant you are casting over them. But most of the time, when the water seems empty of life, it's because the fish are spooked. I firmly believe that even the best fishermen frighten three quarters of the fish in a pool before they even get a fly over them, and not only do you have to contend with your own clumsiness, you have to wonder who has been there before you. A large and shy brown trout that has been frightened in the morning may not feed until the next day, especially if there has not been a heavy hatch of insects to entice him back to feeding. A couple of years ago I was haunting a couple of riffles on the Battenkill early in the morning, fishing nymphs and taking trout with consistent results, as I knew just where the fish were and had figured out what flies would take them. Every so often I would have a morning where I would not take a fish; in fact I would not even bump a fish. I tried to predict why I was not catching anything on certain days—was it the weather, did the hatches change, had the fish moved? One morning I got on the river an hour earlier than usual and met a spin fisherman leaving the river, who told me he had been having great luck on Rapalas three or four mornings a week in the same pools I had been fishing, but he started fishing about three in the morning and usually left right at dawn, a half hour before I arrived. Of course he hadn't caught all "my" fish each time, but he sure stirred up the riffles as he waded through. In the same light, if you fish a pool thoroughly, it's not a great idea to come back to that pool an hour later, unless the pool is so large that you can't wade through the places the trout may be lying in.

If you come around a bend in the river and a heron rises from the water in that curious, silent exit that seems to defy the rules of aerodynamics, or if a flock of mergansers paddle across the surface, or if a kingfisher rattles away from a dead limb, should you stay and

Disturbances like this can make a river seem dead for hours after.

fish the pool anyway? If I were you I would get out of the water and make tracks a hundred yards upstream, before the birds settle down ahead of you and spook even more water. These guys fish for a living, and any trout over a year old will be huddling under a tangle of roots; feeding will be the last thing on their minds.

How to Make a Careful Approach

When prospecting for trout, you don't have the advantage of knowing exactly where the trout are, as you do when fishing to rising fish, so your approach is even more critical. Not only don't you know where they are, but trout that are not actively feeding are more alert to the outside world. Assume that the fish can see you or hear your approach with their lateral line system before you can ever see them, unless the water is extremely clear and you have all the advantages, like the sun at your back and foliage behind you. If you expect me to give you some formulas on a trout's window and blind spot, and how you can calculate exactly how close you can come to a trout's suspected position, you are wrong. Countless times I've tried to approach a trout by determining just where his blind spot is, and I have spooked almost all of them anyway. Rather than carrying a pocket calculator to figure out whether you are in a trout's window or not, concentrate on being stealthy all the time, whether you are in a trout's blind spot or not. You *can* get closer to a trout by approaching a trout from directly behind, but many times stream conditions or the method you have chosen won't allow this approach. Because you are fishing to unseen trout, calculating the window for one suspected position is fruitless, because there might be three unseen trout between you and the place you expect to find one. Keep your profile low and your approach as stealthy as possible.

The most important part of your approach to unseen trout starts before you step into the water. Staying well back from the water, read the water in the entire pool or riffle and figure out where most of the fish are before you even get your feet wet. In a rich stream, where trout may be all over the place, you will have to sacrifice spooking some of the fish when you get into the water, or you can creep along the bank if you decide to fish the pool without entering the water. Then decide on a plan of action for the pool. Let's say you are faced with a pool where you suspect most of the good fish are in the head of the pool, but if you start at the tail you'll spook the smaller trout that live here into the head, causing a chain reaction of spooked fish throughout the pool. (One spooked fish does not always ruin the entire pool, as I have seen frightened trout streak by feeding fish where the feeders keep right on eating, absolutely oblivious to the other fish.) Your plan here might be to cut into the middle of the pool, getting into the middle of the river so that any spooked fish will be forced to run downstream into the tail, as they will seldom run toward you when spooked.

I feel the most important part of approaching a trout is not to push ripples ahead of you when you wade. I'm not sure whether trout hear the sound through their lateral line or are frightened by seeing the ripples, but if you push waves ahead of you any trout within the concentric circles will stop feeding. One way to eliminate this is to stay on the bank, as you can do on most meadow streams. As long as you can keep your profile low and kneel or crawl along the bank, and you don't create any heavy foot falls whose vibrations will telegraph along the bank, you can almost always fish a meadow stream more effectively by staying out of the water. If you have to wade, shallower water diminuates these ripples quicker than deep water, and fast water keeps them from moving upstream, so try to stay in fast, shallow water if you can. In slow pools with a glassy surface, where the ripples radiate in all directions from you, I've learned the hard way that moving slowly downstream, stepping no faster than the current, makes you stealthier than moving upstream. When you move upstream, you have to push against the current, creating waves, but by moving slowly downstream you keep disturbances to a minimum.

You can use a midstream rock or log to an advantage when trying to approach trout. By staying directly below an object, you can use it to break the effect of wading, and you can often wade to within fifteen feet of a trout if there is a rock or log between you and him.

It is always better to kneel or crouch when approaching trout. Easier said than done. Most of us are not physically suited to crouching through six hours of fishing, so it's best to save the

Randall Perkins is using this midstream rock to keep her waves from spreading into the pool above.

crouching for areas of a stream where it is really needed, like the tail of a pool or shallow, slow water. A trout's window does not cut out visibility below a horizon line, but it does compress any object that is low to the water into an almost indistinguishable mess that includes streamside brush and riverbank, so if you move slowly you won't draw attention to your movements. This compression of objects at the bottom of the window also makes it difficult for a trout to determine the distance of an object that is low to the water. You can use this to your advantage by always trying to approach the suspected position of a trout in a straight line, and if you keep your movements low and slow you will be more likely to approach a fish unnoticed.

Dirty water, riffles, and white water all distort a trout's view of the outside world even more, so if you are fishing a riffle, or if the water is not clear, you can get closer to a trout without crouching. We always assume that trout are easier to approach in the early season because they have not been fished over all winter, but I think it has more to do with the fact that the water is usually dirtier early in the season. One year, during the Hendrickson hatch on the Battenkill, our first good hatch of the season, the water was uncharacteristically low. The fish were just as spooky as they normally are in August, and we had to sneak up to each feeding trout as if he was sipping ants and beetles in midsummer.

On cloudy days, early in the morning, or late in the evening, you can get closer to trout because their ability to resolve individual objects is low. By keeping your movements slow, you'll blend into the background. On bright days a trout can distinguish your movements easier, but you can also use bright days to great advantage. A trout's pupil cannot constrict in bright light as your eyes can, and because the iris is fixed trout adjust to changes in light intensity slowly, by the rearrangement of retinal cells. So if the sun is in their eyes, you can approach very close to a fish, again if you keep your sudden movements to a minimum. This is in contrast to a common suggestion to fishermen that you face the sun, so that you don't throw your shadow into the water: throwing a shadow onto a trout *will* spook the fish, but if you can keep the sun at your back and take care not to throw a shadow on the water, you can get close to a trout feeding in bright sunlight.

Your silhouette against the horizon is something to avoid, because it will draw attention to your movements. If you have a choice of wading along a bank that is flat and without any trees or brush, or along a bank that has foliage taller than your profile in the water, always stay to the brushy bank, all other factors being equal. Even better is a day when wind is blowing streamside brush, because your movements can blend into the swaying of the streamside brush. Try to choose the color of your fishing vest and clothing to match the background of a stream. Green is a good color for brushy streams, but tan might be better for blending into summer grasslands in Montana or Wyoming. Bright metal objects that can reflect light like a signal mirror should be avoided, so wear those gadget-holding metal pin-on reels on the inside of your vest.

Trout do get conditioned to movements and objects that might ordinarily frighten them under other circumstances. For instance, fish that live in a bridge pool, with traffic rumbling over a bridge all

Keeping your profile low and near streamside vegetation will help.

day long, are not frightened by the movement of cars and trucks. Yet if you park your car, walk over to the bridge, and peer carefully over the edge, you'll often see every fish in the pool suddenly bolt for cover. There is a place in the Battenkill that is infested with big, white, obnoxious geese that waddle over from a nearby farm, and the trout will continue to feed even when the geese are swimming all over the river. Once I played Pied Piper to a procession of geese, who followed me upstream to a pool they normally don't invade, and it spooked every fish in the pool. Another stream I fish runs through a meadow full of Holsteins, who frequently ramble over to the edge of the river to drink. I've found that if I crouch and make sure my profile rises no higher than a cow's back, and if I amble along, I can get to within ten feet of these trout. I've thought of painting a white T-shirt with black spots, but I will draw the line at getting in line for the evening milking.

Trout also get conditioned to fishermen in the river in places that are so heavily fished that a trout would starve if it were spooked every time it saw a fisherman. In the Beaverkill, the South Platte, the Bighorn, and many other highly pressured rivers, I have had trout feeding almost at my feet, trout that absolutely knew I was there and chose to ignore me as no threat to their health. Fishing a pressured river can lull you into a false sense of security, as Beaverkill fishermen find when they take a side trip to the nearby East Branch of the Delaware. The East Branch gets a tiny fraction of the fishing pressure of the Beaverkill, because it is a more difficult stream, and it is always amusing to see a bunch of Beaverkill regulars stroll into a glassy pool on the East Branch with a stride more suited to a jogging path in Central Park. They spook every fish in the pool and usually return to the Beaverkill shaking their heads in frustration.

A Couple of Rod Tips

Casting can spook trout, and we Americans spend far too little effort in watching where our rod tip is moving. The English, who spend much more time on placid waters, where the trout can see the outside world easier, are more concerned with the visibility of their rod tips. Your rod will always be the object that is most visible to the fish, because it sticks up above your head more than any part of your body. I once fished the Itchen in southern England, an unusual stream in that most of its brown trout are wild and thus spookier than the trout in the Test and other chalk streams. I thought I was pretty sneaky, but my host kept gently reminding me about my rod tip by reaching over and pulling it down from the vertical as we crept along the bank.

Most of us spend too much time false casting. Why take the chance of alerting a trout by waving fly line above its head? To properly approach a trout, you should discipline yourself to no more than three false casts to dry your fly, work out line, and gauge distance. When you can, try to cast on a horizontal plane so that your fly line does not pass directly over a trout's head, and if streamside brush prevents you from making a horizontal cast, try to make your first two false casts off to one side and below the suspected position of a fish, making a small midair correction on the last false cast so the fly lands in the proper spot. Another trick is to use a weight-forward line as it was intended to be used. Most

Sally Swift with great form for spooky trout—polarized glasses, baseball hat, a low but comfortable profile, and a sidearm cast.

fishermen these days use weight-forward lines, but we use them as we would double tapers, and we seldom take advantage of the shooting characteristics of these lines. Instead of false casting with the length of line you need to reach your target, false cast behind your target with five to ten feet less line than you need, then shoot the rest of the line on your final cast. It takes a bit of practice to accomplish this smoothly, but it's worth the effort. These casting tips are doubly important when you are working downstream, when you are not creeping up in a trout's blind spot.

Stalking Visible Trout in a Pool

One of the most challenging and interesting situations in nonhatch fishing occurs when you are stalking trout in a slow pool in a freestone stream, or in a flat-water stretch of a spring creek. Your movements have to be painfully slow, and you really need to find a target rather than fish blind, as in most cases just flogging a slow pool will result in a pool full of neurotic fish, because your casting will spook all of the trout in the pool except those beyond the end of your line. Kneeling or crouching can help in your approach, but by keeping your profile low you won't be able to spot as many fish. If you're fishing with a friend, you can have the other person creep along the bank just behind you, spotting the fish from a higher vantage point—as long as the geography permits this kind of approach, and you trust the other person's ability to be stealthy.

Once you spot a trout, pay close attention to its behavior. An unspooked fish will sway gently in the current, and if the fish darts from side to side or up into the water column, you have a feeder. Choose your best fly—my choice will usually be a small nymph or a terrestrial like a beetle or ant. Your first cast should be just a fraction upstream of the fish and six inches to a foot to one side. Before you cast, try to determine if a feeder favors one side or the other—often it will be feeding to one side and ignoring objects that

Fishing to a visible fish with a spotter is fun for the fisherman and the spotter.

drift on the other. When you make your first cast, watch the trout's reaction intently—other than obviously bolting for cover, as some will do, often the fish will tremble, or suddenly become motionless and sink to the bottom. If the fish just keeps swaying and feeding, keep on presenting the fly, but if its behavior changes in the slightest the fish is alerted—but the game is not over yet, as he has not been frightened enough to run away. Often, if you carefully back up a few steps and stop casting, the fish will resume feeding. If the trout stays stark still and doesn't go back to swaying in the current, you might as well start looking for another fish.

Many fishermen in this situation have trouble distinguishing trout from suckers or whitefish. Unless you are fishing a very rich stream, and unless there are rainbows in this river, a school of fish that hug the bottom and seem to move together as a single organism are likely to be suckers or whitefish. If you spook a trout or a school of trout, they will usually dart for cover quickly, as opposed to a school of suckers or whitefish, which will move away at a more sedate pace. Be prepared to spook most of the fish you see in these circumstances, anyway, and chalk up your mistakes to part of your education—and now at least you know where some trout can be found, for future trips to the same pool.

Prospecting for trout is not just a skill that novice fishermen need to develop, and many fly fishermen go for a lifetime without taking the time to figure out how to catch trout in those more opportunistic times between the hatches. In researching this book, I asked the best fishermen I know what they do when trout aren't rising. One of the most interesting quotes came from Teri Felizato of Torino, Italy, a fly fisherman with over fifty years of experience throughout the world, who has fished with most of the famous fishermen in Europe, including Charles Ritz. When I posed the question to him, he took a long draw on a Parodi cigar, false cast it a couple of times through the air, and said, "In Italy you go to the *osteria*. In France you find a *bistro*. And when in England, you head for the nearest pub."

INDEX